THE ANTHROPOCENE AND THE GLOBAL ENVIRONMENTAL CRISIS

The Anthropocene, in which humankind has become a geological force, is a major scientific proposal; but it also means that the conceptions of the natural and social worlds on which sociology, political science, history, law, economics and philosophy rest are called into question.

The Anthropocene and the Global Environmental Crisis captures some of the radical new thinking prompted by the arrival of the Anthropocene and opens up the social sciences and humanities to the profound meaning of the new geological epoch, the 'Age of Humans'. Drawing on the expertise of world-recognised scholars and thought-provoking intellectuals, the book explores the challenges and difficult questions posed by the convergence of geological and human history to the foundational ideas of modern social science.

If in the Anthropocene humans have become a force of nature, changing the functioning of the Earth system as volcanism and glacial cycles do, then it means the end of the idea of nature as no more than the inert backdrop to the drama of human affairs. It means the end of the 'social-only' understanding of human history and agency. These pillars of modernity are now destabilised. The scale and pace of the shifts occurring on Earth are beyond human experience and expose the anachronisms of 'Holocene thinking'. The book explores what kinds of narratives are emerging around the scientific idea of the new geological epoch, and what it means for the 'politics of unsustainability'.

Clive Hamilton is Professor of Public Ethics at the Centre for Applied Philosophy and Public Ethics, Charles Sturt University in Canberra, Australia.

Christophe Bonneuil is a Senior researcher in History at the Centre A. Koyré (CNRS, EHESS and MNHN) Paris, France.

François Gemenne is a Research fellow at the University of Versailles Saint-Quentin-en-Yvelines (CEARC), France and at the University of Liège (CEDEM), Belgium.

Routledge Environmental Humanities

Series editors: Iain McCalman and Libby Robin

Deborah Bird Rose, University of New South Wales, Australia
Sverker Sorlin, KTH Environmental Humanities Laboratory, Royal Institute of Technology, Stockholm, Sweden
Helmuth Trischler, Deutsches Museum, Munich and Co-Director, Rachel Carson Centre, LMU Munich University, Germany
Mary Evelyn Tucker, Yale University, USA
Kirsten Wehner, Head Curator, People and the Environment, National Museum of Australia

The *Routledge Environmental Humanities* series is an original and inspiring venture recognising that today's world agricultural and water crises, ocean pollution and resource depletion, global warming from greenhouse gases, urban sprawl, over-population, food insecurity and environmental justice are all *crises of culture.*

The reality of understanding and finding adaptive solutions to our present and future environmental challenges has shifted the epicenter of environmental studies away from an exclusively scientific and technological framework to one that depends on the human-focused disciplines and ideas of the humanities and allied social sciences.

We thus welcome book proposals from all humanities and social sciences disciplines for an inclusive and interdisciplinary series. We favour manuscripts aimed at an international readership and written in a lively and accessible style. The readership comprises scholars and students from the humanities and social sciences and thoughtful readers concerned about the human dimensions of environmental change.

Rethinking Invasion Ecologies from the Environmental Humanities
Jodi Frawley and Iain McCalman

The Broken Promise of Agricultural Progress
An environmental history
Cameron Muir

The Biosphere and the Bioregion
Essential writings of Peter Berg
Cheryll Glotfelty and Eve Quesnel

Sustainable Consumption and the Good Life
Interdisciplinary perspectives
Edited by Karen Lykke Syse and Martin Lee Mueller

The Anthropocene and the Global Environmental Crisis
Rethinking modernity in a new epoch
Edited by Clive Hamilton, Christophe Bonneuil and François Gemenne

THE ANTHROPOCENE AND THE GLOBAL ENVIRONMENTAL CRISIS

Rethinking modernity in a new epoch

Clive Hamilton, Christophe Bonneuil and François Gemenne

Routledge
Taylor & Francis Group

LONDON AND NEW YORK

First published 2015
by Routledge
2 Park Square, Milton Park, Abingdon, Oxon OX14 4RN

and by Routledge
711 Third Avenue, New York, NY 10017

Routledge is an imprint of the Taylor & Francis Group, an informa business

© 2015 Clive Hamilton, Christophe Bonneuil and François
Gemenne

British Library Cataloguing-in-Publication Data
A catalogue record for this book is available from the British
Library

Library of Congress Cataloging-in-Publication Data
A catalog record for this book has been requested

ISBN: 978-1-138-82123-1 (hbk)
ISBN: 978-1-138-82124-8 (pbk)
ISBN: 978-1-315-74342-4 (ebk)

Typeset in Bembo
by Swales & Willis Ltd, Exeter, Devon, UK

CONTENTS

FIGURE AND TABLE

Figure

Table

CONTRIBUTORS

Ingolfur Blühdorn is a reader in Politics and Political Sociology at Bath University.

Christophe Bonneuil is a senior researcher in History at the Centre Alexandre-Koyré (CNRS, EHESS and MNHN), Paris.

Dipesh Chakrabarty is a professor of History at the University of Chicago.

Yves Cochet is President of Institut Momentum and Former Minister of the Environment in France.

Jean-Baptiste Fressoz is a senior researcher at the Centre Alexandre-Koyré, CNRS-EHESS.

François Gemenne is a research fellow at the University of Versailles Saint-Quentin-en-Yvelines (CEARC) and at the University of Liège (CEDEM).

Clive Hamilton is Professor of Public Ethics at the Centre for Applied Philosophy and Public Ethics, Charles Sturt University in Canberra.

Alf Hornborg is Professor in the Human Ecology Division, Lund University.

Bruno Latour is a professor at Sciences Po, Paris.

Virginie Maris is a CNRS research fellow at the Centre d'écologie fonctionnelle et évolutive (CEFE), Montpellier.

Michael Northcott is Professor of Ethics at the University of Edinburgh.

Luc Semal is a lecturer in Politics at the Muséum national d'histoire naturelle (Cesco), Paris.

Isabelle Stengers is Professor in the Philosophy of Science at the Free University of Brussels.

Bronislaw Szerszynski is a senior lecturer at the Centre for the Study of Environmental Change and the Department of Sociology, Lancaster University.

1

THINKING THE ANTHROPOCENE

Clive Hamilton, Christophe Bonneuil and François Gemenne

What is the Anthropocene?

Since the atmospheric chemist and Nobel Prize winner Paul Crutzen first mooted it in 2000, a variety of Earth scientists have been arguing that the Anthropocene should be added to the Geological Time Scale. This official scale, determined by the International Commission on Stratigraphy, divides the Earth's 4.5-billion-year history into eons, eras, periods, epochs and ages, with each division of diminishing length and geological significance. After gathering a multitude of evidence from a range of sources, the Commission's Anthropocene Working Group will advise on whether the Anthropocene should be officially deemed the successor to the Holocene. The Holocene is the epoch that began at the end of the last Ice Age some 12,000 years ago, and which stabilised 10,000 years ago at a global temperature that, with small variations, persisted until humans began changing the global climate measurably. A formal decision on whether a new epoch has begun is expected in 2016 or 2017.

The Anthropocene's starting date is a matter of debate. Crutzen and his co-authors initially nominated the beginning of the industrial revolution at the end of the eighteenth century (Crutzen 2002; Steffen et al. 2011). Others have suggested it began with the development agriculture some 7,000 or 8,000 years ago (Ruddiman 2003), although the evidence suggests human impact was not enough to destabilise the Earth system until humans began burning fossil fuels in large quantities. More recently, opinion seems to be converging on the date of 1945, the onset of the 'Great Acceleration' whose impact on the Earth system is unambiguous (Zalasiewicz et al. 2014). That year is also the one in which a layer of radionuclides was spread over the Earth's surface, a layer that will act like a flashing light for geologists of the future. Some Earth scientists argue that the human–induced changes to the Earth system are so great and enduring that, rather than entering a new *epoch* (a relatively minor stratigraphic division), the Earth is now entering a new geological *era*, the Anthropozoic, which succeeds the Cenozoic that arose with the Cretaceous extinction event 65 million years ago (Langmuir and Broecker 2012, 644).

The concept of the Anthropocene has been developed and explored by various disciplines, including atmospheric chemistry, climatology, oceanography and geology. More recently, it has been further elaborated in an interdisciplinary dialogue with historians and social scientists (Hornborg and Crumley 2006; Steffen et al. 2011). Interest beyond the natural sciences is burgeoning because it represents a ground-breaking attempt to think together Earth processes, life, human enterprise and time into a totalising framework. We suggest that it entails three definitional dimensions and two powerful and compelling claims that call for new thinking in the social sciences and humanities.

A first definition of the Anthropocene proposes a new interval in *geological* history. Stratigraphers – geologists who study rock strata – have a centuries-old epistemic culture based on specific, narrow but stringent kinds of evidence to delimit geological intervals (Rudwick 2005). To separate two intervals they usually attribute more value to oceanic sediment series for their consistency and continuity of records. It is in such series that they try to detect major geological turning points ascertained by lithological, palaeontological and isotopic evidence. If the evidence is sufficient, a Global Boundary Stratotype Section and Point, or golden spike, is placed in the record to delimit a new interval. According to this stratigraphic definition, the Anthropocene is, to date, only a potential geological epoch, not yet officially validated. As geologists need to take time to agree on hard evidence, and this hard evidence will have to be found in sediments and rocks, official validation may take some years or decades.

A second definition of the Anthropocene arises out of Earth system science, a domain that assembles a wide array of disciplinary expertise (climatology, global ecology, geochemistry, atmospheric chemistry, oceanography, geology and more) around a shared complex systems perspective on the Earth (Steffen et al. 2005). This Earth system approach, fueled by the dramatic increase in data on the different 'spheres' of the Earth (lithosphere, hydrosphere, cryosphere, biosphere and atmosphere) allowed by Earth monitoring programs, takes a broader view of changes to the Earth than geology traditionally has. This concept of the Anthropocene grows from an interdisciplinary 'Earth system science' perspective that views the Earth as a total entity, stretching from its core to the upper atmosphere, in an unceasing state of flux driven by energy and material cycles. Although 'geological' in its broadest sense, it does not seek evidence only in rock strata. With this wider lens, Earth system science claims that the Earth as a system is experiencing a shift, leaving behind its Holocene state, characterised by several millennia of exceptionally stable temperatures and sea levels, to enter a new Anthropocene state with far-reaching impacts. In this definition, as noted by Jan Zalasiewicz, chair of the Anthropocene Working Group, 'the Anthropocene is not about being able to detect human influence in stratigraphy, but reflects a change in the Earth system' (Zalasiewicz 2014). The words to focus on here are 'Earth system', for to grasp his meaning requires a new way of thinking.

This approach supports the declaration of a new epoch by deploying an array of evidence in addition to stratigraphic evidence, including evidence of anticipated sea-level rise due to anthropogenic warming, large-scale shifting of sediment, rapid rates of species extinction and prevalence around the globe of artificial organic molecules (Zalasiewicz et al. 2012). The well-known work on 'planetary boundaries' dovetails with this approach (Rockström et al. 2009). A tipping point has been reached beyond which 'the Earth system is now operating in a no-analogue state' (Crutzen and Steffen 2003, 253). Here we are no longer talking about the spread of human influence across 'the face of the Earth' (the geographical and ecological approaches that predominated in the twentieth century) but of a shift in the total system (Hamilton and Grinevald 2015).

A third definition of the Anthropocene describes an even wider notion of human impact on the planet, including transformations of the landscape, urbanisation, species extinctions, resource extraction and waste dumping, as well as disruption to natural processes such as the nitrogen cycle. This is what James Syvitski (2012) refers to as 'the cumulative impact of civilisation'. In this usage the Anthropocene represents a threshold marking a sharp change in the relationship of humans to the natural world. It captures the step-change in the quality of the relationship of the human species to the natural world represented by the 'impossible' fact that humans have become a 'force of nature' and the reality that human action and Earth dynamics have converged and can no longer be seen as belonging to distinct incommensurable domains.

If the Stratigraphy Commission, with its narrow remit, were to decide there is not yet enough evidence to declare that the Earth has entered a new geological epoch, the term will continue to be used in the second meaning and a fortiori in the third, even broader and looser, sense. The first definition requires evidence from rock strata while the other definitions are based on data and norms of proof from a wider array of scientific disciplines. The first is descriptive and evidentiary, while the other definitions call in addition for further causal and systemic investigations.

Radically new implications for our worldviews

The Anthropocene thesis is also embodied and embedded in various kinds of grand narratives – a mainstream naturalist narrative, a post-nature narrative, an eco-catastrophist narrative and an eco-Marxist narrative – analysed by Christophe Bonneuil in Chapter 2 of this volume. It seems to us that, beyond the three definitions and these diverse narratives, the Anthropocene thesis makes two powerful and compelling claims that need to be addressed by the social sciences and humanities. First, it claims that humans have become a telluric force, changing the functioning of the Earth as much as volcanism, tectonics, the cyclic fluctuations of solar activity or changes in the Earth's orbital movements around the Sun. Palaeoclimatologists, for instance, estimate that human-induced greenhouse gas emissions may be enough to suppress the glacial cycle for the next 500,000 years (Archer 2009). Whatever the chosen date for this human hijacking of the Earth's trajectory, acknowledging the Anthropocene means that natural history and human history, largely taken as independent and incommensurable since the early nineteenth century, must now be thought as one and the same geo-history (Chakrabarty 2009) – developed further by Dipesh Chakrabarty in Chapter 4 of this volume – with the addition of this new, dominant and willing telluric force. This marks the end of nature as no more than the external backdrop for the drama of human history, and the end of the social-only shackles of modern understanding of society. Modern humanities and social sciences have pictured society as if they were above material and energy cycles and unbound by the Earth's finiteness and metabolisms. Now they must come back to Earth. Their understandings of economy and markets, of culture and society, of history and political regimes need to be rematerialised. They can no longer be seen only as arrangements, agreements and conflicts among humans. In the Anthropocene, social, cultural and political orders are woven into and co-evolve with techno-natural orders of specific matter and energy flow metabolism at a global level, requiring new concepts and methods in the humanities.

The second claim made by the Anthropocene concept and related Earth system science studies is that the human inhabitants of our planet will face, in a time lapse of just a few decades, global environmental shifts of an unprecedented scale and speed, not since the emergence the genus *Homo* some 2.5 million years ago and certainly not in the mere 200,000 years that *Homo sapiens* have been walking the Earth. For instance, the current intensity of biodiversity loss is unmatched since the fifth mass extinction some 65 million years ago that saw some three-quarters of plant and animal species on Earth, including the dinosaurs, vanish. And a climate 4°C hotter by the end of the twenty-first century – every day seeming more like an *optimistic* scenario – has not enveloped Earth for 15 million years. Other parameters – such as human-induced disturbances to the nitrogen and phosphorus cycles, ocean acidification and synthetic chemical pollution – may alone or severally soon reach a tipping point, pushing the Earth – and thus the conditions for life on Earth – into a radically new state (Rockström et al. 2009). So rather than a mere global ecological crisis, the Anthropocene thesis heralds a new geological regime of existence for the Earth and a new human condition. If all humans (and, in particular, the richest 7 per cent to which we the editors belong and who are responsible for half of humanity's global ecological footprint) were to become totally 'green' and all societies adopted 'strong sustainability' tomorrow, it might nevertheless take centuries or, more likely, millennia (if at all) to return to Holocene-like conditions. Meanwhile, living in the Anthropocene means living in an atmosphere altered by the 575 billion tonnes of carbon emitted as carbon dioxide by human activities since 1870 (Le Quéré et al. 2014). It means inhabiting an impoverished and artificialised biosphere in a hotter world increasingly characterised by catastrophic events and new risks, including the possibility of an ice-free planet. It means rising and more acidic seas, an unruly climate and its cortege of new and unequal sufferings. It's a world where the geographical distribution of population on the planet would come under great stress. And it is probably a more violent world, in which geopolitics becomes increasingly confrontational (Dyer 2008). Furthermore, the emergence of the Anthropocene leads naturally to the question of what lies beyond it. Though its starting point is debated, the matter of its end poses fundamental questions: What kind of geological epoch or era will follow the Anthropocene? Will there be a permanent Anthropocene state of the planet with humans steering and engineering the whole Earth system? Is it an epoch in which human activities and the Earth system have reached a new balance, so that humans are no longer the main agents for change? Or is it an epoch in which humans are simply no longer present on the surface of the Earth?

Reinventing a life of dignity for all humans in a finite and disrupted Earth has become the master issue of our time. If we are entering an era beyond the experience of human beings, it is one for which there has been no biological adaptation and no cultural learning or transmission to prepare us for the kind of environmental/geological changes that loom. This constitutes a new human condition. Nothing could call more insistently for new social sciences and humanities research, for the human being who finds itself in this uncertain and radically new age is above all an assemblage of social systems, institutions and representations.

The advent of the Anthropocene challenges some established boundaries between nature and culture, between climate and politics, between natural sciences and the social sciences and humanities. The point here is deeper than a call for interdisciplinarity around hybrid 'socio-ecological' objects. The conception of the natural world on which sociology, political science, history, law, economics and philosophy have rested for two centuries – that of an inert standing reserve of resources, an unresponsive external backdrop to the drama of human affairs – is increasingly difficult to defend. And in an epoch in which 'Gaia' has been reawakened, the social-only conceptions of autonomy, agency, freedom and reflexivity that have been modernity's pillars since the nineteenth century are trembling. The idea of the human, of the social contract, of what nature, history, society and politics are all about – in other words, all of the essential ideas on which these disciplines have been constructed – ask to be rethought.

Nature and culture

The collision of human and Earth temporalities that is revealed by the Anthropocene is a test for the established boundaries of knowledge. From the time of the Bible up to that of the Comte de Buffon, the great French naturalist of the late eighteenth century, human history was understood as largely commensurable with the history of the Earth itself. But within a few decades after Buffon, just as the rise of a new industrial order paved the way for the Anthropocene, a deep divide opened up between the history of humankind and the history of the Earth. For the geologist Charles Lyell, writing in 1830, an intelligent being arriving from another planet would look upon the Earth and 'soon perceive that no one of the fixed and constant laws of the animate or inanimate world was subverted by human agency . . .

[And that] whenever the power of the new agent was withheld, even for a brief period, a relapse would take place to the ancient state of things' (Lyell 1830, 164).

Yet only a year later Jules Michelet, one of the founders of history as a professional discipline, was to write: 'With the world, a war began that will end with the world, and not before: the war of man against nature, of the spirit against matter, of liberty against fatality. History is nothing but the story of this endless struggle.' For him the 'progressive triumph of liberty', of human progress over a static nature, was written into history (Michelet 2013 [1834], 25). So at the moment when both the natural sciences and the social sciences and humanities were being institutionalised and professionalised, setting the cultural stage of industrial modernity, the world was being divided. On one side there was 'Nature', external to society and governed by slow and steady laws, but free of any telos in its history. On the other there was 'Society', teleologically oriented by progress towards a freedom understood as humankind wrenching itself out of any natural determination and limit. The social sciences asserted themselves as science through the elimination of natural causes and constraints in the explanation of the 'social', the 'cultural' and the 'political'. On one side were the 'in-human' natural sciences; on the other were the 'anti-natural' social sciences and humanities, each reigning over a separate dimension of the world.

Inverting the *episteme* of eighteenth-century Enlightenment, the new divide of earthly reality into two dimensions separated temporally, ontologically, epistemologically and institutionally constituted the intellectual enclosures in which the sheep of industrial modernity were kept. These enclosures may also have disinhibited the elite of the industrial and imperial order as they pushed humanity and the Earth into the Anthropocene; after all, if nature was now dead – or disenchanted in Weber's phrase – everything becomes calculable. This divide deserves further attention as the potential cultural impetus for the shift into the Anthropocene epoch (Bonneuil and Fressoz 2015).

Yet now, with the adoption of the Anthropocene concept we have to come back, superficially at least, to a Buffonian view in which human history and Earth history are commensurable and deeply interconnected. This has profound consequences for the way we should now understand and write history. It also implies that some kind of historical mode of thought might have to be reintroduced into the natural sciences. As suggested by Bruno Latour, it might be more fruitful to think in terms of 'geo-stories' or of 'becoming-Earth' (as Deleuze might have said) rather than in terms of the purely natural 'Earth system' (Latour 2013).

Invoking this convergence of natural and human temporalities and processes, some social scientists and philosophers, including Bruno Latour in Chapter 12 of this book, have welcomed the Anthropocene as the end of the Nature/Culture dichotomy. If all places and processes of the Earth are performed by human agency, does it mean that nature is dead and that everything under the sun is a hybrid Earth–society assemblage, a techno–natural cyborg? Is this currently prevailing perspective, in social sciences dominated by post-modern, constructivist and network thinking, a break with modernity? Or is it rather the symptom of a new spirit of capitalism where ontologies have shifted from entities to relations (Boltanski and Chiapello, 2005)? Could it be that this new spirit of modernity obscures and ignores natural limits and our planet's boundaries, not through an externalisation of nature in the way it used to (the old Nature/Culture boundary), but now through the internalisation, digestion or dilution of nature (the new 'NatCult' hybrid network) into technology and the market? In Chapter 10, Virginie Maris defends the otherness and agency of nature against the attempt to abandon them in a new fusion. Indeed, there can be no peaceful relation without acknowledging nature's otherness. In a similar vein, Isabelle Stengers cautions, in Chapter 11, that the language of the Anthropocene that effort-lessly melds science and politics may open up the path for geoengineering.

The end of a Nature/Culture ontological divide proclaimed with the Anthropocene is also a fertile and problematic ground for historians. First of all, it suggests new interdisciplinary work with natural scientists, with deep history cross-fertilising with global history and environmental history. It calls for an integration of socio-ecological metabolisms into the understanding of change and continuity in social order, government and culture. But historians may also question with empirical studies some of the historical assumptions from both natural and social scientists implicitly or explicitly carted around by Anthropocene discourses. One of these is the idea that the moderns, having externalised Nature, were blind to the environmental/geological impacts of the industrial mode of development. In this view a reflexive modernity (popularised by Ulrich Beck and Anthony Giddens) or a reflexive Anthropocene (Steffen et al. 2011) is said to have emerged only in the last few decades. In Chapter 6 Jean–Baptiste Fressoz challenges this, ironically progressist, received wisdom in examining the grammars of environmental knowledge and warnings in the early nineteenth century.

Dipesh Chakrabarty (2009) was one of the first historians to identify the pro-found challenge raised by the Anthropocene to the ways historians frame and write history. In Chapter 4, he extends his analysis, arguing that the story of our neces-sarily divided human lives has to be supplemented by the story of our collective life as a species. This view raises a hot debate with other historians who consider that race, class and gender are not categories belonging to a separate history that supplements the history of an undifferentiated human species transforming the planet's geology. Alf Hornborg argues in Chapter 5 that the industrial path taken by core countries could not have been taken without a systematic unequal ecologi-cal exchange with dominated/peripheral regions of the 'world-system'. Clearly, the Capitalocene/Anthropocene debate, in which dominations, exploitations and dispossessions are at the centre or the periphery of the human forcing of the planet, is only in its nascent stages.

Philosophy confronted

The Anthropocene concept also calls for new inquiries in philosophy. The new interpenetration of human history and natural history in the Anthropocene demands a fresh conception of the human being, beyond all humanist conceptions of 'the rational animal', of the autonomy-seeking creature, and of Kantian ideas of the being with a special capacity of world-making. Clive Hamilton argues in Chapter 3 that the modern project of progressive self-liberation, thrown out of all nature-imposed limits, will be increasingly difficult to sustain as the new geological epoch unfolds. Now freedom must be rethought in the new conditions of post-Holocene instability.

Grand shifts in philosophical understanding are always built on new ontologies, new understandings of the nature of being. Indeed, it is not merely 'understandings' that change; for a Heideggerian that which is understood – the real, the constitution of what is – also changes. In the emerging Anthropocene, there are good grounds for thinking that the nature of reality will undergo a profound transformation. This kind of deep questioning is eerily evoked by Bronislaw Szerszynski in his epilogue to this volume. After all, the arrival of the geologists, with their chisel-point rock hammers, in the middle of the social sciences, means that modernity's rigid division between the subject and the object comes under pressure, at least in relation to those questions that overshadow the future. When human history and Earth history collide, new entities emerge.

At this stage we cannot get a clear view of what those entities will be, although Latour has made a provocative attempt in his 2013 Gifford Lectures (Latour 2013) and Peter Sloterdijk's 'ontological constitution' covering all beings living and otherwise, in which humans must engage with the 'monstrousness of the external', is attractive to some for its new kind of globality (Sloterdijk 2011, 629). Isabelle Stengers' resuscitation of Whitehead provides a 'philosophical' process understanding of the world that has some highly suggestive parallels with the emergent reconfiguring of the Earth due to Earth system science (Stengers 2011). This kind of thinking seems much more fruitful as a means of exploring the Anthropocene than the rationalistic consequentialism of analytical philosophy. Consider, for example, the challenge of the Anthropocene to conventional ethics. If the impact of humans has been so powerful that it has deflected the Earth from its natural geological path, describing the state of affairs as 'unethical' seems to be some kind of category error. We are not arguing that evil lurks behind the Anthropocene (although one could make this case), but we are suggesting that it somehow trivialises the magnitude of what now looms before us to see the new epoch as the result of a failure to act according to a universal maxim or of a miscalculation about how to maximise human welfare. Yes, incredible as it might seem, there are some busily carrying out cost–benefit analyses to decide where we should optimally set the global thermostat, perhaps whether we should engineer the Earth into a new geological era rather than a new epoch. It is not enough to describe as 'unethical' human actions that are causing the sixth mass extinction of species in the 3.7 billion-year history of life on the planet. The attempt to frame such an over-whelming event by mere ethics serves to normalise it, of reducing it to just another 'environmental problem'. Talk of ethics renders banal a transition that belongs to *deep time*, one that is literally Earth-shattering. In deep time, there are no ethics.

 The kind of consequentialist ethics that leads some to regard the Anthropocene as a development to be lamented and avoided (the costs exceed the benefits), others use, on the contrary, to conclude that it represents an *opportunity* for humankind (the potential benefits exceed the costs). For the latter, the new epoch is an invitation to exert uninhibited technological mastery over our planet. In the words of Lowell Wood, the famous Pentagon weaponeer and geoengineering advocate: 'We've engineered every other environment we live in – why not the planet?' So now we see a new breed of 'eco-modernists' joining two words that no one who understands the science ever imagined would be juxtaposed – 'good' and 'Anthropocene' (for a critique see Hamilton 2013, Chapter 8). These optimistic souls brush aside the gloomy prognostications of the Earth scientists to assert that we can create a 'good Anthropocene', a wonderful opportunity for humankind to prove its creative power and finally take its destiny into its own hands. These are the kinds of strategies we can expect to see mobilised to defend and protect the established order as the pillars of modernity crumble. In their belief in human reason, faith in the power of technology and confidence in the nobility of the human quest they are beautifully modern.

Anthropocene politics

As may now be suspected, the Anthropocene poses a challenge to political theory, which used to see political regimes as purely intra-human contracts and struggles. In political science the Anthropocene concept obliges us to embark on a deep reconceptualisation of political agency and democracy. Ingolfur Blühdorn in Chapter 13 begins the process with a commentary on the exhaustion of both the 'objectivist' politics of economics and science and the 'subjectivist' politics of culture and identity. Political theory can no longer externalise the material and energetic metabolism on which the diversity of political systems rests. As Karl Marx had glimpsed with his concept of metabolism, technical *dispositifs* (the 'unsaids' that shape and control our thoughts and behaviour) co-produce a certain social order together with a certain natural order. In his book *Carbon Democracy* (2011), Timothy Mitchell criticises the 'de-natured politics' of the twentieth century and weaves an astute story of the evolution of democratic forms into the history of the extraction and use of coal and oil. Now we must work back from the consequences of the burning of all of that fossil carbon – from a new kind of planet – for our understanding of democracy and how it might evolve.

In political science, environmental issues have been addressed mostly through the prism of international relations and public policies. Scholars such as Oran Young (1994), Robert Keohane (Haas, Keohane and Levy 1993), Scott Barrett (2003) and Jean-Frédéric Morin (Morin and Orsini 2014) have developed theoretical models for the study of international environmental agreements and regimes, while Pierre Lascoumes (Lascoumes and Bonnaud 2014) and Paul Sabatier (1998) have conducted robust analyses of environmental policies. Yet political theory, stuck in the Holocene, has been slow to recognise the Anthropocene and what it means. Most insights have come from philosophers and sociologists such as Bruno Latour, Ulrich Beck and Dominique Bourg. Since the early 2000s, authors like

Andrew Dobson and Luc Semal have sought to renew the discipline in light of the new dispensation.

When environmental movements emerged in the 1970s political sociology considered the environment to be a 'public problem' constructed and promoted by new collective actors. But the Anthropocene idea shows that it is not enough to view the environment as a struggle among humans about nature. Green political theory has emerged in recent years to consider afresh a rematerialised political theory that would no longer externalise nature from its conceptual construction (Dobson et al. 2014). Reconsidering the ideal of strong democracy on a limited planet, in Chapter 7 Luc Semal examines the eco-catastrophist political thought that views the Anthropocene as evidence that there are biophysical obstacles not only to growth, but also to the perpetuation of thermo-industrial civilisation. Michael Northcott, in Chapter 8, reflects on the rhetorical role of catastrophism in the biblical creation-fall story and in today's Anthropocene talk, while Yves Cochet, in Chapter 9, draws on the Girardian notion of mimesis, as well as his own political experience, to argue that catastrophe is unavoidable.

One of the striking paradoxes of the Anthropocene is that, as we appear to have taken control over nature and have become the principal force of its transformation, we also appear ill equipped, and perhaps unable, to govern a world under the influence of these changes. In Chapter 14 François Gemenne reflects on the complex responses we can expect from some of the more vulnerable victims of the Anthropocene. Indeed, the timescale of the Anthropocene goes far beyond what the human experience is able to comprehend. And here lies the real challenge to democracy. Too often we have framed issues of environmental politics as issues of global governance, of international relations, and of balancing competing interests. These all assume that the future is a horizon of limitless progress (conveniently measurable with the yardstick of GDP) in which the only thing that is irreversible is progress itself. We have never thought about how to govern the irreversible. If we cannot reverse the irreversible the Anthropocene should force us to rethink government. This implies that government needs to be thought in terms of geo-politics, or rather of Gaia–politics, that is, the politics of the Earth in the words of Dryzek (2005). Geopolitics can no longer be a matter of understanding relations of power over land and natural resources; it is a matter of thinking the Earth as a political subject. Politics in the Anthropocene is about the collision of the system Earth with the system world, traditionally conceived as the political and social organisation of the former, which served as a background for the latter. This can no longer be the case in the Anthropocene, which signals a new era for geopolitics.

When the environment formally entered the politics of government in the early 1970s with the first international conferences and appointment of environment ministers, the politics were about conservation. Policies sought to create nature reserves and national parks, while laws to protect endangered species were passed (depressingly followed by the suggestion that we have nevertheless entered into the sixth mass extinction). The early conservationist period led to a perceived need for an administration of the environment, a structure of management; nature could not just be conserved, it needed to be managed. This too proved insufficient when the internationalisation of environmental problems became evident. No state alone could deal with them; even a 'superpower' could not solve transboundary pollution, ocean dumping, climate change and the depletion of the ozone layer. So the environment became a matter of international relations, of global collaboration, which unavoidably became mixed up with other problems of global governance, from trade treaties to refugee arrangements and the exigencies of the Cold War. The results were mixed, to say the least.

Yet now the Anthropocene forces us to reconsider it all. Why? Because it's not just our capacity to agree and act collectively that is at stake. Now there is a question about our capacity to make decisions regarding events that are beyond the human experience. That's probably one of the first requirements of the new geological epoch – to extend our ability to think and act beyond human experience. In the case of the big one, climate change, everyone can see that we are floundering. When it comes to collective decisions (the only ones that count in the Anthropocene) it is not just international cooperation, 'global governance', at stake. How to do democracy at home is an urgent question when the timescales of the Earth and the human experience no longer align yet cannot be separated. How can democracy account for very long-term, multigenerational issues that extend beyond the human experience? What should politicians do? How should they speak?

One of the fundamental principles of democracy is that any newly elected government can undo what the previous government has done. This is one reason why crusading governments of left or right attempt to embed their policy shifts in the deepest cultural and institutional foundations. With the Anthropocene, this kind of undoing is no longer possible in the sense that the Earth system, the environment on which life depends, is now on a different trajectory with tremendous momentum. Reversing a carbon price policy would, therefore, mark not an undoing but rather an *acceleration* of the problem. Many future generations have been thrown into the new era. When we entered the Anthropocene, we also entered a long age in which the irreversible must somehow be governed, a permanent state of adaptation, not only to seas that rise on thousand-year scales, but to decision processes where the Earth's future can no longer be known.

This volume is designed to begin the rethinking of the social sciences and humanities prompted by the arrival of the 'Age of Humans', an ironic moniker since modernity has supposedly been the age of humanism. It draws together scholars who have a prescient insight into the significance of the new epoch. Some critique the idea of the Anthropocene from various social science perspectives, while others argue that the Anthropocene demands a re-examination of those very social sciences. As with the arrival of the scientific revolution and then the industrial revolution we expect that it will take many years, more like several decades, for the full significance of the Anthropocene to sink in and bring about the transformations in the social sciences and humanities that we believe are inevitable. We anticipate that the idea of the Anthropocene – not as a geological question but as a human question – will meet resistance, and when not resisted will be framed in a variety of overlapping and competing narratives and worldviews. On the other hand, we find it impossible to have a clear idea of what the most innovative and leading thinkers will be saying in ten or twenty years' time. Bronislaw Szerszynski's poignant epilogue to the volume adds further layers of complexity to the task.

So we hope this book will inaugurate an intellectual journey, one that will be both stimulating and demanding, even if its subject is deeply disturbing. Its difficulty arises from the fact that our societies seem to go on unconcerned. Few people (even among our professional colleagues) have an inkling of the meaning of the Anthropocene; after all, it's hard enough to find people willing to accord full seriousness to the warnings of climate scientists. So as social scientists working today we are like the Earth scientists: we are certain that an enormous transformation is underway, but we can only speculate as to the exact forms that will emerge. Yet, while we may be feeling our way half-blind, we all understand that what is coming is too big to ignore.

References

Archer D 2009 *The Long Thaw* Princeton University Press, Princeton

Barrett S 2003 *Environment and Statecraft: The Strategy of Environmental Treaty-making* Oxford University Press, Oxford

Boltanski L and Chiapello E 2005 *The New Spirit of Capitalism* Verso, London

Bonneuil C and Fressoz J-B 2015 *The Shock of the Anthropocene: The Earth, History and Us* Verso, London

Chakrabarty D 2009 The climate of history: Four theses *Critical Inquiry* 35 197–222

Crutzen P J 2002 Geology of mankind *Nature* 415 23

Crutzen, Paul J. and Steffen, Will 2003 How Long Have We Been Living in the Anthropocene Era? An Editorial Comment, *Climatic Change* 61(3) 251–7

Dobson A Semal L Szuba S and Petit O 2014 Andrew Dobson: Trajectories of green political theory *Natures Sciences Sociétés* 22(2) 132–41

Dryzek J 2005 *The Politics of the Earth: Environmental Discourses* Oxford University Press, Oxford

Dyer G 2008 *Climate Wars* Scribe, Carlton North Vic.

Le Quéré C et al. 2014 Global Carbon Project 2013 *Earth System Science Data* 6 235–63

Haas P Keohane R and Levy M eds 1993 *Institutions for the Earth: Sources of Effective International Environmental Protection* MIT Press, Cambridge, Mass.

Hamilton C 2013 *Earthmasters: The Dawn of the Age of Climate Engineering* Yale University Press, London

Hamilton C and Grinevald J 2015 Was the Anthropocene anticipated *The Anthropocene Review* forthcoming

Hornborg A and Crumley C eds 2006 *The World System and the Earth System* Left Coast Press, Walnut Creek, CA

Langmuir C and Broecker W 2012 *How To Build a Habitable Planet* Princeton University Press, Princeton

Lascoumes P and Bonnaud L 2014 *Le Développement Durable, une Nouvelle Affaire d'Etat* PUF, Paris

Latour B 2013 *Facing Gaia* (http://www.bruno-latour.fr/sites/default/files/downloads/GIFFORD-SIX-LECTURES_1.pdf) Accessed 25 October 2014

Lyell C 1830 *Principles of Geology* Volume 1 John Murray, London

Michelet J 2013 *On History: Introduction to World History (1831)* Open Book Publishers, Cambridge [1834]

Mitchell T 2011 *Carbon Democracy: Political Power in the Age of Oil* Verso, New York

Morin J-F and Orsini A eds 2014 *Essential Concepts of Global Environmental Governance* Routledge, Abingdon

Rockström J et al. 2009 A safe operating space for humanity *Nature* 46 472–5 September

Ruddiman W 2003 The anthropogenic greenhouse era began thousands of years ago *Climatic Change* 61 261–93

Rudwick M 2005 *Bursting the Limits of Time: The Reconstruction of Geohistory in the Age of Revolution* University of Chicago Press, Chicago

Sabatier P 1998 An advocacy coalition framework of policy change and the role of policy-oriented learning therein *Policy Sciences* 21(2–3) 129–68

Sloterdijk P 2011 *Bubbles: Spheres Volume I: Microspherology* Semiotext(e), Los Angeles

Steffen W et al. eds 2005 *Global Change and the Earth System: A Planet Under Pressure* Springer and IGPB, New York

Steffen W Grinevald J Crutzen P and McNeil J 2011 The Anthropocene: Conceptual and historical perspectives *Philosophical Transactions of the Royal Society A* 369 842–67

Stengers I 2011 *Thinking With Whitehead: A Free and Wild Creation of Concepts* Harvard University Press, Cambridge, Mass.

Syvitski J 2012 The Anthropocene: An epoch of our making *Global Change* Issue 78 March 12–15

Young O 1994 *International Governance: Protecting the Environment in a Stateless Society* Cornell University Press, Ithaca NY

Zalasiewicz J 2014 Response to Adrian J Ivakhiv's 'Against the Anthropocene' Blog post (http://blog.uvm.edu/aivakhiv/2014/07/07/against-the-anthropocene/) Accessed 6 November 2014

Zalasiewicz J Crutzen P and Steffen W 2012 The Anthropocene, in Gradstein F Ogg J Schmitz M and Ogg G eds *The Geologic Time Scale 2012* Volume 2 Elsevier, Oxford 1033–40

Zalasiewicz Jan, et al. 2014 When did the Anthropocene begin? A mid-twentieth century boundary level is stratigraphically optimal, accepted by *Quaternary International* (http://dx.doi.org/10.1016/j.quaint.2014.11.045)

PART I

The concept and its implications

2

THE GEOLOGICAL TURN

Narratives of the Anthropocene

Christophe Bonneuil

Stories matter for the Earth. Indeed, the stories that the elites of industrial modernity have told themselves – about nature as external and purposeless, about the world as resource, about human exemptionalism, about progress and freedom as an escape from nature's determinations and limits, about technology as quasi-autonomous prime mover – have served as the cultural origins and conditions of the Anthropocene (Merchant 1980; Descola 2013; Bonneuil and Fressoz 2015). In the same way the kind of stories we tell ourselves today about the Anthropocene can shape the kind of geohistorical future we will inhabit.

William Cronon's seminal reflections on environmental history as storytelling provide insights for the study of Anthropocene discourses. His famous 1992 article, 'A place for stories: Nature history and narrative', compared the ways several historians told of the transformations of the Great Plains from the mid-nineteenth century to the mid-twentieth century, which included the dramatic Dust Bowl event. Some narratives were progressive, others declinist. The former tended to depreciate the Indians' managed prairies as a 'stagnant pool' or 'inhabited wilderness' and viewed wheatfields and railways as improvement; the latter insisted that the Great Plains could not support the demands of greedy settlers and capitalists. The former front-staged settlers' efforts and technologies to tame a resistant and unproductive nature, while the latter emphasised the need for state-led sound ecological management, exemplified by the Dust Bowl.

Similarly, writing the history of the Earth and its inhabitants is always telling a story, a narrative. This entails:

- attributing a certain value to the state of the things at the beginning and at the end of the story;
- selecting a focus and a 'framing' that highlights some actors and phenomena while leaving others in the shadows;

- putting time into sequences, pinpointing certain periods, turning points and key forces, while downplaying others; and
- all this constituting a dramaturgy with implicit or explicit causal factors, with implicit or explicit moral lessons.

If nations, races and classes have for a long time been the objects of countless narratives, the Anthropocene has become, as we shall see, the object of various 'geo-stories', to use the term coined by Latour (2013). Anthropocene science is much more than just stories, but it is stories too. The very first Anthropocene papers from Paul Crutzen in 2000 and 2002 contained also a narrative about how 'we', 'humanity', got here. Steffen et al. (2011a) proposed both a scientific characterisation of the Anthropocene and an explicit historical perspective. Following natural scientists' pioneering narratives, historians, philosophers, social scientists, journalists, politicians, think-tanks and activists have woven stories of the Anthropocene. Each tells a tale of 'how we got here', containing (in the double meaning of the word, allowing and framing) a narrative about the future, about the actors, issues and solutions are most relevant. Here I will examine four grand narratives of the Anthropocene: (1) the naturalist narrative, currently the mainstream one; (2) the post-nature narrative; (3) the eco-catastrophist narrative; and 4) the eco-Marxist narrative.

From hunter-gatherers to global geological force: the naturalist narrative

At the heart of the publications by leading natural scientists such as Paul Crutzen and Will Steffen, as well as in historical writings from John McNeill and Dipesh Chakrabarty, lies a particular storytelling that has now become the dominant Anthropocene discourse in the mainstream scientific and media arenas (Crutzen 2002; Steffen et al. 2011a, 2011b). This story line – widely echoed in popular books and magazines – may be summarised as follows:

> Since about 1800, 'we', the human species, have inadvertently altered the Earth system at a geological scale. *Anthropos* did so through three stages that can best be documented through quantitative global environmental data. The key causal forces are population growth, economic growth and expansion of international exchange. But a revolution (to be compared only to the Copernican or Darwinian revolutions) occurred recently: Earth system scientists have made *anthropos* aware, at last, of the danger. And, if only policy-makers would act on the basis of sound science, these scientists have the knowledge to lead humanity towards a sustainable future.

This narrative entails four key interrelated claims: (1) the front-staging of 'the human species' as the undifferentiated causal force changing the Earth; (2) the recency of environmental consciousness thanks to Earth monitoring science, breaking with centuries of a modern dark age of unconscious impacts; and (3) the erasure of civil society and laypeople as producers of environmental knowledge and solutions, associated with a self-celebration of scientists as shepherds of humankind and of Earth and the advocacy of more science and green technologies to save the planet.

Who is the anthropos of the Anthropocene?

The mainstream narrative of the Anthropocene is straightforward: this is the story of a species that evolved 'from hunter-gatherers to global geologic force' (Steffen et al. 2011b, 741). The 'human–environment interaction' is said to have started 'a few million years ago' when an early *Homo* genus mastered fire and tools allowing for a protein-rich diet that 'gave humans the largest brain-to-body ratio of any animal on the Earth' (Steffen et al. 2011a, 846). That paved the way for the emergence of language and civilisation. But, the story continues, 'the human enterprise' still had little impact on Earth until the end of the eighteenth century when the massive use of fossil fuels transformed the atmosphere, oceans and climate at a global scale. This new energy source increased immensely humankind's power to transform the ecosystems of the world and the vital biogeochemical cycles, provoking a geological derailment of our planet, the more so since the post-1945 'Great Acceleration'. After having been an unconscious 'telluric force' in the first two centuries of the Anthropocene, humankind must now enter a wiser era of 'planetary stewardship'. To help and light up this new path to come, the story goes on:

> Understanding the trajectory of the human enterprise from our long past as hunter-gathers to the Great Acceleration and into the twenty-first century provides an essential context for the transformation from resource exploitation toward stewardship of the Earth System.
> (Steffen et al. 2011b, 746; see also Chakrabarty 2009)

In this Grand Narrative 1, the Anthropocene is therefore more than the name of an epoch in which humankind has become a geological force (the naming practice is an anomaly in the stratigraphic nomenclature: until now, geological divisions were named after their main flora and fauna composition, not after any causal agent). The Anthropocene is not only 'Man's' moment in the history of the Earth; it is also the species' moment in the understanding of human history. A biological category, the 'species' or the 'population', rather than specific social groups bearing situated cultural values and taking particular socio-economic and technical decisions, is elevated to a causal explanatory category in the understanding of human history. A landmark Anthropocene article contains no less than 103 uses of 'Mankind', 'humankind', 'humans', 'humanity', 'our species' or the adjective 'human' – as in 'human influence', 'human enterprise' and so on (Steffen et al. 2011a). This framing of history as the ambivalent odyssey of Man from hunter-gatherer to telluric force, as the epic confrontation between the 'human species' and the 'Earth system', has impressed influential scholars in the humanities and social sciences. Typical of the current geological turn, John McNeill's pioneering and outstanding environmental history of the twentieth century, *Something New Under the Sun*, allocates no more than 30 of 420 pages to 'ideas and politics', while describing at length transformations of the atmosphere, biosphere and other components of the Earth system (McNeill 2000). Similarly, another major historian, Dipesh Chakrabarty, has crowned the biological 'species' (the word appears 51 times in his *Critical Inquiry* article; Chakrabarty 2009) and 'population' categories as the major ones in writing 'the history through which we have evolved to be the dominant species of the planet' (Chakrabarty 2014, 132). In the story of a global 'we', humans – 'thanks to our numbers, the burning of fossil fuel, and other related activities – have become a geological agent on the planet' (Chakrabarty 2009, 209), a story that yields to the Anthropocene's official and naturalistic grand narrative of an undifferentiated humanity uniformly concerned by and responsible for global environmental change.

Clearly, the Anthropocene (which, Chakrabarty noted, annihilates the modern natural history/human history disjunction) disproves human exemptionalism, the nature/culture dualism framing nature as 'a domain of objects that were subject to autonomous laws that formed a background against which the arbitrariness of human activities could exert its many-faceted fascination' (Descola 2013), and the social-only conception of society, each of which have dominated the humanities and social sciences since the dawn of western industrial modernity, and represent cultural drivers of the advent of the Anthropocene. But should we throw out the humanities' baby – its sophisticated critical conceptual apparatus – with the industrial-modern bath water, as the naturalist narrative does?

The naturalising, species-centred Narrative 1 obscures the asymmetries among humans *about* nature – unequal access to environmental goods and exposure to environmental bads – and *through* nature – technical systems organise energy and material flows which co-produce a certain kind of 'second', transformed, nature together with a certain kind of social order, entailing unequal social, racial, gender and geopolitical relations. They are overlooked as secondary compared to the global ecological crisis and the sublime of the Anthropocene's politics of scale. However, key researches in political ecology, environmental history, ecological economics and other interdisciplinary environmental studies have illuminated these socio-ecological asymmetries and how they can generate development pathways that are both ecologically unsustainable and socially unequal (Pomeranz 2000; Peet, Robbins and Watts 2010; Hornborg 2013). In neglecting this evidence and subsuming differentiated environmental responsibilities and sufferings into an undifferentiated 'we, the human species', Narrative 1 has been criticised as an ideology telling a geo-story as if 'human impact' on the Earth were not the result of technical, cultural and economic choices made (unevenly) by specific social groups, organisations and institutions. Thus

> the Anthropocene might be a useful concept and narrative for polar bears and amphibians and birds who want to know what species is wreaking such havoc on their habitats, but alas, they lack the capacity to scrutinize and

stand up to human actions. Within the human kingdom, on the other hand, species-thinking on climate change is conducive to mystification and political paralysis.

(Malm and Hornborg 2014, 6)

Indeed, a serious analysis of the causal chain that led to the current climate disruption cannot separate the curve of greenhouse gas emissions from the historical making of a certain kind of social order, one that entails power asymmetries with a small percentage of humans, a few countries and a few companies accounting for most emissions. It is a social order with a specific kind of political system (cf. the notion of 'carbon democracy', Mitchell 2011) and with those people most affected having had no voice in the economic and technical decision-making that shifted the Earth into the Anthropocene. Narrative 1 tends to explain the current geological shift as an unintentional effect of the 'enterprises' of a black-boxed undifferentiated species, a consequence originally of the human mastery of the fire some hundred thousand years ago, or even – the naturalisation of the Anthropocene being here pushed to its outer limits – of 'the planet's own pyrophytic tendencies', the Earth's own 'combustive imperative' of which 'the recent propensity to tap into sedimented and fossilised biomass is the latest' (Clark 2012, 269).

Clearly, a smarter and subtler Anthropocene studies curriculum is to be recommended, if not for polar bears then at least for those humans who seek scientifically more explanatory (and politically more helpful) socio-ecological dynamics than the black box of the 'human species'. In such a curriculum, the 'anthropos' that triggered and triggers the Anthropocene is not a merely biological agent but the product of complex belief systems, socio-technical trajectories and political–economical dynamics.

A new global environmental consciousness?

'We are the first generation with the knowledge of how our activities influence the Earth System' (Steffen et al. 2011b, 749). So goes the standard narrative: our forefathers embarked on the industrial revolution, the fossil fuel age, the age of empire and the atomic age without knowing the global environmental consequences. Even in the decades after the Second World War 'the emerging global environmental problems were largely ignored' (Steffen et al. 2011a, 850). Our allegedly recent and 'growing awareness of human impact on the environment at the global scale' is an essential trait of the third stage of the Anthropocene (Steffen et al. 2011a, 856). 'By changing the environment we have *unknowingly* declared war on Gaia', as James Lovelock puts it (2006, 13, my emphasis). Grand Narrative 1 declares: 'Earth, forgive us. Once we ignored you, but now we know.' Social theorists such as Ulrich Beck and Anthony Giddens have also yielded to this progressist storyline – from darkness to light, from simple modernity to a second, reflexive modernity.

Recent historical evidence shows that past societies were neither unknowing nor unreflexive; nor were they free from risk controversies about the global environmental impact of their activities. First, right after the Second World

War, the rational management of the biosphere became a concern in bestselling books. It was also a major geopolitical and Cold War issue (Robertson 2012; Bonneuil and Mahrane 2014). Secondly, the age of empires was not a *tabula rasa* of environmental knowledge and warnings. Western elites, seeking to establish their control over the globe – their 'civilising mission' – bemoaned the inefficient and destructive use of the environment by indigenous people and colonised peasant communities (Bonneuil 1997; Drayton 2000; Anker 2001). Western science promised both a more intensive and a more sustainable use of the world's resources. 'Faced with the consequences of over-exploitation, the "civilized" become aware of their abuses and embark on "rational" exploitation' argued Pierre Clerget in 1912 in *L'exploitation rationnelle du globe* (Bonneuil 1997, 77). It was on the basis of his allegedly superior environmental reflexivity and scientific mastery of nature that the white man justified the 'rational exploitation of the globe'. This green, 'sustainable' imperialism was sometimes contested by rural communities in colonial peripheries (Guha 1989a) as well as by some occidental scientists. In 1913 the Director of the Paris Museum of Natural History asked: 'Do we have the right to monopolize the Earth for us alone and to destroy for our own profit to the detriment of generations to come' (Perrier 1913, 210).

Thirdly, global environmental knowledge, reflexivity and controversy were present at the very beginnings of industrialism. In the late eighteenth century a theory of global climatic changed driven by human action (deforestation) was well established. In 1778 Buffon observed that 'the entire face of the Earth bears the imprint of Man's power', which was for him good news since Man, through wise management of the Earth, will 'modify the influences of the climate he lives in and set, so to say, the temperature to the convenient point' (quoted in Bonneuil and Fressoz 2015, 18). But in a context of rapid deforestation and environmental degradation in Western Europe and its American colonies, other scientists predicted less controlled and less favourable global climatic changes. From 1780 to 1840, their work was widely debated and stimulated government initiatives and parliamentary debates (Locher and Fressoz 2012). The early socialist thinker Charles Fourier was not alone when he argued in 1821 that industrial capitalism, if unbound, would alter the entire Earth and its climate (Bonneuil and Fressoz 2015, 227–9). The dawn of the Anthropocene was characterised by a strong reflexivity and knowledge of the intricate links between human activities, human health, good government and the environment (Fressoz, this volume).

In sum, the standard narrative purporting that until recent decades there existed only knowledge about local environmental impacts but no systematic knowledge of global environmental changes does not hold serious historical investigation. If we cease to view the shift into the Anthropocene as an unconscious process, our task is not to understand how global environmental knowledge progressed from original darkness to present awareness, but rather how we entered the Anthropocene *in spite of* rich and global environmental reflexivity. Echoing the growing body of work on 'agnotology' in science studies, the quarter-millennium-long history of the Anthropocene might then be better understood as the history of political and techno-scientific strategies to govern and channel fears and oppositions, and to disinhibit Anthropocenic agency from initial environmental cautiousness (Bonneuil and Fressoz 2015). For sure, scientific knowledge of the Earth as a system has advanced. But in erasing the environmental knowledge and intense socio-ecological struggles of the dawn of industrial times, Grand Narrative 1 depoliticises our past *and present* situation.

A tale of scientific shepherds and green geo-technologies

The view of science slowly lifting the veil of past environmental blindness that pervades Anthropocene Narrative 1 has powerful political implications. It stages science as the *deus ex machina* that was not part of the cultural–political–economical nexus that made the Anthropocene, but which will now guide humankind and save the planet. As Crutzen remarks:

> A daunting task lies ahead for scientists and engineers to guide society towards environmentally sustainable management during the era of the Anthropocene. This will require appropriate human behaviour at all scales, and may well involve internationally accepted, large-scale geo-engineering projects, for instance to 'optimize' climate.
>
> (Crutzen 2002, 23)

This narrative pictures society as ignorant, passive and stuck in 'cognitive dissonance'. Key scientific publications carefully avoid reference to any socio-environmental struggle past or present (such as anti-extractivist campaigns from Alberta to Amazonia) and to any bottom-up initiative (such as the Transition Town, Degrowth or *Buen vivir* movements), as if environmental awareness, initiatives and solutions were only on the side of science rather than flourishing in civil societies. In this telling, the solutions are clear – scientists must take the lead and conjure up new green technologies.

> Given the nature of the problems arising in the Anthropocene, it is little wonder that political leaders, policymakers and managers are struggling to find effective global solutions. There are, however, some innovative approaches. Active adaptive management . . . early warning systems . . . model[ing] complex system dynamics . . . geo-engineering [sulphur particles].
>
> (Steffen et al. 2011a, 856–9)

In short, Narrative 1 tends to reproduce the grand narrative of modernity, that of Man moving from environmental obliviousness to environmental consciousness, of Man equaling Nature's power, of Man repairing Nature.

Repairing Frankenstein's monster: the post-nature grand narrative

Promoted by a heterogeneous network of post-modern, eco-constructivist philosophers, natural scientists, and pro-industry, techno-utopian think-tanks, Grand

Narrative 2 heralds the Anthropocene as the end of Nature. Its more ardent advocates promise a world without nature in a 'good Anthropocene'.

While modernity had promised to emancipate society from nature's determinism, the Anthropocene proclaims the inescapable immersion of human destiny in the great natural cycles of the Earth, and the meeting of the temporalities of short-term human history and long-term Earth history that had been viewed as separated for the last two centuries. This reading argues for the impossibility of continuing to separate 'nature' and 'society'. It shakes the whole architecture of our modern knowledge system and our higher education because of the latters' big divide between the 'two cultures' of (anti-social) natural sciences and (anti-natural) social sciences and humanities.

Narrative 2 shares – and even radicalises – the Promethean tropes of the first grand narrative as well as the belief that environmental awareness or reflexivity is very recent, as if in the past the moderns did not really understand the entangled nature of their interactions with nature. But it departs from Grand Narrative 1 in viewing the Anthropocene as a story of feedback loops, connections, networks and hybridity that cut across most of modernity's boundaries. The new epoch is celebrated as the end of the separation between fact and values constitutive of modern science. It is the end of certainty and the rise of risk, uncertainty and controversy, of socially robust 'mode 2' science. Latour even made us realise that we have never been modern and that science in action is always the negotiation of new hybrid arrangements of nature and society (Latour 2004). By acknowledging our thousands of entanglements with nature, the story goes, our modernity, once non-reflexive about its risks and environmental impacts, becomes 'reflexive', as Beck and Giddens put it. Our knowledge is progressing, as in Narrative 1, so this story is nothing but another avatar of the grand narrative of progress and enlightenment (Fressoz 2007).

At a deeper level, the Anthropocene is welcomed as the end of nature itself. In Latour's philosophically sophisticated version, this means the end of 'Nature 1', uniform and history-less from the atom to the cosmos (Latour 2013). Less sophisticated perspectives argue that there is no such thing as 'wilderness', for humans have always shaped nature. The critique of 'wilderness' previously came from indigenous rights activists and postcolonial and postmodern social scientists (Guha 1989b; Cronon 1996; Descola 2013). Now it is voiced by influential natural scientists and industry representatives. For Peter Kareiva, Chief Scientist for the Nature Conservancy, and his co-authors: 'One need not be a postmodernist to understand that the concept of Nature, as opposed to the physical and chemical workings of natural systems, has always been a human construction, shaped and designed for human ends' (Marvier et al. 2012).

Once made mainstream, the idea that external or pristine nature does not exist and that nature is always a cultural and technological construct has become the battle flag of:

> a new environmental movement – sometimes called eco-modernism, other times eco-pragmatism – that offers a positive vision of our environmental future,

rejects Romantic ideas about nature as unscientific and reactionary, and embraces advanced technologies, including taboo ones, like nuclear power and genetically modified organisms, as necessary to reducing humankind's ecological footprint.

(Shellenberger and Nordhaus 2014)

The end of nature thesis, accusing earlier environmentalism of romantically ide-alising a pristine nature that exists apart from people, and of irrationally rejecting technology as a fix to save the planet, has now become a major storyline for a vari-ety of constructivist-demiurgic projects – the transhumanist project to re-engineer the human species, the (Marxist) accelerationist project to unleash technology's productive forces from capitalist and neoliberal constraints, and the geo-constructivist project of eco-pragmatists, notably at the Breakthrough Institute, to achieve a technical stewardship of the Earth as a whole (Neyrat 2015).

In Narrative 2 eco-pragmatists don't dispute the ecological disruptions associ-ated with the Anthropocene. But nor do they see them as a failure of the modern project to control nature. Several eco-pragmatists promote the 'early Anthropocene thesis' asserting that humans took control of the planet several thousand years ago with the development of agriculture, hence downplaying the radical shift associ-ated with the industrial mode of production and consumption (Shellenberger and Nordhaus 2011, 10). As the eco-pragmatist geographer Erle Ellis argues:

> Recognition of human's huge and sustained influence is now leading to a wholesale rethinking of ecological science and conservation that moves away from humans as recent destroyers of a pristine nature and towards humanity's role as sustained and permanent stewards of the biosphere.
>
> (Ellis 2013, 32)

So eco-pragmatists do not see the Anthropocene as demanding more humility and caution towards the Earth. Rather, they radicalise the Baconian project to artificialise evermore the Earth. In his book *The God Species*, Mark Lynas declares: 'Nature no longer runs the Earth. We do. It is our choice what happens here' (Lynas 2011, 8). For Grand Narrative 2, Nature is dead; everything is human-constructed. There is no alterity, and no limit to the cornucopian dream to engineer the planet into a New Atlantis (Hamilton 2013). As Erle Ellis proclaims: 'We will be proud of the planet we create in the Anthropocene' (quoted in Hamilton 2013, 204). In this narrative, 'we' (the same undifferentiated 'anthropos' as in the mainstream narrative) are the pilots of a hybrid techno-nature.

While criticising the modernisation project and viewing the Anthropocene as a refutation of modernity, Bruno Latour, together with Breakthrough Institute's eco-pragmatists, urges us to 'love our monsters'. He reads Mary Shelley's *Frankenstein* not as a cautionary tale against technological hubris, but rather against irrational fears in the face of technology's side effects. Dr Frankenstein failed not because he created a monster but because he fled in horror instead of repairing and improving him: 'The sin is not to wish to have dominion over nature', goes the story, 'but to believe that this dominion means emancipation and not attachment' (Latour 2011, 24).

Rather than departing from the ideology of dominating nature by technology – a proposition dismissed as 'nihilistic ecotheology' by Shellenberger and Nordhaus (2011, 13) – or appealing to the precautionary principle – portrayed as a 'legal, epistemological monster' by Latour (2011, 23) – this reading normalises technological risks as a necessary part of the human condition.

> Each new act of salvation will result in new unintended consequences, which will in turn require new acts of salvation. What we call 'saving the earth' will, in practice, require creating and recreating it again and again for as long as humans inhabit it.
>
> (Shellenberger and Nordhaus 2011, 9–10)

The post-nature narrative is therefore paradoxical: in claiming the end of nature as an external thing it abandons the central cosmo-vision of western modernity. It challenges the modern conception of freedom as an escape from nature and its limits. From this perspective, Bruno Latour, Donna Haraway, Vinciane Despret, Peter Sloterdijk and Isabelle Stengers, among others, have opened important philosophical avenues for elaborating on how to rethink freedom beyond unbound-ness, how to give political existence to the non-humans we care for and are bound to.

But in refashioning nature as a flexible hybrid amenable to further market and technological deconstruction-reconstruction, and in claiming that 'we' understand better the very nature of nature in a way past societies could not see, the post-nature narrative intensifies and accelerates modernity. It constitutes the new spirit of modernity, based on a hybridist, relational and connectionist ontology rather than a substantial one (Bonneuil 2015).

Tipping points and dystopian collapse: the eco-catastrophist narrative

A third grand narrative may be called eco-catastrophist. Rather than Gaia, its mythological figure of the Earth is Medea, she who went so far as to kill her own children when she was betrayed by her husband Jason. The myth provides an analogy for the collapse of industrial civilisation, with humans devoured by the Earth they betrayed. In the telling of Grand Narrative 3, the move into the Anthropocene is a long story of unsustainable practices, resource depletion, transgressed 'planetary boundaries', and increased complexity creating new vulnerabilities paving the way to tipping points and a planetary state shift (Barnosky et al. 2012; Diamond 2005; Tainter 1988).

The eco-catastrophist narrative views the Anthropocene as an age in which modernity's project of indefinite growth and progress hits the wall of the planet's finitude. Earlier eco-catastrophist warnings, such as the *Limits to Growth* report of 1972, focused on resource depletion, on the limits of the Earth in terms of *stocks*. But there are on Earth enough fossil resources to warm the planet more than 12°C in 2300, as in IPCC's worst-case scenario. Earth systems science and Anthropocene research have therefore added new arguments focusing on *flow* limits of the Earth, that is, the limited capacity of Earth biogeochemical processes to buffer human-accelerated cycles of carbon, water, phosphorus, nitrogen and so on.

This reflects a move towards a more dynamic systems thinking perspective from ecology and Earth system science. The eco-catastrophist narrative draws on these new approaches, developed in the wake of Canadian ecologist C. S. Holling's work on the cyclical development of ecosystems – growth, collapse and reorganisation. Resilience is the capacity of a system to endure such processes without losing its key features and functions. Articulated by mainstream institutions such as the Resilience Alliance, this systems perspective has also been appropriated by socio–ecological movements such as permaculture, Transition Towns and the Degrowth movement. Whether articulated by scientists, policy makers or activists, a feature of this discourse is its non-linear and non-progressist conceptualisation of time and history. While Grand Narratives 1 and 2 rest on a progressist regime of historicity, the eco-catastrophic narrative depicts us not as moving towards the better (better lives, better knowledge, better dominion over nature) but towards limits, tipping points, collapse, violence and wars. In this perspective, contrary to the bright future promised by progressive ideologies of all kinds (from liberals to Marxists, see Hamilton, this volume), political discourse should not avoid speaking collapse to the masses (Hamilton 2010). Acknowledging the possibility of a collapse of the industrial way of life and accepting the limits to growth becomes, in Grand Narrative 3, an opportunity for a more participatory politics and a new post-growth resilient society where life would be based on a lower and simpler material and energetic base, but with more enjoyable, meaningful and egalitarian communities (Semal, this volume). Unlike Narratives 1 and 2, the third tends to look to the local level, where communities make life together, rather than the global one, as the relevant political level to democratically plan such a transition (Hopkins 2008).

While drawing on the first two narratives' scientific knowledge about the state shift of the Anthropocene, and harnessing in a similar way the authority of science to ground its warnings, the eco-catastrophist narrative departs from their faith in new greener technologies to save the planet. It argues for the urgent need to radically change the dominant ways of living, consuming and producing, and rejects the belief in technological fixes that would save the planet within the frame of an unchanged socio-economic system. In the wake of Lewis Mumford, Ivan Illich and E. F. Schumacher's proposals for democratic technologies, it puts forward low-tech – though high-intelligence – solutions (such as permaculture, economic re-localisation, and local community-owned renewable energy) over high-tech solutions (such as transgenic crops, nanotechnology and geoengineering). In the eco-catastrophist Anthropocene narrative, science and technology alone cannot 'save the planet'; environmental reflexivity and social innovations will rather emerge from a dynamic civil society (Hopkins 2008).

The Capitalocene: the eco-Marxist narrative

Grand Narrative 4 can be called eco-Marxist. While Marx theorised on the first contradiction of capitalism, its inability to reproduce the labour force, the eco-Marxist narrative sees the Anthropocene as a result of a second contradiction of capitalism, its inability to maintain nature. The Anthropocene is therefore a story of the unsustainable metabolism of the capitalist 'world-system' within the Earth system (Foster et al. 2010). The concept of world-system was elaborated in the 1970s by Immanuel Wallerstein to account for both the internationalisation of the economy and the asymmetries and division of labour within it (Wallerstein 2004). Rather than the species, *capital* is seen as the driver. Indeed, the value of capital has increased about 134-fold since 1700 while human population has increased about 10-fold (Bonneuil and Fressoz 2015). According to Grand Narrative 4, instead of undifferentiated population and economic growth, processes of dispossession and commodification associated with the logic of capitalist expansion, along with the mechanisms of imperial domination, are the essential causal forces of the geological turn. Some prefer to call the new epoch the 'Capitalocene' and consider it started in sixteenth century with European capitalist expansion (Moore 2015).

It is well known that the rise of industrial capitalism is correlated with a divergence in wealth between nations and social groups. The world's poorest 20 per cent received 4.7 per cent of world income in 1820, but only 2.2 per cent in 1992. Over the same period the share of the top 10 per cent jumped from 43 to 53 per cent (Bourguignon and Morrisson 2002). But is there any causal link between the history of this global economic divergence and the history of the human species as a telluric force? Most natural and social scientists voicing Narratives 1, 2 or 3 have tended to focus only on the final and undifferentiated 'human impact' while implicitly 'black-boxing' the second thread of history. Among them, Dipesh Chakrabarty's argument has the merit of explicitly separating social history from the ecological disruptions of the Earth system.

> It is, ironically, thanks to the poor – that is, to the fact that development is uneven and unfair – that we do not put out even larger quantities of greenhouse gases into the atmosphere than we actually do. Thus, logically speaking, the climate crisis is not inherently a result of economic inequalities – it is really a matter of the quantity of greenhouses gases we put out into the atmosphere that in itself is indifferent to human dramas. Those who connect climate change exclusively to historical origins/formations of income-inequalities in the modern world raise valid questions about historical inequalities; but a reduction of the problem of climate change to that of capitalism . . . only blinds us to questions of human agency that climate scientists – working with visions of pasts and futures on much larger scales – often bring to the fore: our agency as a species or a geophysical force over a period of time much longer than that of capitalism. If we see climate change primarily as a symptom of what's wrong with the capitalist mode of production . . . this analytical strategy is ultimately blind to the inter-twining of human histories with the larger history of the planet and of our place in that history.
>
> (Chakrabarty 2014, 123–4)

Is the Earth–humankind drama separated from and indifferent to the intra-human drama? Paradoxically, this 'indifferentialist' view re-enacts precisely the modern divide between the 'natural' and the 'social' that the Anthropocene disproved. The eco-Marxist narrative emphasises that the technical, economic and social trajectories taken by the core countries of the world-system could not have occurred had they not benefitted from unequal exchange with the dominated regions. Economic historian Kenneth Pomeranz's path-breaking work (2000) has shown that the control of millions of American 'ghost hectares' – the slave-produced cotton imported by England in 1830 that saved 9.3 million domestic hectares of pasture and hay for production of an equivalent amount of fibre from sheep's wool – played a major role in Britain's economic take-off. In 1850, exchanging on the world market £1,000 worth of cotton manufactures for £1,000 worth of raw cotton, Britain gained over 46 per cent in terms of embodied labour and about sixty times in terms of land area (Hornborg 2013, 85–91). Extending this idea of an unequal embodied land exchange, other works have documented the ecological debt of western industrial countries, an 'unequal ecological exchange' through which, in the last two or three centuries, the core countries of the world-system imported more embodied land, more high-quality energy and more material from periphery countries than they exported to them, while exporting more environmental load, waste and entropia to them (Fischer-Kowalski et al. 2014; Tukker et al. 2014; Moore 2015). These works, combining the world-system perspective (understanding uneven global intra-human relations) and Earth system perspectives (tracing and quantifying global material and energy flows in the Anthropocene), suggest that the category of world-system might be more fertile than the species category for productive interdisciplinary work between natural and social sciences.

Conclusion

The point here is not to choose the single best grand narrative for our geohistorical shift. (One could add an eco-feminist perspective as well as many subaltern and non-western narratives.) Each illuminates different aspects in valuable ways and each has its limitations. We need a plurality of narratives from many voices and many places, rather than a single grand narrative from nowhere, from space or from the species. Putting the array of narratives on the table in a reflexive and comparative manner helps to think our new geo-historical epoch rather than being predetermined as Anthropocene (species) subjects. It opens the black boxes of the Anthropocene discourse and repoliticises them.

Diffracting histories and stories helps us reflect on 'who we want to inherit from' (as Isabelle Stengers would put it) in the geo-historical drama of the last quarter-millennium. Which imaginary of nature and of the Earth do we highlight as scientists and scholars? Which subjectivation of the 'anthropos' are we promoting? Are 'anthropos' passive and non-knowing subjects who need to be enlightened and overseen by a techno-scientific elite or are they concerned and active Earth commoners who hold in their reflexive minds, in their creative hands, and in their socio-environmental struggles and initiatives some of the 'solutions' for lives of dignity in the Anthropocene? What role for science, technology and the market do we insert into our stories about the Anthropocene? The various Anthropocene narratives we tell are performative; they preclude or promote some kinds of collective action rather than others, and so they make a difference to the becoming of the Earth.

References

Anker P 2001 *Imperial Ecology: Environmental Order in the British Empire, 1895–1945* Harvard University Press, Cambridge MA

Barnosky A D et al. 2012 Approaching a state shift in Earth's biosphere *Nature* 486 52–8

Bonneuil C 1997 Crafting and Disciplining the Tropics: Plant Science in the French Colonies in Krige J and Pestre D eds *Science in the Twentieth Century* Harwood Academic, Amsterdam 77–96

Bonneuil C 2015 Une nature liquide? Les discours de la biodiversité dans le nouvel esprit du capitalisme, in Thomas F and Boisvert eds *Le pouvoir de la biodiversité* Presses de l'IRD, Bondy

Bonneuil C and Fressoz J-B 2015 *The Shock of the Anthropocene: The Earth, History and Us* Verso, London

Bonneuil C and Mahrane Y 2014 Gouverner la biosphère in Pestre D ed *Gouverner le progrès, gouverner ses dégâts* La Découverte, Paris 133–69

Bourguignon F and Morrisson C 2002 Inequality among world citizens: 1820–1992 *American Economic Review* 92(4) 727–44

Chakrabarty D 2009 The climate of history: Four theses *Critical Inquiry* 35(2) 197–222

Chakrabarty D 2014 Quelques failles dans la pensée sur le changement climatique, in Hache E ed *De l'univers clos au monde infini* Dehors, Paris 107–46

Clark N 2012 Rock, Life, Fire: Speculative Geophysics and the Anthropocene *Oxford Literary Review* 34(2) 259–76

Cronon W 1996 The trouble with wilderness: Or getting back to the wrong nature, in Cronon W ed *Uncommon Ground: Rethinking the Human Place in Nature* Norton, New York 69–80

Crutzen P J 2002 Geology of mankind *Nature* 415 23

Davis M 2001 *Late Victorian Holocausts: El Niño famines and the making of the Third World* Verso, London

Descola P 2013 *Beyond Nature and Culture* University of Chicago Press, Chicago

Diamond J 2005 *Collapse: How Societies Choose to Fail or Succeed* Viking Penguin, New York

Drayton R H 2000 *Nature's Government: Science, Imperial Britain, and the 'Improvement' of the World* Yale University Press, New Haven

Ellis E C 2013 Using the planet *Global Change* 81 32–5

Fischer-Kowalski M Krausmann F and Pallua I 2014 A sociometabolic reading of the Anthropocene *The Anthropocene Review* 1(1) 8–33

Foster J Clark B and York R 2010 *The Ecological Rift: Capitalism's War on the Earth* Monthly Review Press, New York

Fressoz J-B 2007 Beck back in the 19th century: Towards a genealogy of risk society *History and Technology* 23(4) 333–50

Guha R 1989a *The Unquiet Woods: Ecological Change and Peasant Resistance in Himalaya* University of California Press, Berkeley, CA

Guha R 1989b Radical American environmentalism and wilderness preservation: A third world critique *Environmental Ethics* 11 71–83

Hamilton C 2010 *Requiem for a Species: Why We Resist the Truth About Climate Change* Earthscan, London

Hamilton C 2013 *Earthmasters: The Dawn of the Age of Climate Engineering* Yale University Press, London

Hopkins R 2008 *The Transition Handbook* Greenbooks, Foxhole

Hornborg A and Crumley C eds 2006 *The World System and the Earth System* Left Coast Press, Walnut Creek, CA

Hornborg A 2013 *Global Ecology and Unequal Exchange* Routledge, London

Latour B 2004 *Politics of Nature: How to Bring the Sciences into Democracy* Harvard University Press, Cambridge, Mass.

Latour B 2013 *Facing Gaia* (http://www.bruno-latour.fr/sites/default/files/downloads/GIFFORD-SIX-LECTURES_1.pdf) Accessed 25 October 2014

Latour B 2011 Love your monsters, in Shellenberger M and Nordhaus T eds *Love your Monsters: Post-environmentalism and the Anthropocene* Breakthrough Institute, San Francisco 17–25

Locher F and Fressoz J-B 2012 The frail climate of modernity. A history of environmental reflexivity *Critical Inquiry* 38(3) 579–98

Lovelock J 2006 *The Revenge of Gaïa* Allen Lane, London

Lynas M 2011 *The God Species* Fourth Estate, London

Malm A and Hornborg A 2014 The geology of mankind? A critique of the Anthropocene narrative *The Anthropocene Review* 1(1) 62–9

Marvier M Lalasz R and Kareiva P 2012 Conservation in the Anthropocene (http://thebreakthrough.org/index.php/journal/past-issues/issue-2/conservation-in-the-anthropocene/) Accessed 25 October 2014

McNeill J 2000 *Something New Under the Sun: An Environmental History of the Twentieth-century World* Norton, New York

Merchant C 1980 *The Death of Nature: Women, Ecology and the Scientific Revolution* HarperCollins, San Francisco

Mitchell T 2011 *Carbon Democracy: Political Power in the Age of Oil* Verso, London

Moore J 2015 *Capitalism in the Web of Life* Verso, London

Neyrat F 2015 *Enquête sur la part inconstructible de la Terre* (forthcoming)

Peet R Robbins P and Watts M 2010 *Global Political Ecology* Routledge, London

Perrier E 1913 Presidential address *Bulletin de la Société nationale d'acclimatation de France* 60

Pomeranz K 2000 *A Great Divergence: China, Europe, and the Making of the Modern World Economy* Princeton University Press, Princeton

Robertson T 2012 *The Malthusian Moment: Global Population Growth and the Birth of American Environmentalism* Rutgers University Press, New Brunswick

Shellenberger M and Nordhaus T 2014 On Becoming an Ecomodernist. A Positive Vision of Our Environmental Future (http://thebreakthrough.org/index.php/voices/michael-shellenberger-and-ted-nordhaus/on-becoming-an-ecomodernist) Accessed 25 October 2014

Shellenberger M and Nordhaus T eds 2011 *Love your Monsters: Postenvironmentalism and the Anthropocene* Breakthrough Institute, San Francisco

Steffen W Crutzen P and McNeill J 2007 The Anthropocene: Are humans now overwhelming the great forces of nature? *Ambio* 36(8) 614–21

Steffen W Grinevald J Crutzen P and McNeill J 2011a The Anthropocene: Conceptual and historical perspectives *Philosophical Transactions of the Royal Society A* 369(1938) 842–67

Steffen W et al. 2011b The Anthropocene: From global change to planetary stewardship *AMBIO* 40 739–61

Tainter J 1988 *The Collapse of Complex Societies* Cambridge University Press, Cambridge

Tukker A et al. 2014 *The Global Resource Footprint of Nations* (http://exiobase.eu/) Accessed 25 October 2014

Wallerstein I 2004 *World-Systems Analysis: An Introduction* Duke University Press, Durham, NC

3

HUMAN DESTINY IN THE ANTHROPOCENE

Clive Hamilton

Here I put forward eight rhetorical propositions about the Anthropocene and what it means for how we think about the human future.

Proposition 1. Nature has an entirely new character

In all previous instances, transitions from one division to the next in the Geological Time Scale came about because the great forces of nature came together in a particular way, but always unconsciously and unintentionally. In the Anthropocene, the 'human imprint on the global environment has now become so large and active that it rivals some of the great forces of Nature in its impact on the functioning of the Earth system' (Steffen et al. 2011). Unlike geological forces such as weathering, volcanism, asteroid strike, subduction and solar fluxes, this new 'force of Nature' is radically distinct – it contains the element of volition. It expresses will.

Anthropogenic impacts – increases in carbon dioxide in the atmosphere, but also cross-global species invasion, disturbance to the nitrogen cycle and so on – do not just happen but are the consequence, intended or otherwise, of *decisions* taken by human minds. In nature, as we have always understood it, no decisions are made.

If in the Anthropocene humans have invaded the domain of geology we must remind ourselves that the forces at work in geology – physical impacts, chemical reactions, temperature changes and heat conductivity – are forces that behave involuntarily. Humanity is perhaps better described as a *geological power* because we have to consider its ability to make decisions as well as its ability to transform matter. This power as a force injected with *will* is an insight that was turned around by Schiller when he wrote: 'Force is depersonalized will.' Unlike forces of nature, it is a power that can be withheld as well as exercised. In claiming that the geological evolution of the Earth is now infused with human will I am not positing any kind of Teilhardian noösphere; I am saying that, while there is nothing 'behind' the forces of nature (they are just forces), there is something 'behind' human action, will, that can no longer be separated from it in Earth history. This is so even if, as Vernadsky (2005) observed, the riddle of how thought can change material processes remains unsolved.

So for the first time in the Earth's 4.5 billion-year history we have a non-physical force or power mixed in with physical forces. And this new force can be integrated only imperfectly into the system of geodynamics used to explain the geological evolution of the planet. The other forces are, in principle, quantifiable and predictable (notwithstanding quantum mechanics), so that, for example, the next Ice Age is expected to arrive in 50,000 years. The new force can be included only to the extent that human activities are predictable, which lends a new level of unpredictability to the Earth system. (The uncertainty about how this new force will behave is the primary reason for the wide variation in warming projections of IPCC scenarios.) Nevertheless, it now seems certain that as long as humans are on the planet all future epochs, eras, periods and so on will be hybrids of physical forces and this new power. This suggests that modern technological humans should be seen not as a new force to be *added* to the pre-existing natural ones, but as a unique power that in some sense now *infuses* the natural ones and interferes, for good or ill, with their operation.

The inference that the Anthropocene is a profoundly new kind of division in the Geological Time Scale can be reached another way. If the International Commission on Stratigraphy adds the Anthropocene to its geochronology, it will need to decide, on the basis of stratigraphic indicators, whether it is best classified as a geological age, an epoch or a period. Wally Broecker even intimates that it may be an era, the Anthropozoic era (Langmuir and Broecker 2012, 645). Jan Zalasiewicz and his colleagues (2010) suggest that deeming it an epoch – that is, longer than an age but shorter than a period – would be a conservative but appropriate decision; but they go on to add that if society does not respond soon to the signs of climate disruption then it may be necessary to upgrade the Anthropocene from an epoch to a period.

In other words, we are entering a geological episode whose designation depends not only on gathering and evaluating the available data but also on human impacts on the Earth system that *have not yet occurred*. The verdict on the Anthropocene reached by the International Commission on Stratigraphy in the next two or three years could be invalidated not by the *discovery* of new evidence that already exists but by the *generation* of new evidence that will appear in the future. That is impossible for every previous decision concerning the Geological Time Scale.

Proposition 2. Modernity is impossible in the Anthropocene

In 2012 the eminent US climate scientist Kevin Trenberth made a striking statement:

The answer to the oft-asked question of whether an event is caused by climate change is that it is the wrong question. All weather events are affected by climate change because the environment in which they occur is warmer and moister than it used to be.

(Trenberth 2012)

Climate science is now telling us that the modern division of the world into a box marked 'Nature' and one marked 'Human' is no longer tenable. In the climate system the natural and the human are mixed up, not merely added, and their influences cannot be neatly distinguished. Furthermore this is true of the Earth system as a whole, because disturbing the climate inevitably means disturbing all components of the Earth system.

In short, *everything* is now in play. Every cubic metre of air and water, and every hectare of land, now has a human imprint. Just how completely humans have overrun the planet is illustrated by the following astounding fact. Imagine we could weigh all of the vertebrate animals on the Earth's land surfaces. The creatures can be divided into three classes: *wild animals*, covering everything from elephants, camels and polar bears to rabbits, kangaroos and wolves; *domesticated animals*, including cows, sheep, pigs, cats and dogs; and *human beings*. If we weighed them all, worked out their mass measured in millions of tonnes, what would be the percentages falling into each of the three classes?

Canadian scientist Vaclav Smil has performed the calculation (Smil 2011). It turns out that (measured in dry weight) humans account for 30 per cent of the total mass of all animals, and domesticated animals account for 67 per cent. That leaves all of the wild animals on the Earth's surface accounting for no more than 3 per cent. In the words of Smil: 'The zoomass of wild vertebrates is now vanishingly small compared to the biomass of domestic animals.' So peering into the box marked 'Nature' will reveal few wild animals, contrary to the image, created by wildlife documentaries, of endless plains teeming with wildebeest.

What was distinctive of the social sciences and humanities that emerged in eighteenth and nineteenth-century Europe was not so much their aspiration to science but their 'social-only' domain of concern. Sociology, psychology, political science, economics, history and philosophy rest on the assumption that the grand and the everyday events of human life take place against a backdrop of a blind and purposeless nature. Only humans have agency. Everything worthy of analysis occurs in the sealed world of 'the social', and where the environment is taken into account – in environmental history, sociology or politics – 'the environment' in question is the *Umwelt*, the natural world 'over there' that surrounds us and sometimes intrudes on our plans, but always remains separate.

Yet a mere 'taking into account' misses the essence of the new epoch. We can no longer draw a diagram with 'Society' nested within a larger circle marked 'Nature'. The point of the announcement in the year 2000 of the Anthropocene's arrival is that we now live in an epoch in which the human inheres in the total functioning of the natural world. Until this fact is internalised, social science and humanities' scholars will fail to understand the politics, sociology or philosophy of climate change in a way that is true to the science.

If our future has become entangled with that of the Earth's geological evolution then, contrary to the modernist faith, it can no longer be maintained that humans make their own history, for the stage on which we make it has now entered into the play as a dynamic and capricious force. And the actors too must be scrutinised afresh. If on the Anthropocene's hybrid Earth it is no longer plausible to characterise humans as the rational animal or as God's chosen creatures or as just another species, what kind of being are we? Suffice it here to say that with climate disruption upon us the appropriate response to the idea of the human as the rational animal is a loud guffaw.

By the same token, the biologistic account of humans as animals with instincts, drives and selfish genes becomes even more indefensible in the Anthropocene because it is precisely because humans are *not* like other animals that the new epoch has arrived. The human has always been the anomaly, the creature both natural and unnatural. The Anthropocene is so momentous because nature's anomaly is now restructuring nature itself.

Proposition 3. Social scientists must become geophysicists

At the 2012 conference of the American Geophysical Union, geophysicist Brad Werner presented a paper with a blunt title: 'Is Earth f**ked?' (Werner 2012). The author is the Director of the Complex Systems Laboratory at the University of California San Diego, and he posed in a formal conference setting the question many at the meeting have for some time been asking in the coffee breaks. His approach to the question of Earth's future has some unnerving implications for social scientists. He is building a dynamic model known as a 'global coupled human–environmental system' (Werner 2012). In addition to the usual kinds of equations capturing elements of the Earth system, the model incorporates the activities of humans represented in a module he calls 'the dominant global culture', which essentially describes the globally integrated system of resource use and waste generation driven by the insatiable need to grow and the political institutions committed to perpetual expansion.

The essential problem for the Earth – for us – is that there is a mismatch between the short timescales of markets and the political systems tied to them, and the much longer timescales that the Earth system needs to accommodate human activity. The climate crisis is upon us not because markets aren't working well enough but because the market system is working too well in accelerating global energy and material cycles. Technological progress and the globalisation of finance, transport and communications have oiled the wheels of the human-willed components of the planetary system, allowing them to accelerate. Put another way, the tempo of the market's metabolism is much faster than that of the Earth system, yet in the Anthropocene they no longer operate independently.

For Werner, all solutions embedded in the dominant culture – including system–compatible ideas like cost–benefit analysis, global agreements, carbon prices and the structure of interest group politicking – cannot slow the human component of the planetary system. Only radical activism that disrupts the dominant culture – including 'protests, blockades and sabotage' – opens up the possibility that the Earth may not be f**ked.

Dipesh Chakrabarty has characterised the Anthropocene as the epoch in which human history and geological history converge (Chakrabarty 2009 and this volume). Now we have in Brad Werner a geoscientist integrating *human* processes with *Earth system* processes to give us a planetary model in which human and geological history rub up against each other. In the Anthropocene, any geoscientist who models an Earth system that excludes humans is stuck in Holocene thinking; and any social scientist who analyses 'human systems' isolated from Earth system processes is stuck in a world of modernity, the world of the epistemological break, that is no longer consistent with scientific understanding.

While social scientists puzzle over the political and social failures that have brought about irretrievable climate disruption, Werner writes: 'It's really a geophysics problem. It's not something that we can just leave to the social scientists or the humanities.' Before the advent of the new geological epoch such a statement would have been preposterous; but now social scientists in the Anthropocene have no choice but to become geophysicists as well.

Karl Marx famously argued that the historical contradictions within the capitalist system become so acute that the pressure for revolution boils over. He claimed that his theory of revolution is 'scientific'. In truth, the mechanisms of social transformation he identified could never follow a foreseeable path in a messy social-only world. Now we have a theory of revolutionary change with a stronger claim to being scientific, a model of geophysical dynamics that incites protests, blockades and sabotage to overthrow the dominant culture, a model that links geophysics to Naomi Klein's call for social disruption (Klein 2014).

Proposition 4. The iron law of progress has been rescinded

If the Holocene's 10,000-year stretch of climatic constancy made civilisations possible, what does it mean for the Holocene to come to an end? What does it mean for humankind to be entering an era of climatic volatility, with a rate of warming rarely matched in the palaeoclimate record? The most immediate implication is that the principal assumption of the contemporary world, that of endless progress, now looks untenable. We are inclined to forget how deeply entrenched this assumption is; it is the grand narrative that will not die, the storyline of daily decision making in public, corporate and private life.

It has often been noted that utopian political movements are a materialised form of the Christian promise of salvation. As Hans Jonas observed, among utopians it did not take long for the *ideal* of progress to harden into a *law*, a law of history (Jonas 1984, 163). The law of progress allowed those who understood it to know the future; to be a political actor then meant working to bring about more quickly that which is inevitable.

When the ideal became law the champions of social transformation – democrats, Marxists and liberators of all kinds – could believe that history was on their side. That is what it meant to be 'progressive', to side with history, and those radicals who opposed industrial expansion were sent to the margins, where they wallow today. Philosophers such as Hegel provided the dialectic motor for the iron logic of progress, but in the end the proof was there for all to see in the relentless advance of gross domestic product.

But what happens to the ideal of progress when the law fails, or proves to have been true only for an epoch that has now passed? The law can live on only at the price of denying the passing of the age of progress and pretending that the Anthropocene is something for scientists alone to worry about. Although the births of utopias are precipitated by times of great turmoil, all presuppose eventual stability and so the absence of conflict. Yet there will be no stability in the Anthropocene, especially if the expectations of abrupt change (tipping points, feedback effects, extreme events and so on) come to pass. Instead of investing in more growth we will be pouring resources into trying to climate-proof our lives – our cities, our coasts, our infrastructure, our houses and our food supplies. The dominant task will be to protect the gains of the past and manage the effects of climatic insecurity so that they do not spill into conflict. Whether the unfolding era will stimulate new liberation projects – post-Holocene ones – is to be seen.

Proposition 5. Humans can dream of utopia only while Gaia sleeps

On the road to every utopia, entrenched power structures and stubborn 'human nature' have been the hindrances. For utopians victory comes by way of a his-torical rupture, often an act of violence, which overthrows the old structures and forges a 'new man'. But the rupture we now confront is not one of our making, or rather not one we have consciously brought about; it is not one to welcome but one to resist for it renders us less free, less powerful, and less able to build a New Jerusalem. The Moderns became convinced that human destiny would be shaped by what they believed. They believed in the human capacity to transform nature. But in the Anthropocene the Earth has been mobilised; it will not be subdued and now holds our fate in its hands.

Some leading thinkers have begun to grapple with the meaning of the new epoch now dawning and the all-crushing truth of climate science. In *Living in the End Times* Slavoj Žižek takes up the essential question for the left: with the shift to the Anthropocene, 'how are we to think the link between the social history of Capital and the much larger geological changes of the conditions of life on Earth?' (Žižek 2010, 331). Žižek declares that 'materiality is now reasserting itself with a vengeance' over intellectual labour (Žižek 2010, 330). That is true; yet he then reverts to the old social categories of capital and labour. For him the ground has not shifted and the task remains the remaking of the social and economic system to 'solve' the problem, confident that the Earth will obediently follow the programme.

For him, human agency, the first-born child of the Enlightenment, is undiminished: 'one can solve the universal problem . . . only by first resolving the particular deadlock of the capitalist mode of production' (Žižek 2010). Of course, socialist modes of production have proven just as contemptuous of Gaia (Josephson et al. 2013; Shapiro 2001).

Ulrich Beck seems to go much further in recognising that the unintended dynamics of capitalist modernisation 'threatens its own foundations' (Beck 2010, 255). Climate change demonstrates the impossibility of maintaining sociology's separation of social forces from natural ones and enforces 'an ongoing extension and deepening of combinations, confusions and mixtures of nature and society'. Quite so; yet Beck too immediately reverts to the familiar by insisting that climate change must be inscribed into the old categories (Beck 2010, 257; Hamilton 2012). He manages to reframe the destabilisation of the conditions of life on a millennial scale as a golden opportunity to achieve the progressive dream. Let us close our ears, he tells us, to 'depressing' talk of catastrophe and shun the 'negativity' of 'well-meaning green souls'. When the 'world public' (itself a utopian fantasy) wakes up to the fact that we are all in this together 'something historically new can emerge, namely a cosmopolitan vision in which people see themselves . . . as part of an endangered world . . .'. He entertains the poignant wish that a golden era of 'enforced enlightenment' and 'cosmopolitan realism' will dawn. Good luck with that.

Beck is the ultimate Modern whose implicit faith in reflexivity, our rationality, guarantees our autonomous capacity to respond to the world as it is. Yet is not the essential lesson of the climate crisis that reflexive modernisation has failed? The most striking fact about the human response to climate change is the determination *not* to reflect, to carry on blindly as if nothing is happening.

Responding to climate change requires, says Beck, a 'new contract between the managers of risk and the victims of risk in world risk society'. This new contract is little more than a minor rewriting of the terms of the old social contract, one from which the Earth itself, in its new incarnation as the Anthropocene, remains excluded. For Beck, ecology becomes a stimulus to solving poverty, inequality and corrosive nationalism (as long as we transcend the negativity of gloomy greens), but the old Earth lingers as the mere backdrop on which the human drama is played out.

So this is where we are. Modernity uprooted the social sciences from the earth. They became *hydroponic* disciplines, floating in the water of the social, sending out their roots to find nutrients supplied only by what humans do to each other, fed only by culture. But the drawback of hydroponics is that, without soil to act as a buffer, the plants die off quickly if anything goes wrong with the system. In the Anthropocene something is going wrong with the system, but to work out what it is our most prominent social scientists (with some noteworthy exceptions in this book) only know how to consult the hydroponics textbooks, where they find the old answers – change the mixture of micronutrients in the water.

The Moderns, including Žižek and Beck, are like Walter Benjamin's Angel of History, flying into the future but facing backwards, fleeing from a horrible past of suffering and oppression but unable to see the destruction that lies ahead. For them the real is what is left behind and the future is only what the autonomous subject ends up creating. Few progressives have turned around to face the future; and one can see why, for the progressive who turns around can no longer be a progressive. In the Anthropocene, in addition to the past we seek to escape, now we have a future we want to avoid; we are squeezed from both ends, and any new emancipatory project must transcend the progressive categories of the past.

Proposition 6. It's too late to negotiate with the Earth

Under the old social contract individuals agree to abide by the rules while the state agrees to provide order and protect our liberties. Michel Serres has argued we must now negotiate a second contract, a contract with nature (Serres 1995). When we walked away from the state of nature we became a parasite on the planet, he wrote, only recently recognising we are poisoning our host. Reimagining ourselves in a symbiotic relationship is the sole means by which both humans and Earth can survive. Under the terms of this natural contract humanity will reject mastery 'in favour of admiring attention, reciprocity, contemplation, and respect'. The contract will grant nature rights and make reparations.

Michel Serres was writing in 1992, at a time when I would have agreed with him, so I don't want to be harsh. But today we must ask under which constitution does humanity have the power to grant rights to Nature? What can we pay back to the Earth? Is Nature keeping a record of our ecological debt? Do we hear the victim of humankind's rapacity plaintively calling to us for mercy? Can we expect Nature to be grateful if we deign to grant her contractual rights? Is not the imposition of victimhood merely the continuation of domination in another guise?

For two centuries people struggled for equity and justice, for a progressive reading of the social contract. Calling now for a second contract – an agreement of reciprocity and justice between humanity and Nature – projects an eighteenth-century conception of the social onto the Anthropocene Earth – a social world of laws, codes, obligations and penalties, of rights and responsibilities, imposed on an entity that knows nothing of these things. When Serres says we can reach a deal because we understand Nature's language of 'forces, bonds, and interactions' is this not a new and thinly disguised anthropic power grab?

In the two decades since Serres wrote, Earth system science has taught us that the globe to which we graciously offer a peace deal – the passive, predictable victim of our exploitation and neglect – existed only in our imaginations. The enlightened among us desire harmony, sustainability and cooperation, but these aspirations clash with the globe scientists now vividly describe using images of 'the wakened giant' and 'the ornery beast', of Gaia 'fighting back' and seeking 'revenge', a world of 'angry summers' and 'death spirals'. We are in no position to begin signalling our willingness to negotiate a contract with the Earth. Instead of talking restitution should we not be preparing for retribution?

Proposition 7. The Earth is indifferent to our love

The arrival of the Anthropocene has some far-reaching implications for environmentalism. Let me quote an apparently unquestionable claim: 'At the heart of modern environmentalism is the idea that the planet must be saved from further damage by humanity' (Lind 2011). Underlying such a statement is a view that, while humans commit rape and pillage, nature is passive and fragile and always our victim. Yet now we see that the planet has been disturbed from its resting state, jolted out of the exceptional era of climatic stability characteristic of the last 10,000 years. Now it has jumped onto an uncontrollable trajectory that is hazardous to human life. We must no longer see the Earth as a submissive repository for supplying resources or taking wastes, suffering in silence from our rapacity or neglect. The new understanding has been expressed most vividly by palaeoclimatologist Wally Broecker: 'The palaeoclimate record shouts out to us that, far from being self-stabilizing, the Earth's climate system is an ornery beast which overreacts even to small nudges' (Broecker 1995, 213).

If we have wakened the slumbering beast by poking and prodding it, the prudent course is firstly to stop. We cannot put it back to sleep, although the Prometheans hope to anaesthetise it with geoengineering (Hamilton 2013). There is no return to the peaceful conditions of the Holocene, at least not for a thousand years. But to provoke it further, as we continue to do, is foolishness on an epic scale.

So the task of environmentalism can no longer be to save the planet, for the Holocene planet we wanted to save has become something else, not the kind of thing that can be saved or protected. Our task now is to refrain from aggravating further an entity vastly more powerful than we are and whose 'psychology' we barely understand. Yes, the Earth still demands our respect, but it is a respect founded on trepidation rather than love (Stengers 2009). It is prudent, as Bruno Latour reminds us, to regard Gaia not as the all-loving, all-nurturing Mother Earth of the romantics but more like the half-crazed, bloodthirsty and vindictive goddess of the original Greek tales (Latour 2011).

Proposition 8. Modernity will fight to the bitter end

At the dawn of modernity Francis Bacon had a vision – to use science to found 'an empire of man over nature'. Man would use technology to hasten natural processes, a transformative power granted by God and distinctive of humans as creatures. For men like Bacon remaking nature could redeem humankind from the Biblical Fall and the misery of the world that followed. Technology and science would bring about what he named a 'second creation'.

Astonishingly, Francis Bacon was the first to write of hydroponics, in *Sylva Sylvarum* published posthumously in 1627. But it is his fable *New Atlantis* (published in the same year) that had a more enduring influence. In the story a council of wise men, schooled in natural philosophy, oversees the making of a new Eden in imitation of the first act of creation. Bacon referred to the council as Salomon's House or the College of the Six Days Works. The College serves as keeper of the know–how to transform nature. Says the magus: 'The end of our foundation is the knowledge of causes, and secret motions of things; and the enlarging of the bounds of human empire, to the effecting of all things possible.'

New Atlantis was one of the first visions of the perfection of human society by means of the conquest of nature, a kind of *technicae paradisum*. Scientists would become Utopia's midwives, and throughout the history of modern science many of its leading practitioners have been content to assume the role. Fredrik Albritton Jonsson has traced some of the many ways Bacon's ideas were developed and applied, from early improvements in English agriculture to the ideology of manifest destiny that animated the nineteenth–century conquest of the American west (Albritton Jonsson 2014). The vision of a second creation reached its secular zenith in the United States in the post–war decades of the twentieth century, energised perhaps by the undreamed of power of nuclear fission that lay at the core of the military–industrial–university complex. Its deep–rootedness in the American psyche helps to explain why faith in geoengineering is stronger in the United States than in Europe, and perhaps why today some American evangelical Christians have been boarding cruise ships bound for the melting Antarctic where they have been caught broadcasting seeds in the expectation that the freshly exposed continent will blossom into a new Eden.

More seriously, we are witnessing a contemporary recovery of the idea of a second creation in the reframing of the Anthropocene as an event to be *celebrated* rather than lamented and feared. Instead of final proof of the damage done by human arrogance, a new breed of 'eco–modernists' welcomes the new epoch as a sign of our ability to transform and control (Hamilton 2013). They see it not as evidence of humankind's short–sightedness, foolishness or callousness, but as an opportunity for humans to realise their full potential. So American ecologist Erle Ellis (2011a) defends what he calls the 'good Anthropocene'. There are no planetary boundaries that limit continued growth in human populations and economic advance. 'Human systems' can adapt and indeed prosper in a hotter world because we are masters of transformation.

In this emerging view, as we enter the Anthropocene we should not fear transgressing natural limits; the only barrier to a grand new era for humanity is self–doubt. '[W]e must not see the Anthropocene as a crisis,' writes Ellis, 'but as the beginning of a new geological epoch ripe with human–directed opportunity' (Ellis 2011a). For eco–Pollyannas like Ellis, four centuries after Bacon, with modern science and technologies of Earth system engineering we finally stand ready to build the New Atlantis. Ellis is confident: 'We will be proud of the planet we create in the Anthropocene' (Ellis 2011b). Only romantic critics of technology and the gloomy scientists they quote in support stand in the way of the vision's realisation (Hamilton 2014). The eco–modern's determination to look on the bright side of the Anthropocene is reminiscent of Brian's song on the cross at the end of *Monty Python's Life of Brian*.

Just as Bacon understood Nature as a passive object to be manipulated once her secrets had been extracted, and saw the exercise of human creative power facing no constraints, so today's eco-moderns understand the Earth as a 'system' that can be subjugated with knowledge and technological power. In his book *The God Species*, Mark Lynas fulfils the prophecy of the College of the Six Days Works. 'Nature no longer runs the Earth,' he declares. 'We do. It is our choice what happens here' (Lynas 2011, cover).

So the battlelines have been drawn. On one side are those who plan to force Gaia into total submission; on the other are those who believe attempting to do so is the ultimate folly. One hundred and thirty years ago, Nietzsche foresaw our dilemma: 'Inexorably, hesitantly, terrible as fate, the great task and question is approaching: how shall the earth as a whole be governed?' (Nietzsche 1968, 501). Except that in the Anthropocene we begin to see that the Earth as a whole is not an entity that takes kindly to being governed.

References

Albritton Jonsson F 2014 The origins of cornucopianism: A preliminary genealogy *Critical Historical Studies* 1(1): 151–68

Beck U 2010 Climate for change, or how to create a green modernity? *Theory, Culture & Society* 27(2–3) 254–66

Broecker W 1995 Ice cores: Cooling the tropics *Nature* 376 212–13 20 July

Chakrabarty D 2009 The climate of history: Four theses *Critical Inquiry* 35 197–222

Ellis E 2011a Neither good nor bad *New York Times* 23 May

Ellis E 2011b The planet of no return *Breakthrough Journal* 2 Breakthrough Institute, San Francisco

Hamilton C 2012 Theories of climate change *Australian Journal of Political Science* 47(4) 721–9

Hamilton C 2013 *Earthmasters: The Dawn of the Age of Climate Engineering* Yale University Press, London

Hamilton C 2014 The new environmentalism will lead us to disaster *Scientific American* 19 June

Jonas H 1984 *The Imperative of Responsibility* University of Chicago Press, Chicago

Josephson et al. P 2013 *The Environmental History of Russia* Cambridge University Press, Cambridge

Klein N 2014 *This Changes Everything* Allen Lane, London

Langmuir C H and Broecker W 2012 *How to Build a Habitable Planet* revised edition Princeton University Press, Princeton

Latour B 2011 Waiting for Gaia. Composing the common world through arts and politics, A lecture at the French Institute, London, November (http://www.bruno-latour.fr/sites/default/files/124-GAIA-LONDON-SPEAP_0.pdf)

Latour B 2013 Facing Gaia: Six lectures on the political theology of nature, Gifford Lectures on Natural Religion Edinburgh, 18–28 February (http://www.bruno-latour.fr/sites/default/files/downloads/GIFFORD-SIX-LECTURES_1.pdf)

Lind M 2011 Is it time to embrace environmental change? *Salon.com* 13 December

Lynas M 2011 *The God Species: How Humans Really Can Save the Planet* Fourth Estate, London

Nietzsche F 1968 *The Will to Power* ed Walter Kaufmann Vintage Books, New York

Serres M 1995 *The Natural Contract* University of Michigan Press, Ann Arbor

Shapiro J 2001 *Mao's War Against Nature* Cambridge University Press, Cambridge

Smil V 2011 Harvesting the biosphere: The human impact *Population and Development Review* 37(4) 613–36, December

Steffen W Grinevald J Crutzen P and McNeil J 2011 The Anthropocene: conceptual and historical perspectives *Philosophical Transactions of the Royal Society A* 369 842–67

Stengers I 2009 *Au temps des catastrophes: Résister à la barbarie qui vient* La Découverte, Paris

Trenberth K 2012 Framing the way to relate climate extremes to climate change *Climatic Change* November 115(2) 283–90

Vernadsky, Vladimir I 2005 Some words about the Noösphere *21st Century*, 16–21 [1943]

Werner B 2012 Is Earth f**ked? Dynamical Futility of Global Environmental Management and Possibilities for Sustainability via Direct Action Activism, unpublished

Zalasiewicz J et al. 2010 The new world of the Anthropocene *Environmental Science and Technology* 44(7) 2228–31

Žižek S 2010 *Living in the End Times* Verso, London

4

THE ANTHROPOCENE AND THE CONVERGENCE OF HISTORIES

Dipesh Chakrabarty

Anthropocene warming brings into view the collision – or the running up against one another – of three histories that, from the point of view of human history, are normally assumed to be working at such different and distinct paces that they are treated as processes separate from one another for all practical purposes: the history of the Earth system; the history of life including that of human evolution on the planet; and the more recent history of the industrial civilisation (for many, capitalism). Humans now unintentionally straddle these three histories that operate on different scales and at different speeds. The very language through which we speak of the climate crisis is shot through with this problem of human and in- or non-human scales of time.

Take the most ubiquitous distinction we make in our everyday prose between non-renewable sources of energy and the 'renewables'. Fossil fuels we consider non-renewable on our terms but as Bryan Lovell, a geologist who worked as an advisor for BP and is an ex-president of the Geological Society of London, points out, fossil fuels are indeed renewable if only we think of them on a scale that is (in his terms) 'inhuman': 'Two hundred million years from now, a form of life requiring abundant oil for some purpose should find that plenty has formed since our own times' (Lovell 2010, 75).

Paleoclimatologists tell a very long history when it comes to explaining the significance of anthropogenic global warming. There is, first of all, the question of evidence. Ice core samples of ancient air – more than 800,000 years old – have been critical in establishing the anthropogenic nature of the current warming (Solomon et al. 2009, 446 Box 6.2). There are, in addition, palaeoclimatic records of the past in fossils and other geological materials. In his lucid book on the oil industry's response – not always or uniformly negative – to the climate crisis, Bryan Lovell (2010) writes that those in the industry who supplied compelling evidence of the serious challenge that greenhouse gas emissions posed to the future of humanity were geologists, they who could read deep climate histories buried in sedimentary rocks to see the effects of 'a dramatic warming event that took place 55 million years ago'. In the literature, this event is known as the late Paleocene-Eocene Thermal Maximum (PETM).

How far the arc of the geological history explaining Anthropocene warming projects into the future may be quickly seen from the very subtitle of David Archer's *The Long Thaw: How Humans are Changing the Next 100,000 Years of Earth's Climate*. 'Mankind is becoming a force in climate comparable to the orbital variations that drive glacial cycles,' he writes.

> The long lifetime of fossil fuel CO_2 creates a sense of fleeting folly about the use of fossil fuels as an energy source. Our fossil fuel deposits, 100 million years old, could be gone in a few centuries, leaving climate impacts that will last for hundreds of millennia. The lifetime of fossil fuel CO_2 in the atmosphere is a few centuries, plus 25% that lasts essentially forever.
>
> (Archer 2009, 11)

The carbon cycle of the Earth will eventually clean up the excess carbon dioxide we put out in the atmosphere, but it works on an inhumanly long time scale.

Anthropocene warming thus produces problems that we ponder on very different and incompatible scales of time. Policy specialists think in terms of years or decades while politicians in democracies think primarily in terms of their electoral cycles. Understanding what anthropogenic climate change is and how long its effects may last calls for thinking on very large and small scales at once, including scales that defy the usual measures of time that inform human affairs. This is another reason that makes it difficult to develop a comprehensive politics of climate change. Archer goes to the heart of the problem here when he acknowledges that the million-year time-scale of the planet's carbon cycle is 'irrelevant for political considerations of climate change on human time scales'. Yet, he insists, it remains relevant to any understanding of anthropogenic climate change because 'ultimately the global warming climate event will last for as long as it takes these slow processes to act' (Archer 2009, 21).

Significant gaps between cognition and action thus open up in the existing literature on the climate problem, between what we scientifically know about it – the vastness of its non- or in-human scale, for instance – and how we think about it when we treat it as a problem to be handled by the human means at our disposal. The latter have been developed for addressing problems we face on familiar scales of time. I call these gaps or openings in the landscape of our thoughts 'rifts' because they are like fault lines on a seemingly continuous surface: we have to keep crossing or straddling them as we think or speak of climate change. They inject a certain degree of contradictoriness in our thinking for we are being asked to think on different scales at once.

I want to discuss here three such rifts: (1) the various regimes of probability that govern our everyday lives in modern economies, now having to be supplemented by our knowledge of the radical uncertainty (of the climate); (2) the story of our necessarily divided human lives having to be supplemented by the story of our collective life as a species, a dominant species, on the planet; and (3) having to wrestle with our inevitably anthropocentric thinking in order to supplement it with forms of disposition towards the planet that do not put humans first. We have not yet overcome these dilemmas to settle decidedly on any one side of them. They remain as rifts.

In what follows, I elaborate on these rifts with a view to demonstrating that the analytics of capital (or of the market), while necessary, are insufficient instruments in helping us come to grips with the Anthropocene. I will go on to conclude by proposing that the climate crisis makes visible an emergent, but critical distinction between the global and the planetary that will need to be explored further in order to develop a perspective on the human meaning(s) of global warming.

Probability and radical uncertainty

Modern life is ruled by regimes of probabilistic thinking. From evaluating lives for actuarial ends to the working of money and stock markets, we manage our societies by calculating risks and assigning probability values to them. 'Economics,' writes Charles Pearson, 'often makes a distinction between risk, where probabilities of outcomes are known, and uncertainty, where probabilities are not known and perhaps unknowable' (Pearson 2011, 25 n6). This is surely one reason why economics as a discipline has emerged as the major art of social management today. There is, therefore, an understandable tendency in both climate-justice and climate-policy literature – the latter dominated by economists or law scholars who think like economists – to focus not so much on what palaeoclimatologists or geophysicists who study planetary climate historically have to say about climate change but rather on what we might call the physics of global warming that often presents a predictable, static set of relationships of probability and proportion: if the share of greenhouse gases in the atmosphere goes up by X, then the probability of the Earth's average surface temperature going up by so much is Y.

Such a way of thinking assumes a kind of stability or predictability – however probabilistic it may be – on the part of a warming atmosphere that palaeoclimatologists, who focus more on the greater danger of tipping points, often do not assume. This is not because policy thinkers are not concerned about the dangers of climate change; nor because they are ignorant of the profoundly nonlinear nature of the relationship between greenhouse gases and rise in the planet's average surface temperature. They clearly are. But their methods are such that they appear to hold or bracket climate change as a broadly known variable (converting its uncertainties into risks that have been acknowledged and evaluated) while working out options that humans can create for themselves striving together or even wrangling among themselves. The world climate system, in other words, has no significant capacity to be a wild card in their calculations in so far as they can make policy prescriptions; it is there in a relatively predictable form to be managed by human ingenuity and political mobilisation (Weitzman 2009, 26).

The rhetoric of the climate scientists, on the other hand, in what they write to persuade the public is often remarkably vitalist. In explaining the danger of anthropogenic climate change, they often resort to a language that portrays the climate system as a living organism. James Lovelock compares life on the planet to a single living organism. Archer describes the 'carbon cycle of the Earth' as 'alive' (Archer 2010, 1). The image of climate as a temperamental animal also inhabits the language of Wallace (Wally) Broecker who, with Robert Kunzig, thus describes his studies:

> Every now and then . . . nature has decided to give a good swift kick to the climate beast. And the beast has responded, as beasts will – violently and a little unpredictably.
>
> (Kunzig and Broecker 2008, 100)

The vitalism of this prose does not arise because climate scientists are less 'scientific' than economists and policy makers. The vitalist metaphors issue from climate scientists' anxiousness to communicate and underscore two points about Earth's climate: that its many uncertainties cannot ever be completely tamed by existing human knowledge and hence the inherent unpredictability of its exact 'tipping points'. As Archer puts it:

> The IPCC forecast for climate change in the coming century is for a generally smooth increase in temperature. . . . However, actual climate changes in the past have tended to be abrupt. . . . [C]limate models . . . are for the most part unable to simulate the flip flops in the past climate record very well.
>
> (Archer 2009, 95)

It is in fact this sense of a 'climate beast' that is missing from both the literature inspired by economics and that inspired by political commitments on the left. Climate uncertainties may not always be like measurable risks. 'Do we really need to know more than we know now about how much the Earth will warm? *Can* we know more?', asks Paul Edwards rhetorically. 'It is now virtually certain that CO_2 concentrations will reach 550 ppm (the doubling point) sometime in the middle of this century,' and the planet 'will almost certainly overshoot CO_2 doubling'. Climate scientists, he reports, are engaged in the speculation 'that *we will probably never get a more exact estimate than we already have*' (Edwards 2010, 438–9).

'Climate scientists are historians,' writes Edwards, and like historians 'every generation of climate scientists revisit the same data, the same events – digging through the archives to ferret out new evidence, correct some previous interpretation,' and so on. And 'just as with human history, we will never get a single, unshakable narrative of the global climate's past. Instead we get versions of the atmosphere, . . . convergent yet never identical' (Edwards 2010, 431). Moreover, 'all of today's analyses are based on the climate we have experienced in historical time'. Edwards quotes the scientists Myles Allen and David Frame: 'Once the world has warmed by 4°C, conditions will be so different from anything we can observe today (and still more different from the last ice age) that it is inherently hard to say when the warming will stop.'

The first rift that I speak of thus organises itself around the question of the tipping point of the climate, a point beyond which global warming could be catastrophic for humans. That such a possibility exists is not in doubt. Paleoclimatologists know that the planet has undergone such warming in the geological past (as in the case of PETM event). But we cannot predict how quickly such a point could arrive. It remains an uncertainty that is not amenable to the usual cost–benefit analyses that are a necessary part of risk-management strategies. As Pearson explains, 'BC [benefit–cost analysis] is not well suited for making catastrophe policy' and he acknowledges that the 'special features that distinguish uncertainty in global warming are the presence of nonlinearities, thresholds and potential tipping points, irreversibilities, and the long time horizon' that make 'projections of technology, economic structure, preferences and a host of other variables 100 years from now increasingly questionable' (Pearson 2011, 31, 26). 'The implication of uncertainty, thresholds, tipping points,' he writes, 'is that we should take a precautionary approach,' that is, 'avoid taking steps today that lead to irreversible changes' (Pearson 2011, 30).

However, the precautionary principle, as Sunstein explains it, also involves cost–benefit analysis and some estimation of probability. But we simply don't know the probability of the tipping point being reached over the next several decades or by 2100, for the tipping point would be a function of the rise in global temperature and multiple, unpredictable amplifying feedback loops working together. Under the circumstances, the one principle that Hansen recommends to policy thinkers concerns the use of coal as a fuel. He writes: 'So, if we want to solve the climate problem, we must phase out coal emissions. Period' (Hansen 2009, 176). Not quite a precautionary principle but what in the literature on risks would be known as the maximin principle: 'choose the policy with the best worst-case outcome' (Sunstein 2002, 129).

Yet this would seem unacceptable to governments and business around the world, for without coal, which China and India are still dependent on to a large degree (around 70 per cent of their energy supply), how would the majority of the world's poor be lifted out of poverty in the next few decades and thus equipped to adapt to the impact of climate change? Or would the world, scrambling to avoid the tipping point of the climate, make the global economy itself tip over and cause untold human misery? Thus, would avoiding 'the harm' itself do more harm, especially as we do not know the probability of reaching the tipping point in the coming few decades? This is the dilemma that goes with the application here of the precautionary or the maximin principle.

At the heart of this rift is the question of scale. On the much more extended canvas on which they place the history of the planet, palaeoclimatologists see climatic tipping points and species extinction as perfectly repeatable phenomena, irrespective of whether or not we can model for them. Our strategies of risk management, however, arise from more human calculations of costs and their probabilities over plausible human timescales. Anthropocene warming requires us to move back and forth between thinking on these different scales all at once.

Our divided lives as humans and our collective life as a dominant species

Human-induced climate change gives rise to large and diverse issues of justice: justice between generations, between small island-nations and the polluting countries (both past and prospective), between developed, industrialised nations (historically responsible for most emissions) and the newly industrialising ones, and so on. Peter Newell and Matthew Paterson thus express a sense of discomfiture about the use of the word *human* in the expression *human-induced climate change* (just as some, such as Alf Hornborg in this volume, are discomforted by the undifferentiated *anthropos* of the Anthropocene). 'Behind the cosy language used to describe climate change as a common threat to all humankind,' they write, 'it is clear that some people and countries contribute to it disproportionately, while others bear the brunt of its effects' (Newell and Paterson 2010). The climate crisis, write John Bellamy Foster, Brett Clark, and Richard York in their thoughtful book, *The Ecological Rift*, is 'at bottom, the product of a social rift: the domination of human being by human being. The driving force is a society based on class, inequality, and acquisition without end' (Foster et al. 2010, 27).

There are good reasons why questions of justice arise. Only a few nations (some 12 or 14 including China and India in the last decade or so) and a fragment of humanity (about one-fifth) are historically responsible for most of the emissions of greenhouse gases to date. This is true. But we would not be able to differentiate between humans as actors and the planet itself as an actor in this crisis if we did not realise that, leaving aside the question of intergenerational ethics that concerns the future, anthropogenic climate change is not inherently – or logically – a problem of past or accumulated intra-human injustice. Imagine the counterfactual reality of a more evenly prosperous and just world made up of the same number of people and based on exploitation of cheap energy sourced from fossil fuel. Such a world would have been more egalitarian and just – at least in terms of distribution of income and wealth – but the climate crisis would have been worse! Our collective carbon footprint would have only been larger – for the world's poor do not consume much and contribute little to the production of greenhouse gases – and the climate change crisis would have been on us much sooner and in a much more drastic way.

It is, ironically, thanks to the poor – that is, to the fact that development *is* uneven and unfair – that we do not put out even larger quantities of greenhouse gases into the biosphere than we actually do. Thus, logically speaking, the climate crisis is not *inherently* a result of economic inequalities – it is really a matter of the quantity of greenhouses gases we put out into the atmosphere. Those who connect climate change exclusively to historical origins/formations of income inequalities in the modern world raise valid questions about historical inequalities; but a reduction of the problem of climate change to that of capitalism (folded into the histories of modern European expansion and empires) only blinds us to the nature of our present, a present defined by the coming together of the relatively short-term processes of human history and other much longer-term processes that belong to the history of the Earth system and of life on the planet.

Agarwal and Narain's insistence that the natural carbon sinks – such as the oceans – are part of the global commons and hence best distributed between nations by applying the principle of equal access on a per capita basis if the world were to 'aspire . . . to such lofty ideals like global justice, equity and sustainability,' raises, by implication a very important issue – the simultaneously acknowledged and disavowed problem of population (Agarwal and Narain 1991, 5, 9). Population is often the elephant in the room in discussions of climate change. The 'problem' of population – while due surely in part to modern medicine, public health measures, eradication of epidemics, the use of artificial fertilisers, and so on – cannot be attributed in any straightforward way to a logic of a predatory and capitalist West, for neither China nor India pursued unbridled capitalism while their populations exploded. If India had been more successful with population control or with economic development, its per capita emission figures would have been higher. (That the richer classes in India want to emulate western styles and standards of consumption is obvious to any observer.) Indeed, the Indian Minister in charge of the Environment and Forests, Jairam Ramesh, said as much in an address to the Indian Parliament in 2009: 'per-capita is an accident of history. It so happened that we could not control our population' (Ramesh 2012, 238).

Population remains a very important factor in how the climate crisis plays out. For without their having such large populations that the Chinese and Indian governments legitimately desire to 'pull out of poverty', they would not be building so many coal-fired power stations every year. The Indian government is fond of quoting Gandhi on the present environmental crisis: 'Earth [*prithvi*] provides enough to satisfy every man's need but not enough for every man's greed.' Yet 'greed' and 'need' become indistinguishable in arguments in defence of continued use of coal, the worst offender among fossil fuels. India and China want coal; Australia and other countries want to export it. It is still the cheapest variety of fossil fuel. Coal represents around 30 per cent of world energy, a share that is growing. Coal companies in the United States, Australia and elsewhere see enormous export opportunities in India and China, which defend the use of coal by referring to the needs of their poor.

Population is also a problem because both the total size and distribution of humanity matter in how the climate crisis unfolds, particularly with regards to species extinction. Humans have been putting pressure on other species for quite some time now, a fact I do not need to belabour. Indeed, the war between humans and wild animals such as rhinoceroses, elephants, monkeys and big cats may be seen everyday in many Indian cities and villages. That we have consumed many varieties of marine life out of existence is also generally accepted. Ocean acidification threatens the lives of many species (see Hansen 2009). And, clearly, as many have pointed out, the exponential growth of human population in the twentieth century has itself had much to do with fossil fuels through the use of artificial fertilisers, pesticides and pumps for irrigation (Smil 2013, 11–12).

But there is another reason why the history of human evolution and the total number of human beings today matter when we get to the question of species survival as the planet warms. One way that species threatened by global warming will try to survive is by migrating to areas more conducive to their existence. This is how they have survived past changes in the climatic conditions of the planet. But now there are so many of us, and we are so widespread on this planet, that we stand in the way. Curt Stager puts it clearly:

> As Anthropocene warming rises toward its as yet unspecified peak, our long-suffering biotic neighbors face a situation that they have never encountered before in the long, dramatic history of ice ages and interglacials. They can't move because we're standing in their way.
>
> (Stager 2011, 66)

The irony of the point runs deeper. The spread of human groups throughout the world and their growth in the age of industrial civilisation now make it difficult for human climate refugees to move to safer and more inhabitable climes (Denny and Matisoo-Smith 2011). Other humans will stand in their way. Burton Richter puts the point thus: 'The population now is too big to move *en masse*, so we had better do our best to limit the damage that we are causing' (Richter 2010, 2).

The history of population thus belongs to two histories at once: the very short-term history of the industrial way of life – of modern medicine, technology, and fossil fuels as well as of fertilisers, pesticides and irrigation – that accompanied and enabled the growth in our numbers and the much, much longer-term evolutionary or deep history of our species, the history through which we have evolved to be the dominant species of the planet, spreading all over it and now threatening the existence of many other life-forms. The poor participate in that shared history of human evolution just as much as the rich do. In a recent paper the Duke University geologist, Peter Haff, has convincingly argued that it would not be possible to sustain the lives of seven – soon to be nine – billion people on the planet without modern forms of energy and communications technology touching all our lives in some significant ways. Without this network of connections, he argues, the total human population on Earth will collapse to about 10 million. The 'technosphere', he argues, has become the condition of possibility enabling so many of us, both rich and poor, to live on this planet and act as its dominant species (Haff 2013).

Per capita emission figures, while useful in making a necessary and corrective polemical point in the political economy of climate change, hide the larger history of the species in which both the rich and the poor participate. *Population* is clearly a category that conjoins the two histories.

Are humans special? The moral rift of the Anthropocene

Anthropocene warming reveals the sudden coming together of the usually separated syntactic orders of recorded and deep histories of humankind, of species history and the history of the Earth system, revealing the deep connections through which the planet's carbon cycle and life interact with each other and so on. It does not mean that this knowledge will stop humans from pursuing, with vigour and vengeance, our all too human ambitions and squabbles that unite and divide us at the same time.

In their fascinating paper on the Anthropocene, Will Steffen, Paul Crutzen, and John McNeill have drawn our attention to what they call – after Polanyi, I assume – the period of the 'Great Acceleration' in human history, from 1945 to the present, when global figures for population, real GDP, foreign direct investment, damning of rivers, water use, fertiliser consumption, urban population, paper consumption, transport motor vehicles, telephones, international tourism, and McDonald's restaurants (yes!) all began to increase dramatically in an exponential fashion (Steffen et al. 2007).

The year 1945, they suggest, could be a strong candidate for an answer to the question, When did the Anthropocene begin? While the Anthropocene may stand for all the climate problems we face today collectively, as a historian of human affairs it is impossible for me not to notice that this period of so-called Great Acceleration is also the period of great decolonisation in countries that had been dominated by European imperial powers and that made a move towards modernisation (the damming of rivers, for instance) over the ensuing decades and, with the globalisation of the last twenty years, towards a certain degree of democratisation of consumption as well.

I cannot ignore the fact that 'the Great Acceleration' included the production and consumption of consumer durables – such as the refrigerator and the washing machine – in western households that were touted as 'emancipatory' for women. Nor can I forget the pride with which today the most ordinary and poor Indian citizen now possesses his or her smart phone or a fake and cheap substitute. The lurch into the Anthropocene has also been globally the story of some long-anticipated social justice as well, at least in the sphere of consumption.

This justice between humans, however, comes at a price. The result of growing human consumption has been a near-complete human appropriation of the biosphere.

This raises a question that bears striking similarity to the question that Europeans often asked themselves when they forcibly or otherwise took over other peoples' lands: by what right or on what grounds do we arrogate to ourselves the almost exclusive claims to appropriate for human needs the biosphere of the planet?

The idea that humans are special has, of course, a long history. We should perhaps speak of anthropocentrisms in the plural here. There is, for instance, a long line of thinking – from religions that came long after humans established the first urban centres of civilisation and created the idea of a transcendental God through to the modern social sciences – that has humans positioned as facing the rest of the world, as nature. These later religions are in strong contrast, it seems, with the much more ancient religions of hunting-gathering peoples (I think here of Australian Aborigines and their stories) that often saw humans as part of animal life. The humans were not necessarily special in these ancient religions. They ate and were eaten in the same way that other animals did. They were part of life. Recall Durkheim's position on totemism. In determining 'the place of man' in the scheme of totemistic beliefs, Durkheim was clear that totemism pointed to a doubly conceived human, or what he called the 'double nature' of man: 'Two beings co-exist within him: a man and an animal.' And again: 'we must be careful not to consider totemism a sort of animal worship. . . . Their [men and their totems'] relations are rather those of two things who are on the same level and of equal value' (Durkheim 1982 [1915], 134, 139). The very idea of a transcendental God puts humans in a special relationship to the Creator and to His creation, the world.

The literature on climate change thus reconfigures an older debate on anthropocentrism and so-called non-anthropocentrism that has long exercised philosophers and scholars interested in environmental ethics: do we value the non-human for its own sake or because it is good for us? (see Buell 2001, 224–42). Non-anthropocentrism, however, may indeed be a chimera for, as the Chinese scholar Feng Han points out in a different context, 'human values will always be from a human (or anthropocentric) point of view' (Feng Han 2008). Ecologically-minded philosophers in the 1980s made a distinction between 'weak' and 'strong' versions of anthropocentrism. Strong anthropocentrism had to do with unreflexive and instinctive use or exploitation of nature for purely human preferences; weak anthropocentrism was seen as a position arrived at through rational reflections on why the nonhuman was important for human flourishing (Norton 1984, 131–48).

Lovelock's work on Anthropocene warming, however, produces a radically different position, on the other side of the rift as it were. He packs it into a pithy proposition that works almost as the motto of his book, *The Vanishing Face of Gaia*: 'to consider the health of the Earth without the constraint that the welfare of humankind comes first' (Lovelock 2009, 35–6). He emphasises: 'I see the health of the Earth as primary, for we are utterly dependent upon a healthy planet for survival.' What does it mean for humans, given their inescapable anthropocentrism, to consider 'the Earth as primary' or to contemplate the implications of Archer's statement that the world was not 'created specially for us'? I will consider this question in the following and concluding section of this essay.

Climate and capital, the global and the planetary

In his book, *Living in the End Times*, Slavoj Žižek made some interesting criticism of my essay 'The Climate of History: Four Theses' (Chakrabarty 2009). Responding to my points that there were 'natural parameters' to our existence as a species that were relatively independent of our choices between capitalism and socialism and that we therefore needed to think deep history of the species and the much shorter history of capital together, Žižek remarked:

> Of course, the natural parameters of our environment are 'independent of capitalism or socialism' – they harbor a potential threat to all of us, independently of economic development, political system, etc. However, the fact that their

stability has been threatened by the dynamic of global capitalism nonetheless has a stronger implication that the one allowed by Chakrabarty: in a way, we have to admit that *the Whole is contained by its Part*, that the fate of the Whole (life on earth) hinges on what goes on in what was formerly one of its parts (the socio-economic mode of production of one of the species on earth).

(Žižek 2010, 333)

Given this premise, his conclusion followed: we also 'have to accept the paradox that . . . the key struggle is the particular one: one can solve the universal problem (of the survival of human species) only by first resolving the particular deadlock of the capitalist mode of production. . . . [T]he key to the ecological crisis does not reside in ecology as such' (Žižek 2010, 333–4).

That the capitalist or industrial civilisation, dependent on the large-scale availability of cheap fossil-fuel energy, is a proximate or efficient cause of the climate crisis is not in doubt. But Žižek puts capitalism in the driver's seat; it is the 'part' that now determines 'the whole'. My position is different: to say that the history and logic of particular human institutions have become caught up in the much larger processes of the Earth system and evolutionary history (stressing the lives of several species, including ourselves) is not to say that human history is the driver of these large-scale processes.

These latter processes continue over scales of space and time that are much larger than those of capitalism; hence the rifts we have discussed. As Stager and Archer point out, however much the 'excess' carbon dioxide we put out today, the long-term processes of the Earth system, its million-year carbon cycle, for instance, will most likely 'clean it up' one day, humans or no humans (Solomon et al. 2009, 20; Stager 2011, Chapter 2). Which is why it seems more consistent to see these long-term Earth system processes as co-actors in the drama of global warming. This is also suggested by the fact that, unlike the problems of wealth accumulation or income inequalities, or the questions posed by globalisation, the problem of Anthropocene warming could not have been predicted from within the usual frameworks deployed to study the logics of capital. The methods of political economic investigation and analyses do not usually entail digging up 800,000-year-old ice-core samples or making satellite observations of changes in the mean temperature of the planet's surface. Climate change is a problem defined and constructed by climate scientists whose research methods, analytical strategies and skill-sets are different from those possessed by students of political economy.

Once we grant processes belonging to the deeper history of Earth and life, the role of co-actors in the current crisis (playing themselves out on scales both human and non-human) highlights Gayatri Chakravorty Spivak's observation that 'The planet is the species of alterity, belonging to another system; and yet we inhabit it' (Spivak 2012, 338). Spivak was on to something here. Her formulation takes a step towards pondering the human implications of the kind of planetary studies that inform and underpin the science of climate change.

This science drives a clear wedge between an emergent conception of the planetary and existing ideas regarding the global. For even though the current phase of warming of the Earth's atmosphere is indeed anthropogenic, it is only contingently so; humans have no intrinsic role to play in the science of planetary warming as such. The science is not even specific to this planet – it is part of what is called planetary science. It does not belong to an Earth-bound imagination. Our current warming is an instance of planetary warming that has happened both on this planet and on other planets, humans or no humans, and with different consequences. It just so happens that the current warming of the Earth is of human doing. The 'global' of globalisation literature, on the other hand, cannot be thought without humans directly and necessarily placed at the very centre of the narrative.

The scientific problem of climate change thus emerges from what may be called 'comparative planetary studies' and entails a degree of interplanetary research and thinking. The imagination at work here is not human-centred. It speaks to a growing divergence in our consciousness between the global – a singularly human story – and the planetary, a perspective to which humans are incidental. The Anthropocene is about waking up to the rude of shock of the recognition of the otherness of the planet. The planet, to speak with Spivak again, 'is the species of alterity, belonging to another system'. And 'yet,' as she puts it, 'we live on it.' If there is to be a comprehensive politics of climate change, it has to begin from this perspective. The realisation that humans – all humans, rich or poor – come late in the planet's life and dwell more in the position of passing guests than possessive hosts, has to be an integral part of the perspective from which we pursue our all-too-human but legitimate quest for justice on issues to do with the iniquitous impact of anthropogenic climate change.

This chapter was first published in a longer form as Dipesh Chakrabarty, Climate and Capital: On Conjoined Histories, *Critical Inquiry* 41 (Autumn 2014) 2014.
© 2014 by The University of Chicago. All rights reserved.

Note: In the interest of editorial consistency, the author's expression 'global warming' has at times been replaced by 'Anthropocene warming' in this essay.

References

Agarwal A and Narain S 1991 *Global Warming in an Unequal World* Centre for Science and Environment, New Delhi

Archer D 2009 *The Long Thaw: How Humans are Changing the Next 100,000 Years of Earth's Climate* Princeton University Press, Princeton

Archer D 2010 *The Global Carbon Cycle* Princeton University Press, Princeton

Buell L 2001 The misery of beasts and humans: Nonanthropocentric ethics *versus* environmental justice, in his *Writing For An Endangered World: Literature, Culture, and Environment in the U.S. and Beyond* Harvard University Press, Cambridge, Mass.

Chakrabarty D 2009 The Climate of History: Four Theses *Critical Inquiry* 197–222 Winter

Denny M and Matisoo-Smith L 2011 Rethinking Polynesian origins: Human settlement of the Pacific (lens.auckland.ac.nz/images/4/41/Pacific_Migration_Seminar_Paper_2011.pdf)

Durkheim E 1982 [1915] *The Elementary Forms of Religious Life*, trans. Joseph Ward Swain, George Allen and Unwin, London

Edwards P N 2010 *A Vast Machine: Computer Models, Climate Data, and the Politics of Global Warming* MIT Press, Cambridge, Mass.

Feng Han 2008 The Chinese View of Nature: Tourism in China's scenic and historic-interest areas, PhD dissertation, Queensland University of Technology, Brisbane

Foster J B Clark B and York R 2010 *The Ecological Rift: Capitalism's War on Earth* Monthly Review Press, New York

Haff P K 2013 Technology as a geological phenomenon: Implications for human well-being *Geological Society, London,* Special Publications, 24 October

Hansen J 2009 *Storms of My Grandchildren* Bloomsbury, London

Kunzig R and Broecker W S 2008 *Fixing Climate: What Past Climate Changes Reveal About the Current Threat – and How to Counter It* Green Profile, London

Lovell B 2010 *Challenged by Carbon: The Oil Industry and Climate Change* Cambridge University Press, Cambridge

Lovelock J 2009 *The Vanishing Face of Gaia: A Final Warning* Allen Lane, London

Newell P and Paterson M 2010 *Climate Capitalism: Global Warming and the Transformation of the Global Economy* Cambridge University Press, Cambridge

Norton B G 1984 Environmental ethics and weak anthropocentrism *Environmental Ethics* 6 Summer 131–48

Pearson C S 2011 *Economics and the Challenge of Global Warming* Cambridge University Press, New York

Ramesh S J 2012 Climate change and parliament, in Dubash N K ed *Handbook of Climate Change and India: Development, Politics and Governance* Routledge, London

Richter B 2010 *Beyond Smoke and Mirrors: Climate Change and Energy in the 21st Century* Cambridge University Press, New York

Smil V 2013 *Harvesting the Biosphere: What We Have Taken from Nature* MIT Press, Cambridge, Mass.

Solomon S et al. 2009 *Climate Change 2007: The Physical Science Basis* Cambridge University Press, Cambridge

Spivak G C 2012 Imperative to re-imagine the planet, in her *An Aesthetic Education in the Era of Globalisation* Harvard University Press, Cambridge, Mass.

Stager C 2011 *Deep Future: The Next 100,000 Years of Life on Earth* Thomas Dunne Books, New York

Steffen W Crutzen P J and McNeill J R 2007 The Anthropocene: Are humans now over-whelming the great forces of nature? *AMBIO* 36(8) 614–21

Sunstein C 2002 *Risk and Reason: Safety, Law, and the Environment* Cambridge University Press, Cambridge

Weitzman M L 2009 Some Basic Economics of Extreme Climate Change (http://www.environment.harvard.edu/docs/faculty_pubs/weitzman_basic.pdf)

Žižek S 2010 *Living in the End Times* Verso, London

5

THE POLITICAL ECOLOGY OF THE TECHNOCENE

Uncovering ecologically unequal exchange in the world-system

Alf Hornborg

Introduction

The currently unfolding discourse on the Anthropocene represents a convergence of Earth system natural science and what I will refer to as post-Cartesian social science. Both fields suggest that the Enlightenment distinction between Nature and Society is obsolete. Now that humanity is recognised as a geological force, the story goes, we must rethink not only the relations between natural and social sciences but also history, modernity, and the very idea of the human. Indeed, the increasingly inextricable interfusion of nature and human society is incontrovertible, as evidenced not only by climate change but also by several other kinds of anthropogenic transformations of ecosystems.

For decades having believed these circumstances to be self-evident, however, I am surprised by the intensity and also the character of the philosophical import that is currently attributed to them. The theoretical implications of the interfusion of Nature and Society, and the imperative of transdisciplinary approaches to human–environmental relations, were prominent in social-science agendas already in the 1990s (for example, Narain and Agarwal 1991; Haraway 1991; Croll and Parkin 1992; Latour 1993; Descola and Pálsson 1996; Peet and Watts 1996; Escobar 1999). Fields such as environmental anthropology, political ecology, development studies, and science-and-technology studies (STS) were attempting to deconstruct the Nature/Society distinction more than twenty years ago.[1] Rather than embroil ourselves in increasingly obscure deliberations on the possible philosophical implications of this shift, it should now be incumbent on social scientists to try to be as clear as possible about the societal and not least political issues that it raises.

The questions I wish to address in this chapter are: In what sense should the idea of the Anthropocene change our understanding of human–environmental relations, history, and modernity? If post-Cartesian perspectives can help us grasp climate change, how can they simultaneously illuminate the history of technology and development? Do they imply a complete dissolution of the categories of Nature and Society, or merely their reconceptualisation? Is the notion of the Anthropocene an adequate designation for the current period? What are the prospects for humanity surviving the planetary transformations that it has set in motion?

Can we dispense with the categories of 'Nature' and 'Society'?

Let me begin by emphasising that the physical mixing of Nature and Society does not warrant the abandonment of their analytical distinction. Rather, it is precisely this increasing recognition of the potency of social relations of power to transform the very conditions of human existence that should justify a more profound engagement with social and cultural theory. I find it deeply paradoxical and disturbing that the growing acknowledgement of the impact of societal forces on the biosphere should be couched in terms of a narrative so dominated by natural sciences such as climatology and geology.

A prominent role of science seems to be to represent technological progress as 'natural', as if capitalist expansion was founded exclusively on innovative discoveries of the 'nature' of things, and as if the social organisation of exchange had nothing to do with it. Constrained by our Cartesian categories, we are prompted by the materiality of technology to classify it as belonging to Nature rather than to Society. The post-Cartesian solution to this predicament would be to abandon the categories of 'nature' and 'society' altogether. Philippe Descola (2013, 82), for instance, rhetorically asks, 'where does nature stop and culture begin' in an increasingly anthropogenic biosphere. But to acknowledge that Nature and Society are inextricably intertwined all around us – in our bodies, our landscapes, our technologies – does not give us reason to abandon an analytical distinction between aspects or factors deriving from the organisation of human society, on the one hand, and those deriving from principles and regularities intrinsic to the pre-human universe, on the other. For example, the future of fossil-fuel capitalism no doubt hinges on the relation between the market price of oil and the Second Law of Thermodynamics,[2] but I cannot imagine that we have anything to gain from dissolving the analytical distinction between the logic of the world market and the laws of thermodynamics.

Regardless of how we represent them, the laws of thermodynamics have been in operation as long as there has been a universe, billions of years before the origins of human societies. They are an undeniably 'natural' aspect of human existence that pervade everything we do, and yet have not been, and cannot be, the least altered by human activity. In contrast, modes of human social organisation such as markets are ephemeral constructs that can be fundamentally transformed by political decisions or the vicissitudes of history. Yes, thermodynamics and markets are intertwined in fossil-fuel capitalism, but this is no reason to deny that the former belongs to Nature and the latter to Society.

In similar ways, it is possible *in principle* to trace the interaction of factors deriving from Nature and Society. It should be feasible, for instance, to estimate what the concentration of carbon dioxide in the atmosphere would have been today, if the additions deriving from human social processes had not occurred. Human societies have transformed planetary carbon cycles, but not the carbon atoms themselves. If the categories of Nature and Society are obsolete, as it is currently fashionable to propose, this only applies to images of Nature and Society as bounded, distinct realms of reality. At the risk of being unfair to Descartes, I shall follow the convention of referring to such distinctions as examples of 'Cartesian dualism'. It seems trivial to observe that such bounded, distinct realms do not exist (who would today object?), but it remains justified to identify the logic of natural and societal phenomena separately, prior to demonstrating how they interact in practice. The challenge of transdisciplinarity is not to jettison intra-disciplinary expertise, but to acknowledge that several kinds of specialised expertise may be required to understand socio-ecological processes. Such are the difficult but crucial ambitions of transdisciplinary fields like ecological economics and political ecology. The disciplines of physics and economics, for instance, both need their devoted scholars, but it would be mistaken to expect either of them in isolation to provide a full account of fossil-fuel capitalism.

A post-Cartesian perspective on the history of technology?

In consequence with the abandonment of Cartesian dualism in our approach to anthropogenic transformations of the biosphere, we have no less reason to reconsider human economies and technologies as similarly hybrid phenomena interlacing biophysical resources, cultural perceptions, and global power structures. Such insights deserve to be pursued not only at the micro-level of our interaction as individuals with specific artefacts, as advocated by Actor Network Theory (ANT), but more importantly at the macro-level, where the global assemblages of artefacts that I have called 'technomass' (Hornborg 2001) indeed are the very stuff of a highly inequitable world-system.[3] It is in this global sense that the social dimensions of technology are the most interesting. By viewing it as a system-wide totality, we can detect how global power relations are delegated to, and buttressed by, technology. Now that we are addressing the environmental predicaments of the Anthropocene from a truly global perspective, why should we not look at the socio-technical networks that brought us here in the same way?

Conventional historiography depicts the 'Industrial Revolution' as the product of British ingenuity and as a contribution destined to diffuse among all humankind. A scrutiny of the transition to fossil fuels in late eighteenth-century Britain, however, reveals the extent to which the historical origins of anthropogenic climate change were predicated on highly inequitable global processes from the start. The rationale for investing in steam technology at this time was geared to the opportunities provided by the constellation of a largely depopulated New World, Afro-American slavery, the exploitation of British labour in factories and mines, and the global demand for inexpensive cotton cloth (Hornborg 2011, 2013a). It would thus be highly misleading to conceive of the *anthropos* starring in the Anthropocene narrative as the human species (Malm and Hornborg 2014). 'Humanity' as a collective has never been an agent of history, and the technological fruits of the Industrial Revolution continue to be very unevenly accessible to different segments of world society. This uneven distribution of modern, fossil-fuel technology is in fact a condition for its very existence. The promises it held out to humanity were illusory all along: the affluence of high-tech modernity cannot be universalised, because it is predicated on a global division of labour that is geared precisely to huge price and wage differences between populations. What we have understood as technological innovation is an index of unequal exchange.

Let me rephrase this by properly explaining what I mean by 'modern technology'. My point is that the Industrial Revolution was not what we usually think it was. Or rather, it was more. The conditions of technological innovation were radically transformed in the late eighteenth century. We usually think that the decisive factors were engineering science and the adoption of fossil fuels, but none of this would have been possible without the global social processes that made the relative prices of labour and resources on the world market *prerequisite* to 'technological progress' in Europe. If slaves had been paid standard British wages, and depopulated American fields had fetched standard British land rent, I am not sure that there would have been an Industrial Revolution. Up until that historical point, 'technology' was founded on local ingenuity, and understood as such. Beyond that point, and for over two hundred years now, the understanding of technology as founded on mere ingenuity has persisted, but has become highly inadequate. Ingenuity is a necessary but not *sufficient* condition for modern technological 'progress'. Global price relations are systematically excluded from our definition of technology, even though, by organising asymmetric resource flows, they are crucial for its very existence. Much as inexpensive labour and land in colonial cotton plantations were fundamental to the Industrial Revolution (cf. Hornborg 2011, Chapter 5), it remains essential for high-tech society that prices of oil and other resources are manageable. What we have thought of as the history of human inventions is actually the history of rising inequalities within an increasingly globalised economy. When Paul Crutzen (2002, 23) refers to 'James Watt's design of the steam engine in 1784,' evoking our conventional understanding of an ingenious but seemingly random technological breakthrough, neither he nor his readers will be inclined to reflect on the extent to which this 'invention' implicated colonialism and slavery.

I am convinced that Cartesian dualism is at the root of the difficulties we are having in perceiving our technological fetishism. A tenacious illusion of Enlightenment thought is that a boundary can be drawn between material forms and the relations that generate them, and that it is only the latter that can be contested, negotiated, and transformed. I think this kind of distinction – the reification of *things* – is more problematic than the distinction between 'natural' and 'societal' aspects. It is the very essence of capitalist fetishism. The 'moderns' generally perceive tangible objects as given, and as separate from the invisible networks of relations in which they are embedded. Such distinctions alienate humans from non-human nature as well as from the products of their labour, because both are perceived as categories of autonomous objects rather than as manifestations of relations. But it does not require the abandonment of analytical reason to realise that it is as misleading to imagine machines as independent of global price relations and resource flows as it is to imagine organisms as independent of their environments. A tractor without diesel is as inanimate as an organism that has starved to death.

The density of distribution of technologies that are ultimately dependent on fossil fuels by and large coincides with that of purchasing power. These technologies are an index of capital accumulation, privileged resource consumption, and the displacement of both work and environmental loads. After more than two hundred years, we still tend to imagine 'technological progress' as nothing but the magic wand of ingenuity that, with no necessary political or moral implications elsewhere, will solve our local problems of sustainability. Universities throughout the world reproduce this illusion by entrenching the academic division of labour between faculties of engineering and faculties of economics. But globalised technological systems essentially represent an unequal exchange of embodied labour and land in the world-system (Hornborg 2011). The worldview of modern economics, the emergence of which accompanied the Industrial Revolution in the hub of the British Empire, systematically obscures the asymmetric exchange of biophysical resources on which industrialisation rests. This disjunction between exchange values and physics is as much a condition for modern technology as engineering.

Is the notion of the 'Anthropocene' adequate?

The uneven accumulation of technomass visible on satellite photos of night-time lights proceeds by means of a simple algorithm: the more fossil fuels and other resources it has dissipated today, the more it will afford to dissipate tomorrow. This account of our entry into the Anthropocene does not refer to the biological properties of the species *Homo sapiens*, but to a specific form of social organisation that emerged very recently in human history, as a strategy of one segment of humanity to dominate the remainder. This form of social organisation continues to be propelled by the interests not of our species, but of a social category (Malm and Hornborg 2014). As of 2008, less than 20 per cent of the world's population was responsible for over 70 per cent of carbon dioxide emissions since 1850 (Roberts and Parks 2007). An average American today emits as much carbon dioxide as 500 average citizens of some nations in Africa and Asia. It must thus be the work of social science to identify the drivers of rising emissions.

The dominant Anthropocene narrative, of course, does recognise that climate change derives from human activities, but these activities are then viewed as expressions of innate traits of our species. Rather than examine their societal and political drivers as factors that can be transformed, the narrative tends to represent them as natural and inevitable features of our biology. But phenomena such as worldviews, property relations, and power structures are *social* phenomena. They are beyond the horizons of natural science, because they require analytical tools that natural scientists are not provided with.

This is not to deny that human organisms are uniquely equipped to develop capitalism. Our semiotic capacity for abstract representation and language, which had enormous survival value for hundreds of thousands of years of hunting and gathering, finally generated general-purpose money and the globalised economy, which in turn made the Industrial Revolution feasible. The world-systemic events of the eighteenth century were products of a global history of increasing interconnectedness (and inequality) ultimately founded on the human capacity for abstract representation. The big question is whether this capacity will be of any use in redesigning our global economy for survival. To challenge the species-centrism of the Anthropocene narrative is to make two important points that are often disregarded by natural scientists: (1) the incentives, benefits, and negative repercussions of industrialisation are very unevenly distributed among social categories within the human species; and (2) there is nothing biologically inevitable about the institutions and forms of social organisation that we know as capitalism.

Dipesh Chakrabarty (2009) correctly observes that we now need to integrate the history of our species with the history of capital, but he does not provide us with any feasible suggestions on how to proceed. He is completely silent on how our biological capacity for abstract representation (as in language and other semiotic systems) is prerequisite to the very idea of money, and how money was in turn prerequisite to the Industrial Revolution that inaugurated the Anthropocene. But it is precisely through this chain of events that studies of natural and human history, while each reserving its specific arsenal of concepts and methods, can be integrated. Modern technology is the pivot of both, because it implicates both biophysical and socio-cultural dimensions of our increasingly globalised history. Rather than imply that climate change is the inexorable consequence of the emergence of *Homo sapiens*, as suggested by the notion of the 'Anthropocene', I would thus prefer that the geological epoch inaugurated in the late eighteenth century be named the *Technocene*.[4]

It is disturbing that social scientists often seem to be retreating from the playing field defined by Earth system science. Whether intended or not, this is a widespread consequence of the assertion that the distinction between 'natural' and 'social' is obsolete (Latour 1993). This dismal verdict on centuries of social science appears to be geared to the conviction of so-called Actor Network Theory that there is no difference between the agency of human beings equipped with perceptions and intentions, on the one hand, and that of rocks, artefacts, and other non-living things, on the other. This foundational assumption of Actor Network Theory is fundamental also to the approach of Latour (2013) and his followers to the Anthropocene. But let us examine this claim more closely. If humans and their artefacts can be shown to be 'actants' of very different kinds, it might help us retain some of our faith in social science.

In what sense do objects have agency?

In a paper co-authored with primatologist Shirley Strum, Bruno Latour argued that the key difference between the sociality of baboons and that of humans is that human relations can be anchored to partially independent and fixed points of reference beyond the body, such as language, symbols, and – importantly – material objects (Strum and Latour 1987). The fixity of such externalities actually simplifies social life, Strum and Latour suggest, compared to the constant Machiavellian manipulations of baboons. If, to a large extent, artefacts (including technologies) are indeed the substance of increasingly complicated human social relations, Latour's preoccupation with their 'agency' within hybrid networks or 'collectives' is understandable. Yet it raises questions. Most centrally, what is the relation between materiality, sociality, and imagination?

A focus on how artefacts are employed in the construction of human societies addresses a phenomenon that is specific to the human *species*, but it can also illuminate the specificity of the social condition that we know as *modernity*. The distinction between pre-modern and modern political economies hinges on the different roles of human perceptions in the two contexts. In pre-industrial societies, where political economy is about the social organisation of human muscle power, people have to be *persuaded* to exert themselves for the benefit of those in power. The operation of modern technology, however, locally *appears* to be independent of human perceptions. As we consider the role of artefacts in different human societies, a central question is: If material objects are mobilised as agents in systems of socio-ecological relations, what is the difference between their capacity to operate *without* the mediation of human perceptions, on the one hand, and their capacity to operate *by means of* such mediation, on the other? In other words, how do we distinguish between technology and magic?

I will argue that technology is our own version of magic. I define 'magic' as a category of social persuasion mediated by human perceptions but represented as independent of human consciousness. In this sense, I agree with Latour (1993) that 'modernity' is not a decisive break with 'pre-modern' ontologies. The Enlightenment demystification of pre-modern magic and 'superstition' was not a final purge of valid, objective knowledge, but a *provisional* and politically *positioned* one. Its understanding of the nature of economic growth and 'technological progress' has been a successful instrument of expansion for core regions of the world-system for over three centuries, but the multiple crises currently faced by global society are an indication of the approaching bankruptcy of this worldview. On the other hand, I continue to believe that even the illusions of capitalist modernity can be exposed through rational analysis, and I suppose that, in this sense, I continue to have faith in the Enlightenment. We can use the same Reason that gave us modern technology to show that this very technology is a particular kind of magic.

How do we deal with the role of human perceptions in granting agency to 'things'? Let us agree that both *keys* and *coins* have been delegated agency, but of different kinds. Such little pieces of metal can be crucial in providing access to resources, whether by physically opening doors, or by social persuasion. The way these metal objects are shaped – whether as keys or coins – have for centuries determined whether they operate as technology or through magic.[5] Coins and keys illustrate how social relations of power in different ways are delegated to material artefacts. They exemplify how such delegation can either be dependent on, or independent of, human perceptions. They thus make very tangible the distinction that John Maynard Keynes long ago made between 'organic' and 'atomic' propositions, the truth of the former depending on 'the beliefs of agents', whereas the truth of the latter is independent of any such beliefs (Marglin 1990, 15).

A conclusion from what I have argued so far is that there are three fundamental categories of artefacts, defined by the specific ways in which they are delegated agency. The first is local, non-globalised technology, which operates without the mediation of either human perceptions or exchange rates. It is exemplified by keys. The second is 'local magic', which operates by means of human perceptions, exemplified by coins. The third is globalised technology, which *locally* operates without the mediation of human perceptions, but globally relies on exchange rates that are dependent on human strategies and intentions. It could also be called 'global magic', and can be exemplified by machines propelled by fossil fuels or electricity. Globalised technology is 'magic' in the sense that it is a specific way of exerting power over other people while concealing the extent to which this power is mediated by human perceptions.

Political ecology in the Technocene

The discourse on political ecology emerged in the early 1970s as an ambition within several human sciences to relate local ecological dilemmas, primarily in what was then known as the 'Third World', to global political economy. Over the decades, two main lineages of research can be discerned: one acknowledging an objective Nature and a set of actors contesting each other's claims to resources, the other inspired by poststructuralist theory to deconstruct images of Nature as well as the identities and claims of the actors (Escobar 1999). Disarmed by its own relativism, the latter, constructivist approach has predictably yielded fewer substantive challenges to capitalist extractivism. Pursuing constructivism ever deeper into philosophical opacity, the 'political ecology' of Bruno Latour (2004) has been criticised for even more radically disarming political criticism (for example, Wilding 2010; Söderberg and Netzén 2010; Hornborg 2014).[6] The emphasis of the constructivist wing of science-and-technology studies on microsociological case studies of individual actors has gone hand-in-hand with a rebuttal of more inclusive socio-economic power structures like 'capitalism' or even 'society' (Söderberg and Netzén 2010, 100–2).

Following my previous argument, however, we must maintain that only *societies –* organised assemblages of interacting human beings – negotiate meanings, generate relations of unequal exchange, and enable people to exert power over each other. Of course, all these social relations are stabilised through the recruitment of non-human components into their networks, and, of course, they are to a large measure shaped by the specific features of these non-human components, but the driving forces and the glue that reproduce them are irreducibly *social* in the sense that they hinge on the incentives, intentions and agency of interacting human subjects.

All this certainly does not mean that social power does not have material components. On the contrary, it always does. Our challenge as social scientists is to show how these material dimensions of power are systematically obscured in hegemonic discourses and worldviews – for example, how the unequal global exchange of labour energy and other biophysical resources is obscured in mainstream economics, how this unequal exchange is prerequisite to our obsession with 'technological progress', and how 'technological progress' is thus ultimately a fetishised account of the global displacement of work and environmental burdens to social categories with less purchasing power.

The Anthropocene narrative is rapidly gaining ground as our hegemonic discourse and worldview. The question is how we relate to it as social scientists. To the extent that it prepares us to acknowledge the constant interlacing of Nature and Society – the material and the communicative – we can only hope that this vision will not be confined to the study of our changing biosphere and atmosphere, while we remain blind to the interlacing of the material and the social in our globalised technologies. A post-Cartesian understanding of the Industrial Revolution should fundamentally reframe the discourse on political ecology. Rather than dream of advanced technological solutions to problems of ecological sustainability,[7] we would recognise most modern technologies as social strategies for *displacing* problems (labour as well as environmental loads) to areas where labour and environmental degradation are less expensive. Instead of technological utopianism, this radical reconceptualisation of technology should prompt us to critically consider the role of general-purpose money in orchestrating asymmetric transfers of labour power and natural resources in the world-system.

Undoing industrialism: redesigning money to curb globalisation

Given this analysis of the respective roles of capitalism and the species-specific characteristics of *Homo sapiens*, what kind of visions for a sustainable future can it support? Let us first establish that there is no inevitable connection between human biology and industrial capitalism.[8] Our capacity for abstract representation was prerequisite to capitalism, but only by means of the specific sociocultural institution of general-purpose money.[9] It was through the globalised circulation of general-purpose money that all the ingredients of the Industrial Revolution – American fields, African slaves, cotton fibre, British workers, coal, cotton textiles, and so on – were transformed into commensurable and interchangeable commodities. The generalised commoditisation of all this human time and natural space, which made industrialisation possible, is *not* an inexorable consequence of the human capacity for representation. If the economic strategies generating globalisation and indus-trialisation are root causes of the perilous prospects of climate change, it should be theoretically possible to avert this threat by modifying the conditions of economic rationality. It should be feasible, in principle, to organise a monetary system that restricts the interchangeability of products to specific spheres of exchange through the use of special-purpose currencies. This is not to suggest that certain kinds of exchanges should be prohibited, but that the options available to individual actors should encourage transactions that substantially reduce the consumption of fossil fuels and other practices contributing to environmental degradation.

To make this suggestion more tangible, let us imagine that a nation–state seriously wishes to reduce the long-distance transport required to provision its citizens.[10] It could achieve this goal by establishing a special currency, a certain amount of which is provided to its citizens on a monthly basis as a tax-free basic income, but which can *only be used to buy goods and services originating within a certain geographical distance from the point of purchase.*[11] It would serve as a 'complementary currency' in the sense that it did not replace conventional money, only provide an alternative to it. The new currency would tend to circulate within localised circuits of exchange, encouraging the growth of an informal sector alongside the conventional economy. The amount provided to each citizen or household would correspond to basic requirements for survival. The extent to which people wished to continue earning conventional, general-purpose money to enable additional consumption would be a matter of personal choice. A likely scenario would be that most people decided to divide their time between working in the formal and informal sectors. What is beyond doubt is that people would tend to *use* the new currency at least to procure basic necessities such as food, repairs, carpentry and so on, as this would leave more of their conventional income for other kinds of expenditures. Local farmers and other entrepreneurs would be encouraged to accept (tax-free) payment in the new currency for two reasons: they would be able to use some of it to pay for local labour, services, and goods; and, they would be offered the option of converting some of it into conventional money, through the authorities, at beneficial rates.[12] Once in operation, this system would undoubtedly radically reduce the demand for long-distance transport, which is one of the main drivers of climate change (Hornborg 2013b). In the long run, it would not only be more sustainable – reducing energy use, greenhouse gas emissions and waste, while enhancing local cooperation, biodiversity and resilience – but also reduce public expenses for transport infrastructure, environmental protection, health services and social security.

What might prompt a nation–state or other political authority to embark on such a radical transformation of market logic?[13] Obviously, the answer is not sim-ply the revelation that 'free' market trade and the accumulation of technological infrastructure is tantamount to an objectively asymmetric exchange of human time and natural space in global society, or even that these correlates of economic growth are generating disastrous climate change. The vocabulary/cosmology of mainstream economics would no doubt be able to resist such moral and political critique, as it has until now. For that vocabulary/cosmology to collapse, business as usual must itself be under threat. At least two such plausible threats can be envisaged, perhaps in conjunction: a definitive collapse of the global financial system, a breakdown ultimately geared to the rising costs of shrinking supplies of energy and other resources; and, a global ecological crisis such as that evoked by the notion of planetary boundaries. When either or both of these scenarios can no longer be disregarded, reforms that currently seem highly improbable, such as the one advocated here, may be considered in a new light.

To consciously redesign the human sign system that is currently jeopardising the biosphere would be to acknowledge the precise way in which Society and Nature are intertwined, and to act responsibly on that knowledge. It would help humans everywhere to regain a relation to the non-human environment that is local and sentient, rather than continue to conceive of Nature as a global abstraction dissociated from our actions yet threatening to imperil our grandchildren.

Notes

1 The field of political ecology, in particular, has long struggled to reconcile the constructivist approaches predominant in anthropology and human geography, on the one hand, with objectivist approaches to biophysical Nature, on the other (Escobar 1999). Adopting a much longer time perspective, environmental historians have traced our acknowledgement of revolutionary human–environmental interfusion to the late eighteenth century (Locher and Fressoz 2012). Humans have interfered with natural cycles for millennia (cf. Redman 1999), but the scale of interference following the 'Industrial Revolution' is decisively transforming the biosphere.

2 The Second Law of Thermodynamics states that entropy (disorder) will inevitably increase in an isolated system. As the Earth is not an isolated system, this did not pose a problem for the biosphere until humans began relying on finite deposits of fossil fuels.

3 For paradigmatic illustrations of world-system analysis, see Wallerstein (1974–1989) and Frank and Gills (1993). For edited collections attempting to integrate world-system analysis and global environmental change, see Goldfrank, Goodman and Szasz (1999), Hornborg and Crumley (2006) and Hornborg, McNeill and Martinez-Alier (2007).

4 Other alternatives to the 'Anthropocene' include the 'Econocene' (Norgaard 2013) and the 'Capitalocene' (Malm and Hornborg 2014). 'Capitalocene' was coined by Andreas Malm at a seminar in Lund in 2009. It usefully emphasises the role of 'capitalism' in generating transformations of the biosphere, but might raise the objection that various forms of capital accumulation had caused ecological degradation, albeit at a lesser scale, for millennia before the Industrial Revolution (cf. Redman 1999; Frank and Gills 1993).

5 To have agency, coins must be believed to have value. Significantly, the invention of the slot-machine enabled even coins to assume technological functions, alongside the magic that Marx called 'money fetishism'. When we use coins to buy a Coke or enter a public bathroom we might reflect over the fact that magical objects can be converted into technology.

6 Latour's efforts to deconstruct distinctions between subject and object and between Culture and Nature apparently duplicate those of early German Romantics such as Schelling in the period 1797–1806, and they raise the same philosophical objections (Wilding 2010).

7 Among the many costly, resource-intensive, and thus inherently privileged technologies that have been advocated as strategies to reduce (local) carbon dioxide emissions are nuclear power, photovoltaic energy, and carbon capture and storage.

8 In this context of discussing anthropogenic environmental change, I see no reason to distinguish between 'industrial capitalism' and the industrialism of purportedly non-capitalist societies such as the Soviet Union or China.

9 The cultural and historical conditions that promoted the emergence of general-purpose money have been endlessly discussed in economic history, economic anthropology, sociology and philosophy. It will here suffice to observe that its adoption required both the general human capacity for abstract representation and specific socio-cultural circumstances encouraging economic exchange disembedded from local social relations and symbolic systems.

10 To the extent that a single nation-state is able to set a highly successful example, other nations can be expected to follow.

11 This latter requirement, although crucial for the prospect of transforming the logic of money, has so far generally been absent in experiments with complementary and local currencies (e.g. LETS).

12 These rates would be set as a compromise between the entrepreneur's demands and the authorities' loss of tax revenue.

13 Note that the transformative implications for market logic would lie in the differentiation between *scales* of market exchange, rather than in the idea of market exchange as such.

References

Chakrabarty D 2009 The climate of history: Four theses *Critical Inquiry* 35 197–222

Croll E and Parkin D eds 1992 *Bush Base – Forest Farm: Culture, Environment and Development* Routledge, London

Crutzen P 2002 Geology of mankind *Nature* 3 23 January

Descola P 2013 *Beyond Nature and Culture* University of Chicago Press, Chicago

Descola P and Pálsson G eds 1996 *Nature and Society: Anthropological Perspectives* Routledge, London

Escobar A 1999 After nature: Steps to an anti-essentialist political ecology *Current Anthropology* 40(1) 1–30

Frank A G and Gills B K eds 1993 *The World System: Five Hundred Years or Five Thousand?* Routledge, London

Goldfrank W L Goodman D and A Szasz eds 1999 *Ecology and the World-System* Greenwood Press, Santa Barbara

Haraway D 1991 *Simians, Cyborgs, and Women: The Reinvention of Nature* Routledge, New York

Hornborg A 2001 *The Power of the Machine: Global Inequalities of Economy, Technology, and Environment* AltaMira, Walnut Creek

Hornborg A 2011 *Global Ecology and Unequal Exchange: Fetishism in a Zero-sum World* Routledge, London

Hornborg A 2013a The fossil interlude: Euro–American power and the return of the Physiocrats, in Strauss S, Rupp S and Love T eds *Cultures of Energy: Power, Practices, Technologies* Left Coast Press, Walnut Creek 41–59

Hornborg A 2013b Revelations of resilience: From the ideological disarmament of disaster to the revolutionary implications of (p)anarchy *Resilience: International Policies, Practices and Discourses* 1(2) 116–29

Hornborg A 2014 Technology as fetish: Marx, Latour, and the cultural foundations of capitalism *Theory, Culture & Society* 31(4) 119–40

Hornborg A and Crumley C eds 2006 *The World System and the Earth System: Global Socioenvironmental Change and Sustainability since the Neolithic* Left Coast Press, Walnut Creek

Hornborg A, McNeill J R and Martinez-Alier J eds 2007 *Rethinking Environmental History: World-system History and Global Environmental Change* AltaMira, Lanham

Latour B 1993 *We Have Never Been Modern* Harvard University Press, Cambridge, Mass.

Latour B 2004 *Politics of Nature: How to Bring the Sciences into Democracy* Harvard University Press, Cambridge, Mass.

Latour B 2013 *Facing Gaia: Six Lectures on the Political Theology of Nature* The Gifford Lectures on Natural Religion, Edinburgh

Locher F and Fressoz J-B 2012 Modernity's frail climate: A climate history of environmental reflexivity *Critical Inquiry* 38(3) 579–98

Malm A and Hornborg A 2014 The geology of mankind? A critique of the Anthropocene narrative *The Anthropocene Review* 1 62–9

Marglin S 1990 Towards the decolonization of the mind in Apffel-Marglin F and Marglin S eds *Dominating Knowledge: Development, Culture, and Resistance* Clarendon, Oxford 1–28

Narain S and Agarwal A 1991 *Global Warming in an Unequal World: A Case of Environmental Colonialism* Centre for Science and Environment, Delhi

Norgaard R B 2013 The Econocene and the California delta *San Francisco Estuary & Watershed Science* 11 1–5

Peet R and Watts M eds 1996 *Liberation Ecologies: Environment, Development, Social Movements* Routledge, London

Redman C L 1999 *Human Impact on Ancient Environments* University of Arizona Press, Tucson

Roberts J T and Parks B C 2007 *A Climate of Injustice: Global Inequality, North–South Politics, and Climate Policy* MIT Press, Cambridge, MA

Söderberg J and Netzén A 2010 When all that is theory melts into (hot) air: Contrasts and parallels between actor network theory, autonomist Marxism, and open Marxism *Ephemera* 10(2) 95–118

Strum S and Latour B 1987 Redefining the social link: From baboons to humans *Social Science Information* 26 783–802

Wallerstein I 1974–1989 *The Modern World-System* 1–3 Academic Press, San Diego

Wilding A 2010 Naturphilosophie Redivivus: On Bruno Latour's 'political ecology' *Cosmos and History: The Journal of Natural and Social Philosophy* 6 1

6

LOSING THE EARTH KNOWINGLY

Six environmental grammars around 1800

Jean-Baptiste Fressoz

The promoters of the Anthropocene have not only coined a name for a new geological era; they have also proposed a very peculiar history of the last two hundred and fifty years. It goes like this: since 1800, and more intensely since 1945, humanity, taken as an undifferentiated whole, has inadvertently altered the Earth system through population growth and economic development, both supported by an exponential use of fossil fuels. Fortunately, at the end of the twentieth century, on the brink of a global disaster, a small group of Earth system scientists has opened our eyes to the danger. Thanks to them, 'We are the first generation with the knowledge of how our activities influence the Earth System, and thus the first generation with the power and the responsibility to change our relationship with the planet' (Steffen et al. 2011, 749).

The concept of the Anthropocene and its wide, yet critical reception among social scientists could trigger serious historical reflection on the origins of the environmental disaster we live in. Indeed, compared to 'global change' or 'environmental crisis', its greatest merit is to put humanity, time and history at the centre.

'Historicising the Anthropocene' can refer to various intellectual projects. The most obvious and politically urgent is to write a proper history of the new epoch, replacing the rather vague 'anthropos' with the nations and companies, institutions and imaginaries, technologies and ideologies that are the true drivers of the Anthropocene. When confronted with contemporary global issues, the specificity of historical reasoning and the construction of explanatory narratives tend to disappear in favour of a quantitative vision. Global statistics, so central to the Anthropocene thesis, create the image of a global humanity united by carbon dioxide, thereby erasing the incommensurability of responsibilities. Indeed, a quick glance at carbon emissions data reveals that, up to 1980, the *anthropos* of the Anthropocene seems to have a very strong English accent. In cumulative terms from 1800 to 1950, 65 per cent of carbon emissions were emitted by Great Britain and the United States alone. Historically speaking, the Anthropocene could well have been called the Anglocene.

Global statistics are also secondary in the causal order. They only measure and reflect the end results of historical processes that are the true causes of the crisis. History is already well equipped for our new geological era, as many classical objects of the discipline play a prominent role in the advent of the Anthropocene. In disorder and without completeness: the industrial revolution, capital accumulation, world-systems, formal and informal imperialism, wars and the military, unequal exchange, Fordism, consumption, energy transitions, science and reductionism, agnotology, and so on. We need to connect these topics to the quantitative history of the Anthropocene.

Beyond replacing the consensual 'anthropos' with a historically grounded narrative, a second, subtler challenge for history is to refute the narrative of a blind humanity transforming its environment unknowingly. On this point, the official story of the Anthropocene actually rehearses what sociologists of risk and postmodernity explained in the 1980s. Thirty years ago 'we' were already the first generation to understand the threat of the environmental crisis and the dead end of development. Thirty years ago, 'risk society and 'reflexive modernity', like the Anthropocene today, were conceived of as a momentous break in the history of civilisation (Beck 1986; Giddens 1991). Because it distinguishes between a blind past and a present on the way to illumination, the Anthropocene could have the same effect as 'reflexive modernity' in the 1980s: the geological sublime replaces the historically grandiloquent, but in the end produces a similar arrow of time based on the presumed progress of our reflexivity. The Anthropocene could well be one of the last reincarnations of the discourse of progress, which it reformulates as the teleology of humanity becoming reflexive as geological agent. The problem with any prophetic narrative centred on a sudden ecological awareness is that by obliterating the reflexivity of past societies, it tends to depoliticise the long history of environmental destruction. And, conversely, by concentrating on our own reflexivity, it tends to naturalise our ecological concern.

As an antidote, this chapter provides a possible typology of the 'environmental grammars' existing at the dawn of the Anthropocene. These grammars are deeply connected to specific disciplines, from natural history to chemistry and thermodynamics, but, more importantly, they provide rules of conduct towards nature. They discriminate between pure and impure, nature and artifice, safety and danger, sustainability and unsustainability; they blame historical processes and valorise certain modes of life.

I distinguish six of them: *circumfusa*/environment, climate, nature's economy, human–nature metabolisms, thermodynamics and exhaustion. The list is not limiting and other classifications are possible. The aim is less historical than to infuse a bit of modesty in the Anthropocene revelation. While it would be a modernist projection to characterise early Anthropocene societies as 'green', conversely it would be self-indulgent to judge our current environmental concerns and theoretical categories (ecosystem, biodiversity, global warming, biogeochemical cycles, etc.) as the only way to be 'environmentally conscious'. It is also unlikely that the naming of a geological epoch or the advent of a geologically reflexive agent make a revolution in the history human–nature relationship, and even less so in the history of environmental destruction.

Circumfusa/environment

At first glance, the history of the word 'environment' in the public space seems to confirm the thesis of a recent environmental awakening. 'The environment' was institutionalised only in the 1970s with the creation of the US Environmental Protection Agency, ministries of environment in various OECD countries and the United Nations Environment Program (1972). But two points need to be made. First, these new agencies and new departments are responsible for enforcing laws and regulations (such as clean air acts) that have a much longer history (Thorsheim 2006; Massard Guilbaud 2010; Le Roux 2011). Second, the genealogy of the word 'environment' shows that the form of reflexivity it names is actually much older.

In the 1850s 'environment' was used as a synonym for 'surroundings' or 'exterior'. If the environment affects living beings and humans (as stated, for instance, in Carlyle, 1837), the word is not yet used to underline the fragility of nature. In *Man and Nature*, the great American environmentalist book of the 1860s, George Perkins Marsh does not use the word; nor does Eugene Huzar in *The End of the World by Science* (1855), the first catastrophic philosophy of technology. It was Herbert Spencer in *Principles of Psychology* (1855) and *Principles of Biology* (1864) who coined a scientific use for 'environment'. In Spencer's works, environment describes the 'surrounding circumstances' of an organism, that is to say, all the physical influences that affect and transform it.[1] In fact, Spencer, probably getting his inspiration from Lamarck and his notion of *circonstances influentes*, inherits from and gives new life to a fundamental concept of eighteenth-century hygiene, that of *circumfusa* (the 'surrounding things' in Latin). Under this category, doctors included the air, water and places (central to the etiology of neo-Hippocratic medicine) and all the various factors influencing health in general (Fressoz 2009). This *circumfusa*–environment filiation is important to keep in mind because it refutes the common opposition between the old 'environment', as an exteriority out of reach, and the environment of the 1970s, malleable, fragile and therefore eminently political.

In fact, in the eighteenth century, the *circumfusa* are already understood as both in danger and dangerous. Seemingly benign alterations could have dire consequences. For example, Abbé Dubos' explanation for the degeneration of the Romans in antiquity is that the medical constitution of Rome had been altered by the destruction of the sewage system (*cloaca maxima*) and by the multiplication of alum mines in the Latium plain (Dubos 1714). According to the medical and philosophical thought of the eighteenth century, human societies evolve in relation to the atmospheric envelopes they inhabit and help to create. Human action reverberates in the *circumfusa*, which in return change human constitutions (Fressoz 2012).

Given this sanitary sensibility, the fumes, smells and vapours emitted by urban workshops could be extremely threatening. During the eighteenth century and well into the nineteenth, populous and industrious cities were generally considered to be unwholesome places, just like swamps, prisons and ships.

So we have the environmental concerns of eighteenth-century urban institutions. The police were in charge of the good management of urban atmospheres, and the *circumfusa* were some of the main objects of their daily work. In his famous treatise *De la Police* (1699–1704), Nicolas Delamare, a commissaire of Paris, referred to the Hippocratic *Airs, Waters, Places* so as to justify the rule of the police over the city. The threats posed by the *circumfusa* and the preservation of citizens' health legitimated the extension of police powers over almost everything pertaining to urban life – streets and buildings, food supply and quality, waters, airs and workshops.

The crucial point to bear in mind is that industrialisation took place not in a cognitive void, but in spite of prevailing medical theories emphasising the importance of a wholesome environment and the dangers of pollution. In France, industrialisation entailed a profound theoretical and political shift around 1800. First, in 1810, the government passed a decree protecting industrialists from their neighbours' complaints. Factories were submitted to a stringent authorisation procedure, but in exchange could no longer be prohibited or displaced by mere police order. Neighbours who could not hope to see the factories removed, received financial compensation for the environmental damages they suffered.

This financial regulation of environment entailed a second major transformation. A small group of chemists and doctors (in France the first *hygienists* were in charge of granting authorisations to factories) justified the presence of manufacturing by studying statistically the causes of mortality and longevity. They emphasised the importance of social factors over environmental ones. Rejecting neo-Hippocratic environmental medicine, social hygiene allowed *hygienists* and the administration to disregard the medical arguments against industrial pollution.

The frail climate of modernity

Closely related to the notion of *circumfusa*, the idea of climate is also central to understanding early Anthropocene societies. Originally defined as a purely topographical notion (a zone between two latitudes), climate acquires its contemporary meaning (the average conditions of temperature and precipitation in a given place) in the eighteenth century. As meteorologists charted local variations in humidity, winds and temperatures, they also understood the impact of locality upon climates and discovered their transformations over time. The comparison between widely different climates at the same latitude across the Atlantic reinforced the idea that civilisation and deforestation transform the meteorology of entire countries. As climate retains its ability to determine human and political constitutions, what determines the health of populations and social organisations is no longer just the position on the globe, but mundane things – forests and marshes, but also fumes and urban forms – on which society can act for good or ill. Climate thus became in the eighteenth century a crucial epistemic category to reflect upon the consequences of human action on the environment and vice versa (Fressoz and Locher 2012).

Take, for example, the 'epochs of nature' of Georges-Louis Leclerc Buffon (1778). Buffon's seventh and last epoch of the world's history is aptly named 'the epoch of Man'. It is characterised by the advent of humankind as a global force. At the beginning of the Anthropocene, Buffon explained that 'the whole face of the earth today bears the imprint of the power of man' (Buffon 1778, 244). And this influence is even being exerted upon the climate because, by tinkering with the environment, humankind will be able to 'alter the influence of its own climate, thus setting the temperature that suits it best'. For Buffon, humanity's impact on nature is generally positive. He contrasts the fertility of the 'civilised nature' of Europe with the savage, hostile and neglected nature of South America.

This then-common view of climate–society co-production did not only give way to optimistic and demiurgic dreams of nature improvement and climate control. Many early-nineteenth-century authors developed nightmarish visions of anthropogenic climate catastrophe. The issue of deforestation in particular transforms Buffon's optimism into climatic angst. Meteorologists and agronomists refer to plant physiology to incriminate deforestation for all sorts of weather events – harsh winters, droughts, storms and excessive rainfall. Trees and forests, by their constant relationships with the atmosphere, moderate climate – they dry damp locations and moisten dry places and they prevent storms, erosion and flooding. The massive deforestation of the seventeenth and eighteenth centuries, both in colonial settings (Grove 1995) and in Western Europe – the forest cover in France seems to have fallen from 18 million hectares in 1550 to 9 million in 1789 (Pomeranz 2000, 308) – is perceived as a break in the natural and providential order that keeps in balance the water cycle linking the soil and the atmosphere.

Concern about climate change was widespread in European scientific cycles. For instance, after the eruption of the Tambora volcano in Indonesia in April 1815, Europe experienced a series of anomalous seasons and bad harvests. In consequence, learned societies in France, Switzerland and Britain fostered research on climate change, pointing to the possibility of its anthropogenic origin. In France, the debate on climate change is particularly acute as it is blamed by the Restoration government on the Revolution through its sale of aristocrats' woods and the short-sighted exploitation of forests by a new bourgeoisie. In 1821, the Minister for the Interior ordered a national inquiry on climate change and deforestation. In Britain, the enclosures are discussed in relation to climate change. According to the renowned horticulturalist John Williams, the multiplication of hedges, and pastures for animal feed rendered the British climate colder and wetter than in the past (Williams 1806).

Several remarks are in order. First, what is at stake in the first quarter of the nineteenth century is not local anomalies but the global climate. For important commentators, such as Joseph Banks', Secretary of the Royal Society of London, deforestation is altering a global water cycle that connects the tropical seas to the polar ice caps. Secondly, climate change is also conceived of as an irreversible phenomenon questioning civilisation itself. As population growth and the expansion of manufactures entail deforestation, climate changes and the rain stops, thus undermining the possibility of future reforestation. Civilisation is caught in a vicious circle of deforestation and climatic change. In the 1820s, foresters develop a theory about the collapse of the ancient civilisations of the Middle East relying on the climatic effect of deforestation. In the engraving of Figure 6.1, François-Antoine Rauch, a prominent French advocate of forest conservation in the 1820s, depicts the ruins of Babylon now lying in the middle of a desert. It serves as a cautionary tale for the French government; this could be Paris's future if deforestation is not stopped.

Thirdly, in the political and scientific spheres of the early nineteenth century, climate change was not a marginal topic. Because wood remains the main source of energy, climate change interferes with a fundamental choice in land use between forests (and thus wood and factories) and fields (and thus food and population). Climate change was discussed in the French National Assembly in 1791, 1821 and 1836. Anthropogenic climate change was also studied by scientific bodies, ranging from provincial literary societies to the Académie des Sciences in Paris and the Royal Society in London (Fressoz and Locher 2012).

Several processes progressively relaxed these climatic anxieties after 1850. First, the shift from wood to coal as the main source of energy made forests much less central to western European economies and their conservation a less vital issue. Secondly, in the second half of the nineteenth century, as geologists

FIGURE 6.1 François-Antoine Rauch, The Ruins of Babylon *Annales Européennes,* 1824, vol. 4, 17

and astronomers gradually accepted the ice age theory, humanity appeared to be trapped in immense cycles of geological time triggered mainly by astronomical phenomena, without human action having any impact whatsoever. And, thirdly, climate itself lost much of its importance as a determinant of social forms and cultures. At the end of the nineteenth century, sociology and economics were careful to distance themselves from the old climatic determinisms and replace them by their own systems of causality (Fressoz and Locher 2012).

Nature's economy

Historians of scientific ecology have identified the concept of 'nature's economy' as the origin of the contemporary notion of ecosystem. They have also demonstrated its centrality in eighteenth- and nineteenth-century natural history (Worster 1977; Drouin 1997). From Linnaeus to Thoreau, naturalists marveled at the systemic relationships weaving all beings together into a coherent whole designed by God. One objective of natural history was to discover networks of interdependency and to demonstrate the 'symphonic precision of nature'. According to natural theology, every being played a precise function in the maintenance of the natural order. Gilbert White, in his *Natural History of Selborne* (1789), explained that 'the most insignificant insects . . . have much more influence in the economy of nature than the incurious are aware of . . . Earthworms, though in appearance a small and despicable link in the chain of nature, yet, if lost would make a lamentable chasm' (White 1789, 216). In this fully connected world, criss-crossed by chains of dependence and reciprocity, disaster is always looming. In face of nature's infinite complexity, there emerged a feeling of dread and modesty. For Jean–Baptiste Robinet: 'We [humans] and other large animals are vermin of the largest animal that we call Earth' (Robinet 1766).

The concept of nature's economy also led to a renewal of the organic vision of the Earth. Carolyn Merchant argues that in antiquity, the Renaissance and up to the scientific revolution, our planet was conceived of as a living body with its veins and its fluids, its shivering and its diseases. The Earth was a mother that had to be respected. The scientific revolution and the emergence of capitalism led to an inexorable decline of organic cosmology. Nature became a vast mechanism to be explained, mastered and exploited (Merchant 1980). In fact, the vision of a living planet persists long after the scientific revolution. In 1795, Felix Nogaret, a courtesan philosopher, published a popular essay depicting the Earth as an animal (Nogaret 1795). The renowned geologists Eugène Patrin and Philippe Bertrand criticised these direct analogies, but nevertheless advocated the introduction of organic explanations. Considering the Earth as having 'organic functions' helped one grasp the 'intimate connexity of all the phenomena of the globe'. The Earth and other planets in the universe formed a third kind of organism, distinct from plants and animals (Patrin 1806, 315). In 1821, the socialist thinker Charles Fourier took on board organic cosmologies so as to criticise individualism in its relation to nature. Climate change, torrents, silting of rivers, erosion and deforestation were testimonies to a planetary disease caused by individualistic societies unable to regulate their relation with the planet (Schérer 2001). Inspired by Fourier, the French catastrophist philosopher Eugene Huzar also constructed the image of a planet as a living and fragile organism. Man's actions were like wounds inflicted on the Earth-as-body (Fressoz 2007a).

Nature's economy is profoundly reconfigured by the emergence of Darwin's theory of evolution and the refutation of a divine order structuring the natural world. Nevertheless, Darwinism, with the law of evolution and coevolution, and the Malthusian law of the geometric increase of populations produced the image of a fully inhabited nature in which all possible resources were exploited by all the different species. In a preparatory manuscript for the *Origin of Species* Darwin compared nature 'to a surface covered with ten thousand sharp wedges, many of the same shape, and many of different shapes representing different species, all packed closely together and all driven in by incessant blows . . . often transmitted very far to other wedges in many lines of direction' (quoted in Staufer 1987, 208).

The word ecology (*Öekologie*), proposed by Ernst Haeckel in 1867, did not point to a *terra incognita*, but rather renamed and reorganised old traditions in natural history. With the word *Öekologie*, Haeckel wanted to achieve two objectives. First, to suggest that living beings struggled for life, as demonstrated by Darwin, but also that they composed a home, an *oikos*, prospering on symbiosis and mutual help. Secondly, his aim was to integrate in a single discipline two fields of inquiry: the study of the interactions between living organisms (Darwin's theory of natural selection) and the older study of the influence of physical conditions on living beings (climate, soil, and so on). The slow diffusion of the term (one must wait for the International Botanical Congress in 1893 to find the contemporary spelling of ecology) is not a sign of a particular difficulty of supposedly reductionist natural sciences to understand the systemic aspect of nature but was due to the existence of the concept of natural economy which remained very much alive until the late nineteenth century (Worster 1977, 191–5).

Once again, the history of environmental reflexivity is not one of a rising awareness culminating in the Anthropocene revelation. The theme of nature's economy regularly surfaced in socio-environmental struggles of the eighteenth century. For example, in the 1770s in Normandy fishermen complained about glassmakers harvesting kelp (whose ashes, used to produce soda, were highly valued in glassmaking), specifically citing kelp's role in the survival of young fish and the natural economy of the marine world. In a memorandum sent to the Academy of Sciences, they explained that fish spawn in kelp because kelp retained fish eggs, increased the chances of fertilisation and protected the young fish from waves and predators (Fressoz 2012). In the 1950s, such ecological connections were 'forgotten' in the management of fisheries. The principle of the maximum sustainable yield, implemented in international treaties, envisages fish populations as a crop to be harvested. Overfishing is understood as a reversible phenomenon; if catches decrease, the reduction of fishing pressure would quickly re-establish the stocks. Systemic interactions between species and the role of the marine environment were neglected and thus the issue of exhaustion marginalised (Finley 2011).

The metabolic rift

The exchange of matter between human society and nature constitutes a fourth grammar of environmental reflexivity. In the late eighteenth century, a chemical vision of agriculture emerged: as each harvest removed minerals from the soil, soil fertility depended on the return of excreta to the fields. In his *Rural Economy* (1770), Arthur Young reflected upon the right balance between pasture and tillage and the best way to move organic nutrients between plants and animals. The task was momentous: 'if one of the proportions is broken,' Young wrote, 'the whole chain would be affected' (quoted in Warde 2011, 166). The development of a chemical theory of agriculture with Liebig, Dumas and Boussingault increased the complexity of the problem. Liebig's 'law of the minimum' fueled a pessimistic view of soils' future, whose fertility was henceforth determined by the subtle balance of various chemical elements (N, P, K, Ca, Mg, S, Fe, and so on).

Strong concerns were voiced in the nineteenth century about the metabolic rift between city and countryside. Urbanisation, that is to say, the concentration of people, animals and their *excreta*, prevented the return to the land of minerals indispensible to its fertility. Great materialist thinkers, from Liebig to Marx, agronomists, hygienists and chemists warned against both soil depletion and urban pollution. For Liebig, urbanisation and the failure to recycle organic matter would lead inexorably to the collapse of European societies. From his analysis of agricultural metabolism, he formulated a scathing critique of modern agriculture and capitalist globalisation. In a famous angry passage he blamed Great Britain, the major importer of guano and mineral fertilisers, of plundering fertilisers from other countries: 'Great Britain deprives all countries of the conditions of their fertility. . . Like a vampire it hangs on the breast of Europe, and even the world, sucking its lifeblood' (quoted in Brock 1997, 178).

Many socialist thinkers of the mid-nineteenth century discovered the work of Liebig and the whole issue of the metabolic rift. In 1843, Pierre Leroux, an early socialist writer (famous for coining the word 'socialism'), used Liebig's arguments to theorise a social utopia he called the 'Circulus' in which society would live in homeostasis, actively occupied to maintain the cycle of nutrients with land and to minimise material losses in the production process. In the third volume of *Capital*, Marx also criticised the environmental consequences of capitalist agriculture with its large farms breaking up the material cycle between society and nature. According to Marx, there was no possible emancipation from nature, whatever the modes of production; human societies remained dependent on a historically determined metabolic regime, the peculiarity of capitalist metabolism being its unsustainability (Foster 2000).

The fate of excrement was thus at the heart of nineteenth-century debates. Excrement was linked to the social question because impoverished soil fomented famines, pauperism and revolution. It was related to the wholesomeness of urban environments and thus to the question of degeneracy. It involved geopolitical issues as Great Britain and the United States competed for the monopoly of Peru's guano. And it was even related to the fate of civilisations; Rome, according to Liebig, had fallen for failing to manage its excrement properly.

Entropy

With chemistry, thermodynamics (the study of energy's properties and transformations) furnished parallel conceptual tools to study the relationships between human society and nature. Since its inception, the concept of energy has been used to explain economic and social problems (Wise 1990). In the late nineteenth century, it was already possible to construct a quantitative view of the energy fluxes intercepted by plants or extracted from coal and to trace its circulation in the economy. One of the first to conduct such an analysis was the Ukrainian socialist Sergei Podolinsky. Comparing pasture with wheat cultivation he demonstrated that the energy efficiency of agriculture increased with the proportion of animal or human labour input and decreased with the use of machines using coal (Martinez–Alier 1987).

Many authors at the turn of the nineteenth and twentieth centuries proposed a reform of economics and of the economy itself based on the study of energy – Eduard Sacher, *Foundations of Mechanics of Society* (1881), Patrick Geddes, *John Ruskin Economist* (1884), Rudolf Clausius, *On the Energy Stocks and Their Valuation in Nature for the Benefit of Humankind* (1885), and Frederick Soddy, *Cartesian Economics* (1921). These authors shared a very critical view of political economy, which merely considered the monetary value of things. Merely 'chrematistic' (focused purely on monetary wealth) political economy obscured the real problem of economy, namely the material and energy supply of human societies. They also pointed out the discrepancy between the appearance of growing financial wealth and the reality of energy's inexorable dissipation. Geddes, for example, noted that economics accounts only for the energy generated by a steam engine, ignoring the other 90 per cent that is dissipated and forever lost. In *Cartesian Economics*, Frederick Soddy, Oxford professor and Nobel laureate in chemistry, explained that the interest rate was a contingent human convention, which could not contradict for very long the entropy principle to which the capital is subjected. According to him, industrial investment, far from increasing wealth, accelerated the depletion of fossil resources (Martinez–Alier 1987).

Depletion

The historical shift from an organic economy based on wood to a mineral one fueled by coal occurred despite deep concerns about the non-renewability of fossil energy. In 1784 Frederic II (who encouraged the shift from wood to coal) ordered a report on the probable duration of Berlin's coal supply (Sieferle 2001, 185). In 1819, Jean–Antoine Chaptal, a major figure of French industrialisation, estimated that national coal reserves were too limited to be wasted on gas lighting. It was wiser to conserve it for steel production and national defense (Fressoz 2007b). In England in the 1820s, the depletion of certain mines, coupled with parliamentary debates on the export of coal, prompted the first evaluations of national reserves. The House of Lords established commissions on the question in 1822 and 1829. Stanley Jevons' famous treatise, *The Coal Question*, published in 1866, is thus to be read as part of a long-running controversy.

However, two inflections occurred after its publication. First, the debate on exhaustion moved from a geological problem (centred on measuring the reserves) to an economic one concerning estimates of future consumption. Should geometric growth be assumed (as Jevons did) or is it simply arithmetic growth? Secondly, the period is marked by a general anxiety concerning the exhaustion of natural resources. We already mentioned the concerns about the metabolic rift. In 1898, the president of the British Society for the Advancement of Science, William Crookes, warned against depletion of nitrate and guano and the risk of a global crisis in agriculture, which had become dependent on non-renewable resources (Smil 2001, 58). At the same time, US conservationists started a crusade against deforestation and wasteful uses of natural resources more generally, in the context of the end of the frontier (Hays 1999). Geologists also warned about the scarcity of copper, zinc and tin, warnings arising from the beginning of electrification.

The transition from an organic to a mineral economy, the disruption of metabolic cycles and the reliance on non-renewable sources of energy took place despite acute awareness of the future and clear warnings of the unsustainability of the new material regime that had emerged at the end of the nineteenth century.

This troubling fact is well illustrated by the brutal shortening of the time horizon of political actors. In 1860, in the House of Commons, Benjamin Disraeli, an opponent of a free trade treaty with France, argued that the British reserves of coal covered only three or four centuries of national consumption, so it was imperative to put a heavy export duty on coal to maintain British world hegemony in the long term. A probable scarcity in three centuries seemed to justify an economically harmful measure in the present. Conversely, William Gladstone, then Chancellor of the Exchequer and a supporter of free trade, referred to other geological studies estimating that British coal reserves could last for over 1,000 years. British politicians of the era, steeped in classical references and tasked with managing the empire, could see a thousand years into the future!

Compared to coal, the first debates on oil reserves were marked by dramatically shorter time horizons. In the United States, the consumption boom associated with the development of the automobile and the First World War took place despite warnings of the imminent exhaustion of national reserves. In 1918, a report of the Smithsonian Institution explained that it was unlikely that geologists would find new major oilfields in the United States. During the First World War, the director of the US Fuel Administration anticipated US military decline due to the scarcity of oil. In 1921, the US Geological Survey estimated the duration of economically exploitable oil at twenty years at the most (Dennis 1985).

How can we explain the marginalisation of both the 'limits to growth' debate and entropic thinking in the late nineteenth century? On the one hand, concerns about the depletion of mineral resources were circumvented by the globalisation of geological surveying. For instance, in 1913, the international geological Congress of Toronto led to the first quantification of the global reserves of coal. The rather vague definition of 'probable reserves' and the extension of economically recoverable coal at a depth of 4,000 feet (instead of 2,200 previously) allowed a massive overstatement of the resource (six times higher than contemporary estimates!) (Madureira 2012).

More profoundly, the intellectual world gradually lost interest in the material conditions of production. The case of economics, which became the dominant mode of formation of the social elite, is exemplary in this regard. With the marginalist paradigm, economists shifted their focus from the study of productive factors (labour, capital and land) to the subjective states of consumers and producers seeking to maximise their individual utility. From 1870 to 1970, the study of natural resources was confined to a sub-branch of the discipline, resource economics. In 1931, in the fundamental article of this field, Harold Hotelling analysed the situation of a mine owner who seeks to maximise its revenue across time. The problem is no longer that of the secular evolution of a national economy (the problem that Jevons tackled), but more modestly to determine the optimal extraction path of an exhaustible resource at a microeconomic level. The mine is considered as an abstract entity, disconnected from the rest of the production system, a mere store of value, obeying to the same type of economic calculation as a stock portfolio.

At the same time, in the context of the 1930s crisis of overproduction, economic growth was conceptualised not in material terms but as the intensification of monetary exchanges in a given territory. The abandonment of the gold standard in 1930 (that is, the end of the idea that banknotes represent gold) and the invention of gross domestic product by the system of national accounts, completed the dematerialisation of economic thought. After the Second World War, economics had conceived the economy as a closed system, a circular flow of value between production and consumption, cut off from its natural ties.

Conclusion

When thinking historically about the Anthropocene and the mess we are in, we need to bear in mind that the destruction of the environment has occurred not as if nature counted for nothing; on the contrary, it proceeded despite an understanding of its consequences. In the late eighteenth century, industrial pollution darkened the atmosphere in spite of neo-Hippocratic environmental medicine's focus on air. In the early nineteenth century, deforestation continued in spite of the fear of climate change. Later in the century, the use of natural resources intensified in spite of the awareness of their limits and the idea of nature's economy.

The history of the Anthropocene is not the emergence of an 'environmental consciousness', but rather the opposite. The historical problem is to understand how modernity became 'disinhibited' in its relation to nature. This modern disinhibition (Fressoz 2012) is not the result of some fundamental fractures in the Western mind (Christianism and man's mastery over nature, the divide between nature and culture, the mechanistic ontology of the scientific revolution, and so on) but is produced by many strategic devices that emerged during the Anthropocene, many of which are still operating (Bonneuil and Fressoz 2013). We need to take on board the disturbing fact that we entered the Anthropocene knowingly and we need to think the contemporary situation in continuity with the past, less as a threshold in environmental awareness and rather as the culmination of a history of two centuries of conscious destruction.

Note

1   I owe this point to Paul Warde.

References

Beck U 1992 *Risk Society: Towards a new modernity* Sage, London [1986]

Bonneuil C and Fressoz J-B 2013 *L'événement anthropocène* Editions du Seuil, Paris

Brock H 1997 *Justus von Liebig: The chemical gate keeper* Cambridge University Press, Cambridge

Buffon G L L 1778 *Histoire Naturelle Générale et Particulière. Des époques de la Nature* Imprimerie Royale, Paris

Carlyle T 1837 *Sartor Resartus* James Munroe, Boston

Dennis A 1985 Drilling for dollars: The making of US petroleum reserve estimates 1921–25 *Social Studies of Science* 15 (2) 241–65

Drouin J M 1997 *L'Écologie et Son Histoire* Flammarion, Paris

Dubos J B 1714 *Réflexions Critiques sur la Poésie et sur la Peinture* Mariette, Paris

Finley C 2011 *All the Fish in the Sea: Maximum Sustainable Yield and the Failure of Fisheries Management* Chicago University Press, Chicago

Foster J B 2000 *Marx's Ecology. Materialism and Nature* Monthly Review Press, New York

Fressoz J-B 2007a Beck back in the 19th century: Towards a genealogy of risk society *History and Technology* 23(4) 333–50

Fressoz J-B 2007b The gas lighting controversy: Technological risk, expertise and regulation in 19th century Paris and London *Journal of Urban History* 33 729–55

Fressoz J-B 2009 Circonvenir les circumfusa *Revue d'histoire moderne et contemporaine* 56(4) 39–76

Fressoz J-B 2012 *L'apocalypse Joyeuse. Une histoire du risque technologique* Editions du Seuil, Paris

Fressoz J-B and Fabien L 2012 Modernity's frail climate: A climate history of environmental reflexivity *Critical Inquiry* 38 579–98

Fressoz J-B and Locher F 2012 Modernity's Frail Climate: A Climate History of Environmental Reflexivity *Critical Inquiry* 38(3) 579–98 Spring

Giddens A 1990 *The Consequences of Modernity* Polity Press, Cambridge

Grove A T 1995 *Green Imperialism: Colonial Expansion, Tropical Island Edens and the Origins of Environmentalism 1600–1860* Cambridge University Press, Cambridge

Grove A T 1996 The historical context: Before 1850, in Brandt J and Thornes J eds *Mediterranean Desertification and Land Use* Wiley, Chichester 13–28

Hays S P 1999 *Conservation and the Gospel of Efficiency: The Progressive Conservation Movement 1890–1920* University of Pittsburgh Press, Pittsburgh

Le Roux T 2011 *Le Laboratoire des Pollutions Industrielles Paris, 1770–1830* Albin Michel, Paris

Madureira N L 2012 The anxiety of abundance. William Stanley Jevons and Coal Scarcity in the 19th Century *Environment and History* 18 395–421

Martinez-Alier J 1987 *Ecological Economics: Energy, Environment and Society* Blackwell, Oxford

Massard-Guilbaud G 2010, Histoire de la Pollution Industrielle en France, 1789–1914 EHESS, Paris

Merchant C 1980 *The Death of Nature: Women, Ecology and the Scientific Revolution* Harper, San Francisco

Nogaret F 1795 *La Terre Est un Animal* Colson, Versailles

Patrin E M 1806 Remarques sur la diminution de la mer *Journal de physique* 60 316

Pomeranz K 2000 *The Great Divergence: China, Europe and the Making of the Modern World Economy* Princeton University Press, Princeton

Robinet J B 1766 *De la Nature* Volume 4 Van Harrevelt, Amsterdam

Schérer R 2001 *L'Écosophie de Charles Fourier* Anthropos, Paris

Sieferle R P 2001 *The Subterranean Forest: Energy Systems and the Industrial Revolution* White Horse Press, Cambridge

Simmons D 2006 Waste not, want not: Excrement and economy in 19th-century France *Representations* 96 73–98

Smil V 2001 *Enriching the Earth* MIT Press, Cambridge Mass.

Staufer C 1987 *Charles Darwin's Natural Selection* Cambridge University Press, Cambridge

Steffen W et al. 2011 The Anthropocene: From global change to planetary stewardship *AMBIO* 40 739–61

Thorsheim P 2006 *Inventing Pollution: Coal, Smoke and Culture in Britain Since 1800* Ohio University Press, Athens, Ohio

Warde P 2011 The invention of sustainability *Modern Intellectual History* 8 153–70

White G 1789 *A Natural History and Antiquities of Selborne* Bensley, London

Williams J 1806 *The Climate of Great Britain* Baldwin, London

Wise N 1990 Work and waste: Political economy and natural philosophy in 19th century Britain *History of Science* 27 221–60

Worster D 1977 *Nature's Economy: A History of Ecological Ideas* Cambridge University Press, Cambridge

PART II

Catastrophism in the Anthropocene

7

ANTHROPOCENE, CATASTROPHISM AND GREEN POLITICAL THEORY

Luc Semal

Since it was coined and described by Paul Crutzen and Eugene Stoermer (2000), the notion of the Anthropocene has been growing in influence in the fields of social science and environmental studies. Now that several papers and books have been published to explain the reasons why many biophysical indicators support the existence of a new geological epoch characterised by human impact, this new notion of the Anthropocene is increasingly used to capture the broad idea that the course of life on Earth has taken a radically new direction. In that sense, the notion of the Anthropocene may be an important didactic contribution for expressing the fact that, despite endless anti-science controversies about the reality of climate change and global change, something fundamental has shifted in the Earth system; there is indeed 'something new under the sun' (McNeill 2000).

Nevertheless, despite its pedagogical force, this notion is today at its early stage of development and is therefore appropriated in problematically heterogeneous ways. One reason may be that not all geologists and stratigraphers accept the arrival of the Anthropocene; officially, according to the scientific standards of 2015, we are still living in the Holocene. This is not necessarily an issue in itself, for it may be that official recognition of the new epoch is granted within the next two or three years – that is to say, tomorrow on the scale of geological time. But this lack of official recognition also goes with a lack of conceptual stabilisation, leading to the coexistence of numerous interpretations of the notion. The problem becomes obvious when, while use of the term creates the impression that all stakeholders are talking about the same thing, highly contradictory significations of the Anthropocene emerge in social discourses.

This chapter does not claim to define what this new epoch of ours actually is, but it will discuss the specific question of *the potential duration and ending of the Anthropocene*. Crutzen and Stoermer (2000, 18) address this issue briefly when they write that 'mankind will remain a major geological force for millennia, maybe millions of years, to come'. The main question here will be to consider the political issues around whether humankind will remain for such a long time the *active* geological force it is today, or whether it will be simply an *inertial* geological force subsequent to just a few decades of intensive fossil fuel burning. Those political issues can be studied through the lens of green political theory, that is, a branch of political science that studies the specificities of environmental politics in the modern political landscape, and tries to explain why and how the global ecological crisis could or should contribute to renewing our analysis of the democratic project (Dobson et al. 2014).

According to Dobson (2007), green political thought is characterised by the conviction that there are limits to growth, which are a biophysical obstacle to the eternal perpetuation of thermo-industrial civilisation. Since the beginning of the twenty-first century this argument has somehow been renewed by the peak oil and 'peak all' hypotheses, which have been politicised by green mobilisations such as the Degrowth and the Transition Towns movements (Semal 2012). Peak oil should be understood as a process beginning with a rising trend in energy prices, which already contributes to worsening fuel poverty today, and leading later to the decline in effectively available energy amounts. As conventional oil resources run out, their decline is temporarily compensated by the rise of unconventional sources of oil and gas. However, this shift in energy sources already contributes to the rising trend in prices and to the ensuing economic downturn (Murray and King 2012). In the long run, there may be no substitutable resource to compensate for the unconventional fossil fuel resources when they too run out. Furthermore, the rising trend in energy prices should lead to a rising trend in the price of other resources, such as metals, which need more and more energy to be extracted, in the same way that unconventional fossil fuels need more and more metals to be extracted, leading us from peak oil to peak all (Bihouix 2014). According to this hypothesis, the path from peak oil to peak all can be regarded as a limits-to-growth *realisation* process.

From a green political theory perspective, the seminal idea of limits to growth should lead us to envision possible boundaries to our current active geological agency, as resource depletion may very well make us cease to be a geological force. This may happen within decades, and certainly less than two centuries, a very short time on the geological scale. Cheap fossil energy has been the early Anthropocene fuel, giving humankind an unprecedented power enabling the rise of thermo-industrial civilisation. Expensive energy is already becoming the late Anthropocene fuel, and its depletion raises the question of whether humankind does or does not have the technical ability to remain an active geological force for more than a few decades.

After a brief scene setting, this chapter will explain why the current stage of 'Great Acceleration' is now leading us to a new, final stage that we may call the *late Anthropocene*. It will argue that various conceptions of the late Anthropocene currently coexist and can roughly be divided between *continuist* and *catastrophist* ones. The continuist conceptions are Promethean in nature, based on 'techno-fix' solutions such as geoengineering technologies, while the catastrophist ones argue that humankind does not have the technical capacity to remain for long an active geological force. Nor does it have the moral aptitude to become a conscious one. Catastrophist conceptions of the Anthropocene, by contrast, envision its coming final stage as *a global energy descent*, which may last less than a century after which humankind would have to live for millennia with the inertial, potentially titanic consequences of its past, that is, the meteoric decades of energy exuberance. Such an outcome would be *an unprecedented democratic challenge*, as modern democratic societies implicitly rely on a story of collective, perpetual progress and emancipation that may find its limits with the end of cheap energy in a globally deteriorating environment. If we are to discuss this issue, then some current catastrophist mobilisations, such as Degrowth or Transition Towns, can offer useful insights, as they provide two of the more ambitious attempts to frame a democratic debate for a possibly desirable post-growth condition set in the late Anthropocene energy descent.

This chapter may, therefore, be read as a contribution to a green political theory analysis of the Anthropocene, understood as an epoch characterised by global overshoot and the ensuing realisation of limits to growth. It aims at developing a rationally catastrophist conception of the Anthropocene, by arguing that humankind may not have the energy resources to remain an active geological force for more than a few decades – or a century or two at most. The finitude of energy resources is highlighted by the peak oil and peak all hypotheses, according to which the cumulative depletion of all fossil resources will contribute first to the global slowing of growth, and then to its replacement by some kind of global degrowth. The end of cheap energy and the end of growth would not mean the immediate end of the Anthropocene, but may mark the beginning of a substantial decrease in our geological agency. Of course, this is not to say that the end of cheap energy will be the solution to the numerous challenges, as global warming would probably be out of control before all fossil fuel resources run out. But it is an invitation to analyse the potential becoming of the Anthropocene in a green political theory perspective, that is, in a finite world, with finite resources, and with limits to growth.

Anthropocene – its beginning and its ending

Scene setting

Although there is no consensus at the moment for a precise definition of the Anthropocene, it is commonly agreed that it is a new geological epoch in which humankind rivals geological forces in influencing the course of the Earth, and represents an unprecedented convergence of the history of humankind and the history of the Earth (Chakrabarty 2009). We might as well write 'humankind' in inverted commas, as Andreas Malm and Alf Hornborg (2014) effectively argue that the term tends to conceal some huge intra-species inequalities, inequalities that play a vital role in explaining the social origins of the global, geological shift on which we have embarked (see also Hornborg in this volume). Here, however, the focus is on another ambiguous aspect of the Anthropocene notion, the question of the new epoch's potential length. This ought to be a decisive question for anyone trying to explain what the Anthropocene is and what may be the material and political consequences of this epoch for our societies.

Several theories have already been advanced about the inauguration of the Anthropocene (Crutzen and Steffen 2003). Propositions that identify an 'early' Anthropocene, starting, for example, with the emergence of agriculture, prove unhelpful operationally, for the Anthropocene would then be in effect the renaming of the Holocene. Crutzen (2002) proposed 1784 as a starting year, the year James Watt invented his steam engine and unlocked the potential for a massive expansion of fossil energy use. However, 1784 is merely a symbolic date, for it was decades before industrialised countries, and after them globalised societies, could massively expand technologies based on fossil fuel combustion (Gras 2007). Steffen et al. (2007) later argued that it seems more appropriate to distinguish a first stage of the Anthropocene (the 'industrial era', roughly 1800–1945) and a second stage, the latter characterised by the sudden global spread and acceleration of a previously more localised, emerging phenomenon (dubbed 'the Great Acceleration', 1945–c.2015). This distinction emphasises the fascinating *abruptness* of the geological shift entailed by the Anthropocene, but it also raises some awkward questions: How long will this 'Great Acceleration' last? What is to happen after 2015? Will there be an extension of the second stage, the emergence of a third stage, or a shift towards *something else* beyond the Anthropocene?

Despite their importance for understanding the material consequences of the Anthropocene, these questions are rarely raised. According to Steffen et al. (2007, 618–20), the 'Great Acceleration' already seems to be reaching critical tipping points, so that we may soon enter a third stage of the Anthropocene. They suggest calling this third stage of the Anthropocene 'stewards of the Earth system?', with a question mark that highlights the uncertainty of such an ambiguous denomination. They also identify three broad practical and philosophical approaches to this third stage: (1) a 'business-as-usual' scenario potentially leading to global collapse; (2) a 'mitigation' scenario leading to a more sustainable society; and (3) a 'geoengineering' scenario leading to a risky attempt to intentionally manipulate global-scale Earth system processes. They do not risk suggesting an approximate date for the end of the Anthropocene or for the end of its third stage.

Four hypotheses for the end of the Anthropocene

It is tricky to propose an inquiry into such a huge topic as the convergence of the history of Earth and the history of humans. However, the risk is worth taking if we want to consider what this third stage may look like, how long it may last, and what might come next. While there can be no settled answer to these questions we can identify several hypotheses based on the various current narratives about the Anthropocene. To identify those narratives and turn them into hypotheses, two burning questions should now be raised. Is the Anthropocene expected to be a short or a long geological period? And is the current convergence between

Earth and human histories meant to endure, or will they separate again? The first question, I will suggest, appears to be mainly a sophisticated *naming* problem, while the second refers to a truly decisive distinction between *continuist* and *catastrophist* conceptions of our future. Of course, we already know that the inertial effects of current human activities will last for many millennia; so what is at stake here is to know whether 'humankind' will have the capacity to remain an *active* geological force for long, rather than becoming just an *inertial* one. If humankind does remain an active geological force over the long term it would probably be the sign of a real, definitive and enduring convergence of human and Earth histories. If it doesn't remain an active force, the convergence will be a relatively short and temporary one, followed by a new divergence process. Crossing those two issues, the length of the Anthropocene and the length of the convergence, four basic hypotheses can now be advanced. These are presented in Table 7.1.

TABLE 7.1 Four hypotheses about the Anthropocene, its potential duration and its possible ending

	Brief Anthropocene (a few decades or centuries)	*Long Anthropocene (many centuries or millennia ahead)*
Definitive or enduring convergence between human and Earth histories	<u>H1:</u> Anthropocene is the brief, current geological epoch when 'humankind' became a blind geological force. **This epoch will soon be followed by another one (still to be named) in which 'humankind' will become an enduring, conscious geological force** through the discovery of abundant and clean energy, and through the mastering of climate engineering technologies.	<u>H2:</u> Anthropocene is the current, long geological epoch which started when 'humankind' became a blind geological force. **This epoch will now continue for centuries as 'humankind' will soon learn to remain a geological force (albeit a conscious one)** through the discovery of abundant and clean energy, and through the mastering of climate engineering technologies.
Brief, temporary convergence between human and Earth histories	<u>H4:</u> Anthropocene is the brief, current geological epoch characterised by an unprecedented, massive and brief burning of fossil fuels (the current few decades during which 'humankind' temporarily rivals geological forces). **This epoch will soon be followed by another one (still to be named) characterised by centuries of resource scarcity in a highly destabilised climate and a heavily deteriorated environment** (inertial consequences of a past, temporary human ability to rival geological forces).	<u>H3:</u> Anthropocene is the current, long geological epoch, which was inaugurated by an unprecedented, massive and brief burning of fossil fuels (the current few decades during which 'humankind' temporarily rivals with geological forces). **This epoch will now continue for centuries of resource scarcity in a highly destabilised climate and a heavily deteriorated environment** (inertial consequences of a past, temporary human ability to rival geological forces).

The late Anthropocene: catastrophist *versus* continuist hypotheses

A rational, scientific approach to catastrophism

In the study of Earth history there have been enduring controversies about the pace of change in geological transformation and biological evolution. One of the most important discussions has long counterposed *catastrophist* thinkers – who argued that Earth and life transformations could only be explained by intermittent, catastrophic events – and *continuist* or *gradualist* thinkers – who argued that those transformations occurred very slowly, without catastrophes, over very long geological timescales. Catastrophist thinkers were commonly accused of letting religious beliefs colour their scientific work. The hypotheses that massive disasters had shaped life on Earth did indeed frequently refer to the biblical Flood and to the creation of Earth by God only a few millennia ago. After Darwin had formulated the theory of evolution and published it in 1859, catastrophist theories were for a long time disqualified.

In recent decades, however, some scientists have demonstrated that on certain occasions catastrophic events have played a decisive role in the Earth's transformations. The most powerful argument was the discovery of a meteoric crater near the Mexican shore, which led to the belief that the sudden, catastrophic impact of an asteroid may have contributed to what is now known as the Earth's fifth mass extinction, the end of the dinosaurs and many other forms of life, 65 million years ago, an event marking the shift from the Mesozoic to the Cenozoic (Alvarez 1997). If this hypothesis is correct, it implies a more complex history of the Earth during which slow transformations (well explained by continuist theories) can sometimes be punctuated by massive disruptions better explained by catastrophist arguments. It is not a victory of catastrophist theories over continuist ones but a scientific rehabilitation of *some* catastrophism, for rare occasions where continuist arguments fail to explain a sudden and massive shift in Earth history.

Today, the irruption of the Anthropocene should cause us to question deeply the way we think about catastrophism, continuism and the current pace of Earth transformations. If 'humankind' truly did become a geological force within just a few decades, do continuist theories have the power to describe what is now happening on our planet? Or would it be more appropriate and more reasonable to conclude that we are now living in one of these rare times that would better be explained by catastrophist arguments? The four hypotheses identified in Table 7.1 suggest some highly contradictory interpretations of the Anthropocene, some of which happen to remain continuist in a strange way (H1 and H2), while others are clearly catastrophist (H3 and H4).

Continuist and catastrophist interpretations

In the last chapter of *Earthmasters*, Clive Hamilton (2013) explains why, for some scientists and politicians, the irruption of the Anthropocene should be regarded as good news. While acknowledging that humankind has been acting as a blind geological force during the last decades, risking unprecedented global chaos, they believe that this situation is an opportunity for 'humankind' to achieve its destiny, which is to take control of the Earth system and to create the conditions for a 'good Anthropocene'. This is clearly a Promethean interpretation of the new geological epoch based on the conviction that our technical ingenuity will not only save us from potential global chaos, but even enable us to extend our history of growth and progress for ages, probably thanks to the deployment of massive climate engineering technologies and the discovery of new sources of abundant, cheap energy.

In the table, hypotheses H1 and H2 clearly refer to this kind of Promethean conception; after having been a blind geological force for a few decades 'humankind' now has the opportunity and the technical capacity to become an enduring *conscious* geological force, potentially in perpetuity. The distinction between H1 and H2 is primarily a matter of naming. H1 stresses that the Anthropocene will be a short geological epoch followed by another still to be named, and characterised by human control of the Earth system. H2 suggests that this coming time of conscious global mastery should rather be regarded as a further stage in the same Anthropocene. H1 and H2 share the same idea that 'humankind' will *remain* a geological force for ages, not simply because of the inertia due to its current carbon emissions but *actively* and *consciously*. They both refer to the same *continuist* story in which the Anthropocene is regarded as just another passing stage in a long, continuing history of progress, growth and development, another step in humankind's technological domination of nature.

By contrast, H3 and H4 appear to be *catastrophist* hypotheses suggesting that the current geological impact of 'humankind' will be materially impossible to maintain for long. Indeed, this human geological irruption may be regarded as *meteoric*. Sixty-five million years ago the collision of the asteroid with Earth was a very brief event, but its inertial effects were both colossal and enduring, contributing to a mass extinction and a dramatic reorientation of the Earth system. Nowadays, because of the finitude of those resources, the massive burning of fossil fuel cannot last for more than a few more decades, the blink of an eye in geological time. However, its effects on the Earth system will last for millennia. The main anticipated consequence of this pulse of carbon into the atmosphere is an alarming warming of the climate, although much more is at stake, including the sixth mass extinction of biodiversity (Barnosky et al. 2011).

Once again, the difference between H3 and H4 is mainly a subtle matter of naming. H3 assumes that the Anthropocene is an epoch inaugurated by a few decades of massive fossil fuel burning, potentially followed by millennia of inertial global change that should still be named 'Anthropocene'. H4, in contrast, suggests that this coming *age of consequences* should be given a *different* name because *anthropos* will already have ceased to be an active geological force at that time. Even so, H3 and H4 share the same fundamental presumption, that *'humankind' will not remain an active geological force for long* because there are unavoidable limits to its power on Earth, not least the finitude of fossil resources but also the human mind's inability to fully understand and master something as complex as the Earth system. Those two hypotheses are clearly anti-Promethean ones, for they rely on a fundamental scepticism about technological solutions and insist that industrial growth over the last decades will prove to be the historical exception, a one-off event in the history of the Earth made possible by the easy accessibility of fossil fuels. To put it in another way, H3 and H4 are *green political* conceptions of the Anthropocene.

Green political thought and catastrophism in the late Anthropocene

Limits to growth, catastrophism and the Anthropocene

According to Andrew Dobson (2007), the conviction that there are limits to growth was a seminal idea in the emergence of a distinctly green strand of political thought in the 1970s. He argues that because this fundamental idea was something 'that other ideologies could not "swallow" without getting very severe indigestion', and because this original idea may radically change the way we envision the future of our societies, ecologism should be regarded as an ideology in its own right (Dobson et al. 2014). The idea of limits to growth is rooted in a characteristically green critique of technology. There cannot be *any* decisive technical solution to the global ecological crisis. Techno-fix speculations generate false hopes and illusions that are dangerous because they divert us from searching for more modest, social responses to global environmental degradation. Dobson stresses two additional distinctive features of ecologism. One is its ecocentric set of moral values, reflecting the tendency to accord intrinsic value to non-human beings or entities, a tendency that cannot be found in any other contemporary political ideology. The second is its bioregional conception of the 'good society', rooted in both a resource-limited and a democratic critique of globalisation.

If the anticipation of limits to growth was a distinctive feature of green political thought in the 1970s and early 1980s, it became less apparent as green political thought was progressively mainstreamed (Dobson 2009). Indeed, the emergence of 'sustainable development' and the process of institutionalisation led many green parties, movements and organisations to defend less radical options, such as 'green growth'. However, the advent of the Anthropocene challenges this mainstreaming process as this new epoch can be interpreted as the beginning of the *realisation* (rather than the mere *anticipation*) of the limits on growth. It may also prompt us to consider a more *catastrophist* green political thought, not in the sense of a pointless preoccupation with global disaster, but as an ambitious political thought explicitly rooted in the catastrophic, geological shift in which our globalised societies are henceforth embedded.

The notion of catastrophism is discomforting because it is frequently associated with an irrational fear of disasters, if not to a pathological attraction to doom-mongering. But from a scientific viewpoint, there can be some very cogent uses of the notion in certain rare circumstances. And considering the gigantic scale of what is at stake, it can convincingly be argued that the global ecological crisis *is* one of those rare circumstances. The recent arrival of the Anthropocene should lead us to push this intuition further, and to try understanding how this new geological epoch may contribute to framing a rationally catastrophist analysis of the interactions between societies, energy and climate (Grinevald 2007; Steffen et al. 2011).

An eco-catastrophist critique of late Anthropocene scenarios

Returning to the four hypotheses of Table 7.1, it is now possible to select the most apposite one from an ecologist and catastrophist perspective. First, if ecologism assumes that there are limits to growth then H1 and H2 should be regarded as fantasy. Of course, there may be some climate engineering experimentations in the coming decades, maybe even massive ones, but such experiments would never enable humankind to achieve a decisive *mastering* of the Earth system. Given the complexity of the Earth system and the inevitability of unintended effects, the climate engineers would first have to turn themselves into God-like creatures – omniscient, omnipotent and perpetually benevolent (Hamilton 2013). Moreover, to remain the geological force it is today 'humankind' would have to find some new, abundant sources of energy as a substitute for the rapidly depleting fossil fuels that have temporarily given us this unprecedented, titanic power over the Earth. From the point of view of ecologism, such Promethean fantasies can never be realised because of the tragic reality of limits to growth. Sooner rather than later, those limits will materialise, inevitably truncating humankind's function as an active geological force and condemning it to live in a world of irreversibly depleted resources and climate chaos, marked by the colossal inertial consequences of a brief period of energy exuberance – a classical vision of eco-apocalypse.

By contrast, H3 and H4 both appear to be far more consistent with ecologism's conviction that there are limits to growth. Humankind has become a temporarily active geological force, but will not stay one for long, despite all of its technological ingenuity. The current, massive burning of fossil fuels is but a *fleeting interlude* in geological time – an intermission with a potentially huge chain of consequences, but an interlude all the same. With this in mind, H4 appears more pertinent than H3 because it better captures the *meteoric* character of the current socio-natural processes we now inhabit, as well as the uniqueness and transience in *socio-natural history* of the geological force we make use of today. In H4, the Anthropocene is the brief, current geological epoch characterised by an unprecedented, massive and transient era of fossil fuel combustion, the *few decades* during which humankind rivals geological forces for influence over the Earth system. This epoch will soon be followed by *something else that is still to be named*, but is expected to take the form of centuries of resource scarcity in a highly destabilised climate and a heavily debased environment.

Summed up this way, H4 encapsulates a conception of the Anthropocene that is both green, because it is consistent with the idea of limits to growth, and catastrophist, because it acknowledges the major geological shift we are embedded in. To be more precise, in such a vision the Anthropocene *is* the catastrophic process that leads us to something else, one hard to anticipate but certainly radically different to all we've known. It is a socio-natural process that can't be captured in a single date but which may be defined by some tipping points and some dangerously accelerating processes. At the end of the process, one way or another humankind will probably no longer be an active geological force.

Next, we take a further step in this eco-catastrophist conception of the Anthropocene by attempting to say more about the possible stages of the process.

Catastrophist activism and its contribution to democracy in the late Anthropocene

Stage 3 of the Anthropocene: the coming energy descent (c.2015–?)

Since the beginning of the twenty-first century, there has been a strong revival of interest in the limits to growth within green political thought. This has been due largely to the politicisation of peak oil and peak all themes by some extra-institutional green movements, such as the Degrowth movement (initially French) and the Transition Towns movement (initially British) (Semal 2012; Sinaï 2013). According to those movements, peak oil and peak all should be regarded as catastrophic processes that are beginning to make real the long-anticipated limits to growth. After several decades of economic and energy growth, this process is now bringing us to a dangerous 'energy descent', a descent that is expected to lead to a post-oil and post-growth world to which our societies will have to adapt in one way or another. In that sense, such movements can be regarded as green, *catastrophist* mobilisations, because they have been developing a political theory of the economic and geological shifts to be precipitated by the peaks.

The way those movements envision the coming energy descent matches the catastrophist conception of the Anthropocene as a meteoric process. In this conception, the 'Great Acceleration' (stage 2) is now reaching critical tipping points; peak oil and peak all may be some of those, because the acceleration process always needs more cheap energy. As stage 2 is coming to an end, it should be followed by a global energy descent that may last several decades, a period that may be regarded as stage 3 of the Anthropocene during which humankind will have less and less access to cheap energy. This third stage may also be called the 'late Anthropocene', as it could be its final stage. Without access to massive amounts of cheap energy, humankind may lose its ability to rival geological forces. By the end of the energy descent, something else would succeed the Anthropocene. This 'something else' would be radically different both from the Holocene and from the Anthropocene, because there is no turning back once huge, irreversible phenomena like these are in play.

Beyond the Anthropocene: Eremozoic, Soterocene or Apocalypse?

If, during the *late Anthropocene*, humankind burns all available reserves of fossil fuel on Earth the outcome would be the same as in the 'business-as-usual' scenario described by Steffen et al. (2007, 619), with potential civilisational collapse, enduring climate chaos and a sixth mass extinction. After such a dramatic change in the Earth system, stratigraphers of the future may identify not merely a new epoch, or even a new period, but a new *era* in the geological time scale. As in the Cenozoic, inaugurated 65 million years ago by a meteoric catastrophe and a fifth mass extinction, it would come to an end with another meteoric catastrophe causing a sixth mass extinction. Envisioning such a scenario, Edward Wilson (2006) coined the idea of *Eremozoic*, literally, the era of the desert. A hot Earth era would be the inertial consequence of the very short epoch during which humankind once challenged the forces of nature.

During the energy descent, however, substantial mitigation efforts may be undertaken so that some kind of self-limitation principle prevents the extraction of all available fossil fuel resources. If so, the current catastrophic process may be slowed and its outcome may be postponed – for as long as this self-limitation principle is adhered to. In such a scenario, the end of the Anthropocene may give way to another geological epoch, characterised by collective precaution in an already heavily deteriorated environment, and which may be called *Soterocene* – the epoch of precaution, in reference to the Greek goddess Soteria exhumed by Hamilton (2013). It would be an epoch rather than a period or an age, but no one could be certain how long it would last.

The Eremozoic and Soterocene share the same eco-catastrophist assumption that humankind will remain an active geological force for a long time, as we are already beginning to face the realisation of limits to growth. Humankind will remain an *inertial* geological force for many millennia, so the Earth system will eternally be marked by the consequences of the meteoritic process called the Anthropocene. As far as future generations are concerned, the Soterocene scenario may be a relatively happy one, or at least the happiest one given the harsh, material constraints of a post-Anthropocene world. By contrast, the Eremozoic scenario appears much closer to an eco-apocalyptic novel, perhaps worse if we take into account the nuclear threat and its possible role in precipitating the era of the desert.

Because they focus on the material consequences of peak oil and peak all, the contemporary catastrophist mobilisations actively contribute to collective reflection on post-growth societies (Jackson 2009). One of the main questions in post-growth debates is whether modern, democratic societies have the ability to survive without the implicit promise of perpetual progress and development enabled by cheap energy and material affluence. Historically, the use of fossil fuels has shaped modern democratic societies (Mitchell 2011), including our conception of freedom. In Chakrabarty's words, 'the mansion of modern freedoms stands on an ever-expanding base of fossil-fuel use' (Chakrabarty 2009, 208). So depletion of fossil resources would be likely to have a strong impact on democratic theories and practices (Villalba 2010). This should lead us to question the capacity of democratic societies to maintain themselves during the late Anthropocene energy descent, as well as in the world that would probably follow.

Catastrophist mobilisations such as Degrowth and Transition Towns have nevertheless contributed to formulating a democratic response to the coming energy descent. In a rather counter-intuitive way, by acknowledging the finitude of fossil resources and the need to anticipate a post-growth future, they have managed to inspire very dynamic local deliberation processes. In a catastrophist conception of the Anthropocene, such 'degrowing' communities may have a crucial role to play during the energy descent of the late Anthropocene. They highlight the narrow margin for manoeuvre in which democratic societies may have to evolve by trying to invent the best possible way out of the meteoric process, towards something like the Soterocene rather than towards the Eremozoic. Their contribution to current debates over the Anthropocene may be to underscore that humankind may not have the ability to remain an active geological force for long but still must plan for the time beyond the Anthropocene as the millennial consequences of that brief era play out in the Earth system.

Acknowledgements

Thanks are due to Mathilde Szuba and the members of Momentum Institute (Paris) for earlier discussions on this topic. Thanks to the editors for their comments and suggestions.

References

Alvarez W 1997 *T. Rex and the Crater of Doom* Princeton University Press, Princeton
Barnosky A D et al. 2011 Has the Earth's sixth mass extinction already arrived? *Nature* 471 51–7
Bihouix P 2014 *L'Age des Low Tech. Vers une civilisation techniquement soutenable* Seuil, Paris
Chakrabarty D 2009 The climate of history: Four theses *Critical Inquiry* 35 197–222
Crutzen P J 2002 Geology of mankind *Nature* 415 23
Crutzen P and Steffen W 2003 How long have we been in the Anthropocene era? An editorial comment *Climate Change* 61 261–93
Crutzen P J and Stoermer E F 2000 The 'Anthropocene' *IGBP Newsletter* 41 17–18
Dobson A 2007 *Green Political Thought* Oxford University Press, London and New York
Dobson A 2009 'All I left behind' – the mainstreaming of ecologism *Contemporary Political Theory* 8 (3) 319–28
Dobson A, Semal L, Szuba S and Petit O 2014 Andrew Dobson: Trajectories of green political theory *Natures Sciences Sociétés* 22 132–41
Gras A 2007 *Le Choix du Feu. Aux origines de la crise climatique* Fayard, Paris
Grinevald J 2007 *La Biosphère de l'Anthropocène: Climat et pétrole, la double menace. Repères transdisciplinaires (1824–2007)* Georg éditeur, Genève
Hamilton C 2013 *Earthmasters: The Dawn of the Age of Climate Engineering* Yale University Press, New Haven
Jackson T 2009 *Prosperity Without Growth: Economics for a Finite Planet* Earthscan, London
Malm A and Hornborg A 2014 The geology of mankind? A critique of the Anthropocene narrative *The Anthropocene Review* 1(1) 62–9
McNeill J R 2000 *Something New Under the Sun: an Environmental History of the Twentieth-century World* W.W. Norton, New York

Mitchell T 2011 *Carbon Democracy: Political Power in the Age of Oil* Verso, London and New York

Murray J and King D 2012 Oil's tipping point has passed *Nature* 481 433–5

Semal L 2012 *Militer à l'Ombre des Catastrophes: Contribution à une théorie politique environnementale au prisme des mobilisations de la décroissance et de la transition* Unpublished PhD thesis Department of Politics, Université de Lille II

Sinaï A ed 2013 *Penser la Décroissance. Politiques de l'Anthropocène* Presses de Sciences-Po, Paris

Steffen W, Crutzen P J and McNeill J R 2007 The Anthropocene: Are humans now overwhelming the great forces of nature? *Ambio* 36 (8) 614–20

Steffen W, Grinevald J, Crutzen P J and McNeill J R 2011 The Anthropocene: Conceptual and historical perspectives *Phil. Trans. R. Soc. A* 369 842–67

Villalba B 2010 L'Écologie politique face au délai et à la contraction démocratique *Écologie et politique* 40 95–113

Wilson O 2006 *The Creation: An Appeal to Save Life on Earth* W.W. Norton, New York

8

ESCHATOLOGY IN THE ANTHROPOCENE

From the *chronos* of deep time to the *kairos* of the age of humans

Michael Northcott

Scottish geologist James Hutton invented the idea of deep or geological time. He developed his theory based on long observation of soil erosion and rock strata in Scotland and was the first scientist to argue that soil erosion, combined with pressure from the ocean, creates new layers of rock which, over geological time, are pushed up through the visible land surface by subterranean heat. His theory was first presented at the nascent Royal Society of Edinburgh in 1785. He had worked as a farmer and a mineralogist in Scotland for thirty years and had arrived at the conclusion that rocks were primarily formed from eroded soils that, under pressure from the ocean, turned into sedimentary rock, and by extrusions of magma from the Earth's hot inner core (Repcheck 2003). Since these processes could be seen to occur in the present, Hutton judged that their incremental effects must have taken millions of years to reproduce the arrangements of rocks presently visible on Earth. Against the reliance of his scientific contemporaries and predecessors on an intergenerational estimate of the beginning of time from the biblical record of the creation and succeeding generations, Hutton argued that only a vastly deep temporal history could have achieved the present state of which he could 'find no vestige of a beginning, no prospect of an end' (Hutton 1788). Time, and not a divine creator, had therefore produced the Earth as humans now observe it and hence, and even more controversially, it was 'vain to look for anything higher in the origin of the Earth' (Hutton 1788).

The principal evidence for Hutton's proposal was his observation of soil erosion on his farmland in the Scottish Borders. His other source of evidence was the veins of granite and other rocks that were visible in the midst of older sedimentary rocks. Hutton theorised these were molten rock thrust up by magma from deep below the Earth's surface that had subsequently cooled and hardened. His theory was most clearly evidenced at Siccar Point on the North Sea coast south of Edinburgh, where Old Red Sandstone (Devonian and 350–400 million years old) meets limestone (Silurian and 420–440 million years old) at right angles, creating a 'T' formation

(Playfair 1822). Geologic 'unconformities', such as that at Siccar Point, and others he observed at Glen Tilt and Cumbria, were not individual instances of exceptional events but examples of the uniform operation of Newtonian-style physical laws that operate in the present and have always so operated. Geologic 'unconformities' indicate the Earth as presently constituted is a living 'Earth system' which has been uniformly created, and is still being created, by living processes which over long time periods change its appearance and constituent parts.

Hutton's thesis was received with considerable scepticism since it contradicted the established scientific view that the Earth was no more than 6,000 years old. Only one geologist before Hutton had challenged traditional intergenerational chronology. The dating of the Earth at 6,000 years old originated in a theological interpretation of the first Hebrew creation story in Genesis 1 which described the creation of the Earth as having taken place over 'six days'. Another Hebrew text, Psalm 90:4, proposed that 'one day is as a thousand years' from a divine perspective and hence Jewish theologians, writing in the Jewish Talmud in the second century of the Christian era, proposed that each day of creation correlated to a thousand years of human and creaturely history.

Christian theologians Julius of Africanus and Eusebius of Caesarea adopted this chronology in the second and third centuries of the Christian era (Hendel 2013). It was later adopted by early modern theologians, including Martin Luther in Germany, the English Bishop Ussher, and by historians. Luther and Ussher proposed only slight variations to Julius' chronology in order to keep the 'six millennia' extending beyond the then present into the near future (Fuller 2001).

Hutton's chronology was almost universally resisted, both for its departure from established geological science and chronology, and for its theological implications. Hutton was criticised for sponsoring atheism, since his theory suggested that the Earth was the result of mechanical processes over long time periods and not of direct divine creative actions, as the biblical record was said to indicate. Hence not until the publication in the mid-nineteenth century of Charles Lyell's *Principles of Geology* was Hutton's chronology accepted, and opposition to it dispatched in scientific and most theological circles.

Not only did Hutton's deep time chronology displace divinity from Earth history beyond its primeval beginning; it also displaced humanity. Although Nicolai Copernicus had argued that the Earth was not at the centre of the universe, as Ptolemaic cosmology had held, Copernicus did not challenge humanity's central place in Earth's history (Northcott 2014). Christian chronology from the second century of the Christian era had mapped human intergenerational history onto Earth history with only slight variations in calendric enumeration for more than 1,500 years before Hutton. It was universally believed in Christendom, therefore, that there were three ages of the Earth: the first was the era from the Creation to Christ (BC); the second was the era from the birth of Christ to the present and near future (AD); and the third was the eschaton which would herald the Last Judgement, and the return of Christ to the Earth to inaugurate 'a new heavens and a new Earth', as predicted in the New Testament Book of Revelation.

After Hutton, the history of the Earth is divided into a much longer set of eras that had nothing to do with God, Christ or humanity, and which extend back over roughly four billion years. In all of these eras, apart from the Holocene, which roughly corresponds to BC and AD combined, humans were either completely absent or very epiphenomenal. However, it is still the case that the Christian division of human history and Earth history until the present into two eras – Before Christ and Anno Domini – remains culturally dominant. The two best-known 'eras' in popular culture are still eras in which human history and Earth history are aligned, and the division between them remains the estimated date of the birth of Jesus Christ. The only concession to contemporary secularism is that the BC and AD nomenclature have been revised to BCE and CE where 'C' stands for 'Common' rather than Christ and E for Era. There are alternative faith-based calendars, but the BC/AD two-era chronology is so influential that it is represented in astronomic clocks, digital computers, and printed and online encyclopaedias and history books. The enduring role of the birth of Christ in dividing human history into two calendric eras may explain why a significant minority of individuals still leave school in Western Europe, and the United States, believing the Earth is only 10,000 years old.

Rehumanising deep time

Hutton's deep time chronology bifurcated Earth and human history and the cultural implications of this are not fully appreciated by those who propose that a 'new universe story' that resituates human consciousness in deep time will facilitate greater identification between humans and the rest of the 'natural' world than the old intergenerational creation story (Berry 1999). Knowledge of deep time, while it may provoke wonder at the 'abyss of time' that Hutton opened up, also generates a sense of the epiphenomenal character of human history as compared to the history of life on Earth. If the passing of human generations, and the birth of children and grandchildren, is so peripheral to Earth history, it may be said to be unreasonable to argue, as climate scientists and some evolutionary biologists now do, that humans are capable of significantly influencing the course of natural history.

Hence Hutton's deep time chronology underwrites the refusal – particularly prominent in Anglo-Saxon cultures – to acknowledge that humanity may be passing critical thresholds in her influence on species and the climate. For deep time futurists, twenty-first- and twenty-second-century anthropogenic climate change represents a mere blip in the future history of the planet, and decisions about fossil fuel use or deforestation have minimal import in this longer view (Stager 2011). Hence the claim that geological time provides the basis for a new sacred universe story that promotes greater care for the Earth than the intergenerational story from Adam and Christ to the present may be erroneous. On the contrary the deep time frame indicates that human beings have no influence on the history or future of life on Earth and hence, as climate science refuseniks argue, it is foolish to propose they should take responsibility for the future of a planet in whose history neither they nor their gods have any significant agency (Sideris 2013).

Instead of looking back into deep time to stimulate ecological consciousness, some Earth scientists argue that the best way to provoke care for the future is to remap Hutton's geological history onto the recent and near future history of humanity. Paul Crutzen, Will Steffen and others propose that scientists name the recent intergenerational history of increased anthropic influence on the Earth system as a new geological epoch that they call the Anthropocene (Crutzen and Stoermer 2000). The date of 1784 is chosen for the commencement of this new 'age of humans' because the widespread adoption of James Watt's condensing steam engine facilitated the large-scale mining of coal and drove the factories and workshops, ships and trains of the Industrial Revolution. Atmospheric deposits from the vast scale of burning of the subterranean deposit of sunlight produced a global change in the 'vast machine' of the Earth's climate because it altered the heat exchange between the Earth's surface and the sun. By trapping more of the heat of the sun reflected from the Earth's surface within the atmospheric envelope of the planet humanity has, since 1784, displaced other terrestrial and extra-terrestrial global change generators – such as the amount of solar activity or volcanic eruptions – as the dominant progenitor of global changes within what Hutton first called the Earth system.

Pressure from Earth scientists for the recognition of a new geological era involves a judgment about scientific rhetoric. Crutzen and others intend that consciousness of this new era will assist an urgent transition to a more responsible shaping of Earth's habitat (Crutzen and Stoermer 2000). The first two hundred years of the Anthropocene, if its beginnings are coterminous with the age of steam (Robin and Steffen 2007), is the period in which humanity's pursuit of scientific progress through taking charge of Earth's carbon store unintentionally changed the atmosphere. Some call this the 'bad Anthropocene' (Szerszynski 2012), although atmospheric change was an unforeseen double effect of coal and oil-based development so it is unreasonable to consider this morally bad until consensus was reached on climate science in the 1980s. As Earth science educates the public and politicians about the increase in human powers over the Earth system, scientists hope that humans will transition to a more responsible exercise of those powers. And advocates of the Anthropocene intend that its recognition will sensitise modern humans to their moral obligations to future generations and to other creatures. Hence this ethics for the Anthropocene represents a revival of human duties to other species and to future generations that were attenuated in the industrial 'age of machines'.

Eco-modernists and libertarians argue that if the Anthropocene is indeed a new geological epoch, then it is merely the extension of the powers over life on Earth which the stable and relatively warm climate of the Holocene gave to humans in the development of agriculture, and its influence over animals, plants and soils (Ruddiman 2005). What some call the 'good Anthropocene' on this account represents an era in which technologically enabled humans achieve the maximal freedom to shape life processes and Earth's habitats after their aspirations and desires (Nordhaus and Shellenberger 2007). For others recognition of the 'good Anthropocene' paves the way for new forms of Earth engineering by an empowered global technocratic elite. In this perspective human beings are now 'in the engine room of the Earth System' and must intervene in whole planet processes to maximise human welfare and reduce any harmful Earth system effects from human activities such as the use of fossil fuels (Schellnhuber 1999). Since the 1980s scientists have been conscious that there is no part of the Earth that is untouched by industrial engineering, and as humanity is now capable of transforming the planet 'self-conscious intelligent management of the Earth is one of the great challenges facing humanity as it approaches the twenty-first century' (Allenby 1999). Humanity's new agential control over the Earth system requires a more purposeful re-engineering of Earth systems. In this perspective humanity needs to form clear intentions about desired planetary and climate states, and then use Earth system engineering and global meteorological governance to bring them about. Given the failure of carbon politics to mitigate fossil fuel burning and deforestation, a growing minority of natural scientists, along with engineers from the oil and gas industries, propose that it will be necessary intentionally to engineer the Earth system to reduce the heating potential of present and future greenhouse gas emissions (Hamilton 2013).

Both ecomodernists and would-be geoengineers describe the Anthropocene as a new evolutionary moment – an anthropic epiphany – in which human beings are at last in the driving seat both of human and natural history. In this vein the Anthropocene fosters not humility but arrogant hubris of the kind that recalls the cosmological assumptions of the Baconian vision of science as redemption. But a third approach suggests that the Anthropocene, far from enhancing human intentionality and agential interaction with the Earth, threatens to reduce it and hence to undermine the modern scientific imaginary of the human control of nature. If rising sea levels inundate cities and ports, and droughts destroy much presently viable cropland, the Anthropocene will turn out to be an era in which human power over nature is greatly reduced. In these circumstances nature will have wrested back control over the boundary between land and sea from human defences, and over agricultural lands from the irrigation schemes, terracing and crop rotations of farmers.

Contestation over the implications of the Anthropocene raises questions about its cultural meaning. For Schellnhuber, the passing of Earth from the Holocene to the Anthropocene represents a second Copernican revolution (Schellnhuber 2009). The Copernican turn decentred humanity from the cosmos, and reduced the perception of human influence over the Earth and the skies, a displacement that was deepened by the Huttonian deep time narrative. Whereas premodern humans thought of the weather as something they could influence, or which carried messages for them from the ancestors and heavenly beings, moderns inhabit a mechanistic universe in which the heavens reveal no meaningful messages about human behaviours, and in which human behaviours do not affect the climate (Northcott 2014). Recognition of the Anthropocene, therefore, involves acknowledgement that the refusal of premoderns to split nature from culture was wise, and that after a mechanistic interlude of five hundred years the 'age of humans' brings 'natural' and 'human' history back together again (Chakrabarty 2009). Recognition of the Anthropocene also recovers the intergenerational character of historiography – both natural and human – before Hutton. This has a particular cultural resonance with the ethical description of efforts to mitigate anthropogenic climate change in terms of duties to future generations who will inherit a less stable, less fertile and less biodiverse Earth habitat if fossil fuel use and deforestation are unabated (Page 2007; Hansen 2009).

Anthropocene as apocalypse

Earth scientists' advocacy of the recognition of the Anthropocene is of a piece with a larger turn to apocalyptic language – the 'end of nature', 'Earth without us', the 'storms of my grandchildren', the 'revenge of Gaia' – in environmental discourse (McKibben 1989; Weisman 2008; Hansen 2009; Lovelock 2007). The Greek word 'apocalypse' means 'unveiling' and the announcement of the Anthropocene is intended to reveal that because of his or her greatly extended technological powers, and the range and scale of his or her interventions, *Homo industrialis* has become a geological force who is changing life on Earth through a range of Earth system-level interventions. The announcement of the Anthropocene as an epoch which heralds ecological cataclysm unveils a future in which geologists, coming upon sedimentary strata from 1768 onwards, will be able to identify a stratigraphic 'golden spike' which indicates a range of anthropogenic modifications in the atmosphere, biota, oceans, soils and species of the planet. These changes will manifest in the fossil record which will reveal a marked rise in species extinction, 100–1,000 times faster than the background rate and the global distribution of exotic species into non-native ecosystems, and in the prevalence of artificial organic molecules including polyaromatic hydrocarbons and carbon isotopes from fossil fuel combustion in the atmosphere and marine sediments, and artificial radionuclides from atomic bomb tests.

The claim that the industrial revolution commenced a new geological epoch is closer to the literary genre of science fiction than of natural scientific writing. Like Asimov's *I Robot* or Piercey's *Woman on the Edge of Time* the Anthropocene narrative is an 'archaeology of the future' which involves the attempt 'to transform our own present into the determinate past of something yet to come' (Jameson 2005). The science fiction character of the term Anthropocene was demonstrated in Szerszynski's multimedia presentation entitled 'The Onomatophore of the Anthropocene' at the Thinking the Anthropocene conference in Paris in 2013 (Szerszynski this volume). Szerszynski depicted a future 'Commission on Planetary Ages' that deliberates on the human claim and agrees to its designation. Science fiction adopts a different temporal frame to most literature in that it describes how humanity, Earth and species developed from the perspective of an imagined future, so the near future becomes the imaginary past. This approach is often used in environmental literature, and most influentially in *Silent Spring*, in which Rachel Carson looked back from a potential future where 'no birds sing' to the political, chemical and biological events and processes that had led to that novel situation (Carson 1962). The book, perhaps the most influential environmental text ever written, provoked a mass environmental movement in the English-speaking world, which led to a political and regulatory thrust against pesticides and other synthetic chemicals which threatened species extinction and human health. In the United States the book prompted the establishment of the Environmental Protection Agency in 1970. In Europe national-level regulation of synthetic chemicals was underwritten by the establishment of the European Chemical Agency and REACH. But there has been no equivalent concerted international action against climate changing emissions of carbon dioxide from burning fossil fuels, or against the large-scale industrial interventions which are leading to the sixth wave of species extinction in Earth history (Leakey 1996); hence the mobilisation, again, of apocalyptic discourse, though this time at the Earth system level.

Environmental apocalyptic takes up the literary imaginary and rhetorical timbre of Jewish and Christian apocalyptic in secular mode (Buell 2003). The genre of apocalyptic emerged in the historical context of the Babylonian exile of Israel. The gift of the land is described in the history books of Israel as having occasioned the redemption of Israel's ancestors from imperial slavery in Egypt, and opened up the possibility of a novel covenantal and federal polity in which distributive justice and political participation were underwritten by land-sharing arrangements and legal restraints on debt and economic inequality (Northcott 2013). Exile from the land was a momentous rupture with this redemptive narrative and its legal and political instruments. While the Exile seemed to close down the possibility of future redemption, the Hebrew prophets discerned in the cataclysm a new revelation which transformed the Israelite story into a story about the potential redemption of all peoples, and potentially all species in Isaiah's imaginary of a peaceable kingdom where wolves and lambs 'lie down together' (Isaiah 11:6).

John of Patmos took up this apocalyptic reading of history in the context of the harsh persecution of Christians by Nero in the first century of the Christian Era. In the Book of Revelation John described persecution as herald of a near-term cataclysmic end of the Roman-dominated world order. He prophesied that those who remained faithful to the message and worship of the Incarnate Christ through the coming Armageddon would be vindicated at the end of time as the redeemed inhabitants of a 'New Heaven and a New Earth' in which peace would reign between the nations and creatures and peoples would be redeemed from destruction. The concluding and paradigmatic image of Revelation is of the 'tree of life', a reference that recalls the Exile of Adam and Eve from the Garden of Eden. In the restored Earth 'the river of the water of life' flows from 'the throne of God and of the Lamb through the middle of the street of the city' and there grows 'on either side of the river, the tree of life with its twelve kinds of fruit' and 'the leaves of the tree were for the healing of the nations' (Revelation 22:1–2).

In Christian history the vision of a New Heaven and New Earth, and peaceable relations between peoples and species, shaped the imaginary of desert ascetics who ministered to lions and were ministered to by wolves at the mouths of their hermetic caves (Bratton 1993). Over centuries monastic gardens, herbariums, hospitals and universities gradually transformed human interactions with non-human creatures. Through the domestication of animals, bee-keeping, herbal medicine, plant breeding, wetland drainage, wind and water mills, Christian monks fostered new bodies of knowledge and new institutions and practices that underwrote progress in agriculture, arts and crafts, in human health, in scientific knowledge and technological capacities, and in Earth care (Ovitt 1987). This progress was underwritten by the apocalyptic imaginary of Revelation and the restoration of Paradise, so that for the Elizabethan Renaissance scholar Francis Bacon the scientific method had the potential to usher in a 'New Atlantis' and a 'Novum Organum' in which human life would be redeemed from hunger, illness, plague and suffering (Bacon 1844).

In promoting the idea of divine Providence as leading history towards the restoration of Paradise on Earth, Christian eschatology underwrote belief in discoverable scientific laws of a mechanistic universe, and in the human capacity to use scientific knowledge to sustain agricultural, economic and technological progress (Schwartz 2000). But the eschatology of the Anthropocene indicates an era in which human arts and technologies have reached a crescendo of power and influence over the Earth system so as to destabilise Earth system relationships between humans and other creatures. This new era indicates not the perfection of nature but a new and even more fateful Exile from Paradise than the ancestral journeys from Eden to Egypt, or from Jerusalem to Babylon. In this new Exile masses of humans will die from drought, hunger or plague, while the lucky few will inhabit technologically advanced towers on high ground near the former ice-covered Polar regions, or they will seek life support elements such as water and carbon on other planets as the Earth overheats and the land area is variously flooded or turned to desert, and gradually becomes uninhabitable.

The announcement of the Anthropocene represents a portentous reversal of the Christian apocalyptic. The new epoch's apocalyptic timbre is closer to that of nuclear winter than the New Heaven and New Earth of Christian salvific eschatology, and indeed the first herald of the Anthropocene, Paul Crutzen, had earlier worked on the Earth system consequences of large scale thermonuclear war (Crutzen and Birks 1982). In the New World of the Anthropocene no heavenly being will intervene to redeem the humans from Exile, and wolves will not make peace with monks. In the Anthropocene only large-scale changes in human interventions in the Earth system, and in particular the planet-wide substitution of wind, water and solar power for fossil fuels, and the replanting of forests, can stave off ecological apocalypse. But the announcement of the Anthropocene, and the accumulation of scientific evidence of the biogeochemical signals that herald its coming, have yet to unleash such large-scale changes.

The Anthropocene as *kairos*

The Greeks have two words for time: time as *Chronos* indicates the successive cyclical passing of day and night, moment by moment, generation by generation; time as *Kairos* indicates moments in time which herald great or sudden change, or the need for change, in the flow of events and the passage of history. This distinction between *Chronos* and *Kairos* is evident in a discussion Christ had with the rabbis about the difference between weather signals and the 'signs of the times':

The Pharisees and Sadducees came, and to test Jesus they asked him to show them a sign from heaven. He answered them, 'When it is evening, you say, "It will be fair weather, for the sky is red." And in the morning, "It will be stormy today, for the sky is red and threatening."' You know how to interpret the appearance of the sky, but you cannot interpret the signs of the times. An evil and adulterous generation asks for a sign, but no sign will be given to it except the sign of Jonah.

(Matthew 16:1–4)

In this passage the cycle of morning and evening, and the seasonal cycles of weather, represent time as *Chronos* while the phrase 'signs of the times' represents time as *Kairos*, which is elsewhere described as the 'time of judgement' and 'the time for repentance' (Smith 1969). For the Christians of the first and second centuries the Incarnation of Christ inaugurated a new messianic era in which the promised redemption of all peoples, and species, had moved close, and this was symbolised in the nativity story of Christ being born among animals as well as princes. The birth of Christ, and the events of his public ministry, crucifixion and resurrection, therefore represented a *Kairos* moment in which salvation had come near, and for which humans could ready themselves through repentance and a new way of life in the time that remained before the end of time.

The Christmas festival, celebrated at the time of the northern winter solstice, represents an annual, chronological reminder of the intergenerational reading of history as *Kairos* and not merely as *Chronos*. In every heart, in every year, the Christ-child seeks a way in as the author of the carol 'Once in Royal David's City' suggests. But in the post-Christian culture of capitalist consumerism Christmas has morphed from the festival of the Incarnation of light in cosmic darkness into a fossil-fuelled festival of consumption where neon lights and LCD screens displace candles and incense. This ritual turn also symbolises the bifurcation of human history from natural history that Hutton's invention of deep time inaugurated. After Hutton, the birth of Christ is no longer the era-defining moment Christians once imagined. Instead human beings inhabit just a few millennia of a 4.5 billion-year history and successive eras are brought about by earthly and heavenly agencies such as volcanoes and solar activity. Era after era followed each other for billions of years before human births and deaths, human intents or purposes. Against this predominantly non-human *Chronos*, the recent fifty-year expansion in human consumption of fossil fuels, fresh water, forests, minerals and rocks, known as the Great Acceleration (Steffen et al. 2007), represents a mere cosmic blip in the abyss of time. Hence climate denialists and Gaian realists are both comforted by the *Chronos* of deep time.

It is perhaps inevitable that natural scientists, inheritors of the Baconian paradigm of nature as machine, would seek to reunite human and Earth history by the discovery of an apocalyptic *Kairos* moment not in the birth of a child but in the invention of a machine, Watt's condensing steam engine. It is doubtful, however, that such an artificial rhetorical device will have the cultural power to reunite the histories of humans and the Earth. The mechanistic and stratigraphic science fiction of the Anthropocene lacks poetry, and it lacks hope. But the announcement of the Anthropocene resembles other *Kairos* moments and it therefore contains a salvific possibility; in near-term repentance, in concerted human efforts to reduce deforestation and fossil fuel extraction, and to 'transition' to a mode of civilisation that lives off the renewing capacities of the Earth system, and ends unsustainable consumption. Analogously, the failure to embrace this possibility is often linked in climate apocalyptic, as in the film *Age of Stupid*, to the rhetoric of the judgement of future generations on present-day inaction to prevent the coming climate cataclysm. Here again Anthropocene apocalyptic mirrors that of the New Testament. Christ's parable of the Last Judgement at the end of time distinguished between two peoples: on the right hand of God were the 'sheep' who had used their time on Earth to relieve the suffering of their fellow humans, while on the left hand were the 'goats' who had ignored it (Matthew 25 31–46). The Anthropocene is already revealing itself as a time of increasing suffering: for Bangladeshi fishers, Syrian and Somali farmers, arctic bears and tropical salamanders. Creaturely and personal suffering will increase in the near-term of the Anthropocene.

The announcement of the Anthropocene represents recognition that this increase in suffering is a *Kairos* moment, which requires urgent action to reduce industrial humanity's impacts on the Earth system and hence the suffering of future persons and species. In this vein, the Anthropocene may be said to recover, after a 200-year interlude a historical narrative of human and Earth history which acknowledges their mutually constitutive relationship, and a narrative moreover in which, as in New Testament history, future generations will act as judge on those who inhabit the present moment and fail to read and respond to the signs of the times.

On the other hand, and more hopefully, the Anthropocene may also be said to facilitate a recovery of an ethic of love between persons who are distant across space or time. The Christian ethic of 'stranger love' was encapsulated in Christ's paradigmatic parable of the Good Samaritan who rescued the stranger by the wayside caught among thieves. And from this parable arises the concept of third party responsibility for injured persons, or tort in Western legal history (Bankowski 1994). Large-scale interventions to reduce present and future third-party harms from industrial activities mediated by the Earth system are more likely to have ethical suasion when they are described as hopeful and transformative responses to the *Kairos* moment of the announcement of the Anthropocene, as works of love for future generations and species, and not as props to the chronological but unsustainable growth of the present human economy into the near-term future.

References

Allenby B 1999 Earth systems engineering: The role of industrial ecology in an engineered world *Journal of Industrial Ecology* 2 73–93

Bacon F 1844 *Novum Organum or True Suggestions for the Interpretation of Nature* William Pickering, London

Bankowski Z 1994 How does it feel to be on your own? The person in the sight of autopoesis *Ratio Juris* 7 254–66

Berry T 1999 *The Great Work* Random House, New York

Bratton S P 1993 *Christianity, Wilderness, and Wildlife: The Original Desert Solitaire* University of Scranton Press, Scranton, Penn.

Buell F 2003 *From Apocalypse to Way of Life: Environmental Crisis in the American Century* Routledge, New York

Buell F 2010 A short history of environmental apocalypse, in Skrimshire S *Future Ethics: Climate Change and Apocalyptic Imagination* Continuum, London, 13–36

Carson R 1962 *Silent Spring* Houghton Mifflin, New York

Chakrabarty D 2009 The climate of history: Four theses *Critical Inquiry* 35 197–222

Crutzen P J and Birks J W 1982 The atmosphere after a nuclear war: Twilight at noon *Ambio* 11 114–25

Crutzen P and Stoermer E F 2000 The 'Anthropocene' *Global Change Newsletter* 41 17–18

Fuller J 2001 Before the hills in order stood: The beginning of the geology of time in England *Geological Society London*, Special Publications 190 15–23

Hamilton C 2013 *Earthmasters: The Dawn of the Age of Climate Engineering* Yale University Press, New Haven

Hansen J 2009 *Storms of My Grandchildren: The Truth About the Coming Climate Catastrophe and Our Last Chance to Save Humanity* Bloomsbury, London

Hendel R 2013 The Oxford Hebrew Bible: Its Aims and a Response to Criticisms *Hebrew Bible and Ancient Israel* 2(1) 63–99

Hutton J 1786 *A New Theory of the Earth* William Creech, Edinburgh

Jameson F 2005 *Archaeologies of the Future: The Desire Called Utopia and Other Science Fictions* Verso, London

Leakey R 1996 *The Sixth Extinction: Patterns of Life and the Future of Humankind* Random House, New York

Lovelock J 2007 *The Revenge of Gaia: Earth's Climate Crisis and the Fate of Humanity* Basic Books, New York

McKibben B 1989 *The End of Nature* Random House, New York

Nordhaus T and Shellenberger M 2007 *Break Through: From the Death of Environmentalism to the Politics of Possibility* Houghton Mifflin, New York

Northcott M 2013 Whose danger, which climate? Mesopotamian versus liberal accounts of climate justice, in Rozzi R Pickett S Palmer C Armesto J and Callicott J eds *Linking Ecology and Ethics for a Changing World: Values, Philosophy, and Action* Springer, New York 241–50

Northcott M 2014 *A Political Theology of Climate Change* SPCK, London

Ovitt G 1987 *The Restoration of Perfection: Labor and Technology in Medieval Culture* Rutgers University Press, New Brunswick NJ

Page E 2007 *Climate Change, Justice, and Future Generations* Edward Elgar, Cheltenham

Playfair J 1822 Biographical Account of Dr James Hutton, in *The Works of John Playfair* William Constable, Edinburgh

Repcheck J 2003 *The Man Who Found Time: James Hutton and the Discovery of Earth's Antiquity* Simon and Schuster, London

Robin L and Steffen W 2007 History for the Anthropocene *History Compass* 5 1694–1719

Ruddiman W F 2005 *Plows, Plagues, and Petroleum: How Humans Took Control of Climate* Princeton University Press, Princeton NJ

Schellnhuber H J 2009 'Earth system' analysis and the second Copernican revolution *Nature* 402 Supplement: C19–C23

Schwartz H 2000 *Eschatology* Eerdmans, Grand Rapids MI

Sideris L H 2013 Science as sacred myth? Ecospirituality in the Anthropocene age, in R Rozzi et al. eds *Linking Ecology and Ethics for a Changing World: Values, Philosophy, and Action* Equinox, Dordrecht 147–62

Smith E 1969 Time, times and the right time: Kairos and Chronos *The Monist* 53 1–13

Stager C 2011 *Deep Future: The Next 100,000 Years of Life on Earth* Thomas Dunne, New York

Steffen W Crutzen P J McNeill J R 2007 The Anthropocene: Are Humans Now Overwhelming the Forces of Nature? *Ambio* 36 614–21

Szerszynski B 2012 The End of the End of Nature: The Anthropocene and the fate of the human *Oxford Literary Review* 34 165–84

Szerszynski B 2015 Commission on Planetary Ages Decision CC87966424/49, this volume

Weisman A 2008 *The Earth Without Us* Random House, New York

Zalasiewicz J and Williams M 2008 Are we now living in the Anthropocene? *GSA Today* 18 4–8

9

GREEN ESCHATOLOGY

Yves Cochet

Traditionally, apocalyptic texts announced both the dramatic end of the present time and the promise of a new world. For both the Christian and Marxist traditions, to refer to only two Western ones, this abrupt changeover – the 'Doomsday' or the 'Revolution' – would establish a new world order based on a new kind of humanity, less adversarial than the previous one, a melioristic mutation of the species. Contemporary environmental catastrophism is less enchanting (Catton 1980; Dupuy 2004; Barnosky et al. 2012; Meadows 2013). It claims that a critical transition of the biosphere will happen before 2050 without simultaneously proclaiming the hope of a better world thereafter.

Material evidence of the ecological apocalypse

Let us first illustrate our catastrophe hypothesis with two examples from contemporary scientific research. The first example comes from a 2004 book summarising the research of the International Geosphere–Biosphere Programme (IGBP), which was launched in 1986 with the intention of studying changes that affect the Earth system as a result of human activities (Steffen et al. 2004). The second is a survey on the state of the planet and its future, written by twenty naturalists, and published in 2012 by the journal *Nature* (Barnosky et al. 2012). The Fifth Assessment Report of the IPCC provides corroboration (IPCC 2013).

All these studies establish alarming findings; the threats are real and serious. Of course, humanity has faced local environmental problems in the past, and solved or ameliorated them. But the novelty of the present situation is the global and simultaneous nature of the threats. Today, humanity is like a telluric force affecting major biogeophysical cycles and jeopardising the Earth system as a whole, and we cannot accurately predict the Earth's future path.

The paper in *Nature* introduces additional concepts in an attempt to better understand what is happening in the biosphere (Barnosky et al. 2012). Traditional research in scientific ecology, which is often satisfied by linearly projecting past trends into the future, can no longer account for the climatic or biological disorders observed today. Complex interactions, feedbacks and unlikely disruptive effects have to be taken into account. It has already been observed that a local ecosystem could be subject to abrupt and irreversible switches from one state to another after crossing critical thresholds. For example, the eutrophication of shallow lakes or seashores after pollution by excessive nitrate or phosphate nutrients can cause clear water rich in vegetation and fish to be quickly replaced by turbid and stinking water with the explosion of phytoplankton and oxygen depletion (Carpenter et al. 1999). In 2009 the 'green tides' in the bay of Saint-Michel-en-Grève (Brittany, France) even caused the death of a horse and rider due to asphyxiation by hydrogen sulphide fumes from decaying algae.

Is it feasible to go from the local to the global to form the hypothesis that the Earth system itself could be subject to a similar critical transition, a shift from one state to another unknown to all human experience, one that is rapid and irreversible? This is what the authors of the *Nature* article postulated after examining a series of characteristic warning signals sent by the stressed atmosphere, oceans and lands. These forces are well known: population growth and resource depletion associated with the transformation and fragmentation of natural habitats, the extraction and exuberant consumption of fossil fuels, climate change, and the pollution of air and water. All these mechanisms now far exceed the biocapacity of the Earth, that is to say, its ability to supply resources and absorb wastes continuously. In other words, the ecological footprint of humanity exceeds the available space, so that today we need a planet and a half to sustainably support our consumption levels (acknowledging, of course, the widely disparate ecological footprints between nations and among social classes).

In summary, the current Earth system is subject to global, objective, systemic, accelerated, anthropogenic, unpredictable and unregulated phenomena, phenomena characteristic of the Anthropocene. Why are such stunning findings not sufficient to change public policies, from the local to the international? More than the force of the biogeophysical realities themselves, I believe that it is the denial of recognition of the magnitude and gravity of the situation that makes the global collapse, the Apocalypse, plausible. Predicting collapse is on much more solid ground than naming a date for it; but it is likely to be much sooner than most people believe. Such a future stands in stark contrast to the standard, and convenient, assumption that the future will evolve without a rupture.

Let us be clear: I am not saying that this 'Apocalypse' will be a rapid and spectacular global biogeophysical disaster. Rather it is likely to be the result of financial, economic and political collapse. But, like the 2008–9 recession after the fall of Lehman Brothers (Hamilton 2009), it will be caused mainly by the intolerable degradation of the Earth system, including the scarcity of resources. According to Kunstler (2012), it would involve each of the following components:

- The stock market suffers a crash bigger than that of 2008.
- Several large banks go bankrupt.
- The electrical system at the regional level fails repeatedly, with cascading consequences for trade.
- Fossil fuels are in short supply.
- The Internet is practically dead, with catastrophic business impacts.
- Airlines are inaccessible to the vast majority and transport is mostly rudimentary and restricted to short distances.
- Many schools, colleges and universities close.
- Public hospitals are unable to operate and social security collapses.
- Many other activities cease; the financial and technology sectors grind to a halt.
- Obtaining food and drinking water is the main activity of almost everyone. Home gardens proliferate, but hunger and malnutrition spread.
- The politicians are powerless and the majority of the population is led by local unelected leadership.

The 'ostrich' policy

Why is it that, even among scientific and political ecologists, the approach of the Apocalypse and the orthogonal changes of behaviour and decision making that should follow are not the primary concern, the political priority, and the individual and collective obsession? After all, the problem is the survival of humanity. Along the route of my political journey – first as member of the French National Assembly, then as France's Minister for the Environment and now as a Member of the European Parliament – I have seen the denial of the coming disaster expressed in many ways by many actors. The first, arising from cognitive dissonance (the discomfort arising from facts that contradict one's firm beliefs), is to consistently underestimate the importance of the ecological catastrophe.

But the way this is done has evolved over the past forty years, according to Dennis Meadows (2013). In the 1970s, the critics said: 'There are no limits. Anyone who thinks that there are limits just does not understand anything.' In the 1980s, it became clear that there are limits so they said: 'Well, OK, there are limits, but they are a long way off. We do not have to worry about them.' In the 1990s, it was recognised that the boundaries are not so remote; it was a decade of fruitful scientific work on the damage to ecosystems, for example. So proponents of growth said: 'You know, maybe there are limits that will be reached soon, but we do not need to worry about them because markets and technology will solve the problems.' In the last decade, it became apparent that technology and the market will not make the problems disappear (they have done nothing for climate change except make it worse). So the response has changed once again: 'Well, OK, but it is still necessary to support growth, because only growth will provide the resources we need to deal with problems growth causes.'

Marxists also practice denial when they interpret the situation simply as the result of the excessive power of oil corporations. This is not mistaken but it does not solve the issue of the impact of the ecological disaster on the life of oil corporations and their owners. Indeed, if the hypothesis of the Apocalypse caused by ecological collapse is true, then in its most extreme form there will be no survivors in the transformed Earth system – no fortresses where the world's wealthy elite can shield themselves from system breakdown. While the poor will suffer more from this breakdown as it is occurring, in the end, in a state of global collapse, there are no bourgeois and proletarians.

The neoliberal kind of denial (one of its most virulent forms) takes comfort from the belief that nothing can stand in the way of 'consumer preferences', consumers with an unquenchable thirst for energy and resources. The leaders of private companies have told me: 'Go and preach degrowth to the European masses and [their *coup de grâce*] to those in emerging countries.' They add, mischievously: 'And get yourself re-elected by campaigning against economic growth and for a project of happy frugality.' Indeed, the question is about the contradiction between the short time frames of elective democracy (at most a few years) and the long term (decades) for the implementation of a radical political programme aimed at reducing the risk of global collapse. The philosopher Jean-Louis Vullierme summarised this contradiction:

> It is virtually impossible to counter radical ecological risk simply by taking a decision. It is not socially acceptable to create a war economy before the war, or to take drastic measures affecting our way of life before being confronted directly with a disaster whose effects have begun to manifest obviously to the collective gaze. In other words, the most enlightened of us could only be prepared by thinking about policies whose implementation would be post-Apocalypse.
>
> (Vullierme 2013)

Specular interaction

Let us deepen the question of denial by presenting an anthropological hypothesis, one conveyed by Vullierme (1989), who philosophises on the nature and evolution of societies. The social psychology that structures societies is partly an emergent phenomenon that occurs when individuals meet; it is also a generic process of their constitution, of human nature itself. The human being is shaped by the world that existed previously and is also a modeller in the world by the actions he or she undertakes. Thus, the child enriches her capacity to model the world by experiencing the differences between herself and the world as she models it. By my bodily postures and words and through my actions, I act on the world by issuing traces or signs of my model of the world and I retrofit the model based on the answers that I receive.

Actually, it is not one model of the world I have but a modelling scheme, a matrix of alternative models, allowing me to generate somewhat different models. My everyday life, bathing in the stream of pure experiences, takes place as a constant alternation of models of the world, reorganising each time my whole being in the world. A sketch: for a while I practice my profession of repairer of clocks; then I meet friends for lunch and discuss the proposed extension of the Parisian boulevards tramway; I go back to work on my springs while looking forward to an evening dinner with my son; I leave my shop to hug my girlfriend tenderly; I see my son for dinner, and then I attend the meeting of my local green group to prepare for the next elections. In all these situations, and a thousand other possibilities, it is the same person who paints his life by tapping into its range of models of the world that corresponds to his experience of that kind of situation.

These models are evolving, disparate, and even contradictory. Such an individual – fragmented, but who accepts this fragmentation – is everyman and everywoman. The human being is multidimensional, colourful and ambiguous. Yet in the neoliberal world, this design is opposed to the one-dimensional vision of *homo economicus,* the poor soul who is reduced to a rational, unitary self always seeking consistency and maximising its usefulness. It is also an object in the Marxist conception of the mass-produced individual whose conscience is entirely determined by the position it occupies in class relations.

If there is a human nature, it develops in interaction with others. If there is a society, it emerges from the interactions between individuals. This hypothesis is called *specular interaction.* I become myself by exchanging with others models of the world formed in these exchanges. So society is a system of mutual perceptions among individuals; I imagine how others represent things and myself. In other words, individual models of the world owned by someone, including the model itself, are derived from models of the world owned by others, including the model that others have of me. What determines the behaviour of an individual is the system of models that refer to this individual. This is an evolutionary scheme capable of generating multiple models corresponding to all situations encountered. No two individual patterns are identical, of course, but they tend to adapt to each other by the multiplication of social opportunities to respond to the behaviour of others. This allows everyone to predict and anticipate the actions and the reactions of others, which is the foundational coordination capacity of any lasting society. The mirroring of models is what ensures the unification of societies. Specular distinction is what makes their essential diversity and is the starting point for social ecology. The hypothesis of specular interaction allows us to bury the old epistemological debate over the priority of the individual or of society. They mutually shape each other.

According to René Girard (1972), this loop is powered by imitation or mimesis. But in specularity, the imitation is imitation of the same and imitation of the different, *duplicative* mimesis and *distinctive* mimesis. Specularity deals with the intersections of representations of the world that everyone develops gradually in intersubjective dealings. Children (and adults!) have this ability to model the world; they learn to imitate others as well as to distinguish themselves from others. So they develop a set of representations of the world, including a representation of themselves in the eyes of others (the others are our mirrors, thus the word 'specular'). Within a human community, each individual being is placed in the same position as others. Duplicative mimesis tends to bring matching representations of the world of each other, in particular the representation that others have of my representation of the world, so that other people's reactions to my actions are neither unpredictable nor dangerous. Duplicative mimesis binds a community more closely within shared values, principles and common behaviours. At the same time, distinctive mimesis ensures diversity without which contagious undifferentiation creates social chaos of pure rivals and general violence in the community – 'the war of all against all', as Thomas Hobbes put it.

Denial of collapse

Let us review the denial of global collapse in the light of specular interaction among citizens (Cochet 2009). A citizen whose ecological model of the world is sufficiently well informed is sometimes willing to change her lifestyle. But she does not think about her behaviour alone, but also about her image in the eyes of others. If she were the sole judge, she would change her habits to reduce her ecological footprint. This is probably true for the majority of our fellow citizens, who are more or less aware of environmental disaster. If it were enough to add up individual wills to change behaviour, the ecological paradise would reign long over the world. But this will not occur because, according to our hypothesis, the will is not the first reality, but is derivative from the reality of specular interaction. The individual, aware of the disaster, does not ask if he wants to change his own life; he would do so only if a number of others would too. Everyone being placed in the same situation, the disaster will be avoided, not in response to the will of all but through their cross-representation, that is to say, based on the expectations that everyone has of the effective capacity of those around him to change their lives. Many historical examples – dictatorships, for example – show that a situation can be opposed by almost all yet persist; the desire for change is not enough. Yet the social dynamics are sometimes unpredictable due to specular interaction, so these situations may also change rapidly.

Here we find a social system whose development, like some natural systems discussed above, may shift abruptly to another state once certain limits are exceeded. So even in seemingly simple situations of specular interactions, the overall dynamics are vital (Granovetter 1978). According to the initial conditions of the situation, and exogenous shocks that can befall societies, the trajectory of social dynamics and the final situation may be very different. Specularity is producing social self-organisation. It can give rise to qualitatively new societies, impossible to imagine by reducing the analysis of society solely to its components.

Psychology of decision makers

What about the denial of collapse among policy makers? In my experience as a minister and policy maker I have seen that the specular dynamic carries on inexorably, describing the beliefs and actions of political actors, which are built on their interactions with rivals for positions. If one of these political actors, such as Barack Obama, were suddenly converted by Dennis Meadows to an understanding of the impending ecological disaster, he would seek to test the credibility of his new belief in the eyes of various political actors. Otherwise he would lose his authority. His political acts would be determined less by the strength of his new conviction than by his evaluation of the strength of that belief among rivals and friends. Unsure of this strength and fearful of criticism by rivals, he will not be motivated to translate his new belief into strong political action.

Propagation of belief in impending ecological catastrophe can only be slow in a world gripped by political rivalry, so much so that even if all world leaders had a revelation and found themselves suddenly inhabited by a belief in imminent ecological catastrophe, they would doubt themselves if their rivals and friends did not share their belief. Everyone could know of the impending disaster, but it may be that no one knows that others know. Everyone would notice the backlash against anyone publicly disclosing or hinting at their convictions, so that none are willing finally to unveil it. Moreover, acting on the belief would radically disrupt public policies by demanding changes in patterns of production and consumption in industrialised societies. Citizens would need to accept radical changes in their lifestyle. So the denial of collapse may not be due to everyone's unreasonableness or ignorance but to the way specularity plays out in a society.

Specular interaction leads to the impossibility of an early consensus on complex and controversial issues. The exact dimensions of environmental issues escape our senses; they are often quite technical so that our opinions are mediated and shaped by experts, scientists and various other third parties. Scholars can agree on basic questions and answers in specific areas – such as the rate of carbon dioxide increase in the atmosphere, or what is the minimum number of anchovy in the Bay of Biscay that can be taken sustainably – but discrepancies between scientists may emerge because ecology is a complex area and the replicability of experimental results may be low or impossible. It is then necessary to introduce models of studied reality, based on choices that are not always technical. Within each model, the conclusions are certain, but the choice between models is not. The findings of a model may contradict those of another. When model results are harbingers of social change then it is ideology (based on a political model of the world) that will guide decision makers, most towards a path consistent with a capitalist-productivist way of thinking, occasionally toward 'happy degrowth' (such as the 1987 Montreal Protocol on Substances that Deplete the Ozone Layer). Each will have his or her own experts. But in the end policy makers must make the decisions themselves under certain constraints, including electoral, fiscal and international ones. These constraints are, of course, highly specular, and generally see decisions made that are at odds with any personal conviction about ecological disaster. The orientation towards the truth is psychosocial rather than based on reason and evidence. As Galileo knew, one cannot be right and alone in a specific area, in a given society.

So, the collapse seems inevitable not because scientific knowledge of its approach is uncertain but because the social psychology of human life does not allow the right decisions to be made at the right time. We are reaching the limits of the planet in many ways and at the same time. There are often several ways to solve a local or a circumscribed problem, but facing many global dangers together makes the burden of implementing solutions so high that denial is the natural response. It is this denial that ensures that Apocalypse is near.

References

Barnosky A D et al. 2012 Approaching a state shift in Earth's biosphere *Nature* 486 52–8

Carpenter S R Ludwig D and Brock W A 1999 Management of eutrophication for lakes subject to potentially irreversible change *Ecological Applications* 9 751–71

Catton W R 1980 *Overshoot: The Ecological Basis of Revolutionary Change* University of Illinois Press, Urbana

Cochet Y 2009 *Antimanuel d'écologie* Bréal, Paris

Crutzen P and Stoermer E F 2000 The 'Anthropocene' *IGBP Newsletter* 41 17–18

Dupuy J P 2004 *Pour un catastrophisme éclairé. Quand l'impossible est certain* Seuil, Paris

Girard R 1972 *La Violence et le Sacré* Grasset, Paris

Granovetter M 1978 Threshold models of collective behavior *American Journal of Sociology* 83(6) 1420–43

Hamilton J 2009 Causes and consequences of the oil shock of 2007–08 *Brookings Papers on Economic Activity* Spring 2009 215–59

IPCC 2013 *Climate Change 2013: The Physical Science Basis. Contribution of Working Group I to the Fifth Assessment Report of the Intergovernmental Panel on Climate Change* Cambridge University Press, Cambridge

Kunstler J H 2012 The Collapse Wager, blog post http://http://cluborlov.blogspot. fr/2012/08/the-collapse-wager.html Accessed 9 July 2014

Meadows D L 2013 Il est trop tard pour le développement durable, in Sinaï A ed *Penser la Décroissance, Politiques de l'Anthropocène* Les Presses de Sciences-Po, Paris 195–210

Steffen W et al. 2004 *Global Change and the Earth System: A planet under pressure* Springer-Verlag, New York

Vullierme J-L 1989 *Le Concept de Système Politique* Presses Universitaires de France, Paris

Vullierme J-L 2013 Personal communication with the author

PART III

Rethinking politics

10

BACK TO THE HOLOCENE

A conceptual, and possibly practical, return to a nature not intended for humans

Virginie Maris

Introduction

Life on Earth is going through an unprecedented crisis, often referred to as the sixth mass extinction. Human activities affect virtually all taxa and biomes of the planet. If species extinctions are the most visible manifestation of this global disaster, others, like the degradation and fragmentation of natural habitats, global deforestation and defaunation, and the acidification of oceans, are no less critical and, at least for some of them, no less irreversible. Parallel and somehow independent of this ecological crisis, the concept of nature has drawn harsh criticism over the past thirty years. Today, environmentalists, scientists and policy makers scrupulously avoid this term, preferring to address conservation issues by talking about 'biodiversity', 'environment' or even 'ecosystem services'. Nature, as a reality as well as a concept, could thus be declared to be dead, and the mere idea of the Anthropocene is nothing but the confirmation that we now live in a wholly human-made world.

However, my purpose in this chapter is to show that, more than ever, we need to reinvestigate and revivify the idea of nature. The aim is not to exhume a zombie but to argue that, despite some convincing arguments to abandon the unified, idealised and somehow sterilising concept of Nature (with a capital 'N'), there is still room for a creative representation of nature, natures, and natural entities and processes. More specifically, there are three features of the non-human world that offer a sound basis to characterise nature: its externality, its otherness and its agency. Taking them into account in the way we consider and protect biodiversity should be a great asset in facing the present environmental crisis.

The circumstances of the death

To begin, as forensic scientists, let's take the time to examine the circumstances of the so-called 'death of nature'.

First, the scene of the crime – a blurred dichotomy

The dichotomy between culture and nature, humans and non-humans, tradition-ally lies at the heart of Western culture. Lynn White Jr accused this dualism of constituting the root of our ecological crisis (White 1967). Many contemporary environmental ethicists conflate anthropocentrism with this strong separation of human beings from the rest of the world (Sylvan 1973; Callicott 1987). Yet it should be noticed that more than the dichotomy itself, it was the concomitant hierarchy between humans and the rest of living beings that gave rise to the radical appropriation and deterioration of the natural environment. The ambition of this chapter is to maintain the separation between humans and nature while rejecting the domination of the former over the latter. To make the argument I will present and reject the two strategies that have been used to undermine the Nature/Culture dichotomy – the one that claims that nature is nothing but a product of culture and the one the claims that culture is nothing but a natural process. I will then offer an alternative consisting of the reassessment of a natural world independent of culture and human ends.

The acculturation of nature

On one hand, the acculturation of nature stems from the assumption that there is no nature; there are only ideas of nature. This deconstruction of the concept of nature has taken different forms over the past decades. I briefly sketch three of them: the ecofeminist criticism, the anthropological criticism and the sociological criticism.

In *The Death of Nature: Women, ecology and the scientific revolution*, Carolyn Merchant criticises the strong association between women and nature made by Western culture after the scientific revolution (Merchant 1980). For the ecofemi-nist, Western science and its political extension into modern capitalism have been a historical enterprise to subjugate and dominate both women and nature. The mere concept of nature is thus so tinged with anthropocentrism and patriarchism that it would be better to avoid it. Merchant suggests we find a less gendered concept, such as an ethic of partnership, in order to assess the numerous interdependencies between humans and non-humans.

Based on a thorough anthropological study of diverse cultures around the world, Philippe Descola (2013) shows how the idea of a nature external to and separated from human beings is historically and culturally constructed, specific to Euro-American modernity, which is characterised by what Descola calls a 'naturalist epistemology'. Far from being universal, the nature–culture dualism is the fruit of a provincial worldview that operates a separation and a hierarchy between human beings and all other living things. The aim of Descola in *Beyond Nature and Culture* is to provide an appropriate epistemology for anthropology that does not impose ill-suited homogeneous categories on varying cultures. However, beyond this epistemological issue, his thorough study of the genealogy and partiality of the concept of nature offers good reasons to try to overcome the traditional dualistic worldview that no longer fits with our environment and our knowledge.

In a different vein, Bruno Latour (2004) has argued that what stands for a smooth and unequivocal concept of nature is rather an inextricable composition of hairy objects, hazardous hybrid things that carry with them a slew of social and cultural excrescences. For Latour, the concept of nature is not only an empty one, since nothing in the world could be properly designated as 'nature', but is also not operative and represents a threat to political action. Indeed, as long as nature is considered to be the immutable hierarchy of beings, subsuming everything in a continuous chain from the stars to the underground bacteria, the defence of nature could mean nothing but the offence of politics. Politics has nothing to do with any so-called 'natural order'. For Latour, politics has to do with the complex and embedded real-life situations in which balance of powers, individual wills, knowledge uncertainties and plural experiences articulate around particular collectives in which social and natural entities are inseparable. However, contrary to Latour, who proclaims the 'death of nature', one can try to revise the old modernist vision of nature in order to capture the strong intuitions at stake when nature's advocates engage themselves in its defense while avoiding the anti-political claim to come back to a 'natural order'.

The naturalisation of culture

By contrast, the naturalisation of culture is essentially due to more or less fruitful human sociobiological reductions (Wilson 1975). Indeed, the application of evolutionary theory to social behaviour allows for the blurring of the distinction between what is considered a natural process and what is properly cultural. An essay by Boyd and Richerson (1988) offers an ambitious attempt to apply evolutionary theory to cultural transmission. For them, cultural transmission (that is, transmission by means of communication, learning, imitation and so on) is not essentially different from genetic transmission, and it could be studied and explained through the same evolutionary lens. Thus even if the evolution of human cultures is based much more on cultural transmission than genetic heredity, the difference between human societies and non-human societies is more one of degree than a qualitative one.

In both cases, the separation between human beings and nature is blurred in favour of a continuum of more or less anthropogenic beings and matters-of-facts. The concept of nature has been harshly criticised as an artificial way to separate humans and non-humans, one mainly founded on an old-fashioned Western dualist worldview. Today, the consensus is growing that the dichotomy between Nature and Culture should be abandoned in favour of a more holistic conception of the human/non-human relationship. So much for the background scenery; now what of the evidence?

Second, the evidence – a tame Earth

The place for nature on Earth is dwindling. Today there are more than seven billion humans occupying two-thirds of the planet's land surface (Mittermeier et al. 2003). The remaining parts of the planet, while not used by humans, are either under permanent ice (one-third) or threatened by diverse human activities like agriculture, logging, mining, pollution and so on (one-half). Almost all the coastal ecosystems are heavily influenced by human activities. No marine area is unaffected by human influence, and over 40 per cent is strongly affected by factors like pollution, fishing, species invasions and climate change (Halpern et al. 2008).

If nature is thought of as wilderness or as the spatial portion of the Earth immune from any human influence, it might be the case that the only remaining nature has to be found in the highest mountains, the deep sea and the ice sheets, which, unfortunately, are all threatened by anthropogenic global warming. As anticipated by Bill McKibben (1989) more than twenty-five years ago, we are witnessing 'the end of nature'. There is no longer something like a true nature independent of human influence. But obviously nature cannot be reduced to wilderness or pristine nature, and most of us would agree that walking in a second-growth forest, bird watching in a saltpan or hiking in a mountain pasture have something to do with nature, even if all these habitats are heavily influenced by human activities.

Third, the suspects – no one is innocent

Now, let's browse the suspects. First, in the role of the innocent culprit we could mention the naturalists themselves. Those who traditionally used to care for nature have been prompt to abandon their cherished baby in favour of the more serious and scientific-sounding concept of 'biodiversity' (Takacs 1996). The neologism, coined by Walter G. Rosen during one of the first scientific meetings dedicated to biological diversity, was kept by Edward O. Wilson for the title of the proceedings (Wilson 1988). It soon became a rallying cry for scientists to alert the public and policy makers to the unprecedented crisis of the diversity of life on Earth. 'Biodiversity' is generally defined as the diversity of life at its different levels of organisation. Despite the scientific and formal flavour of the term, there is no single measure or theoretical appreciation of biodiversity, but rather a constellation of heterogeneous and sometimes contradictory concepts depending on the scale and the level of organisation – species richness, genetic variability, phylogenetic diversity, alpha, gamma and beta diversity, and so on. The profusion of definitions is not an issue for scientists themselves, who can make explicit which facet of biodiversity they refer to in their works. But it may give the public the impression that the protection of nature, requalified as biodiversity conservation, is a matter of science more than a social and political issue.

Second, in the role of the unexpected accomplices, some of those who could have been the natural allies of nature conservation turned out to be harsh detractors. Environmentalism is all but a homogeneous field. The concern for nature preservation has been attacked by some environmental philosophers as misanthropic (Bookchin 1995) or imperialistic (Guha 1989). In the political arena, the green parties have often neglected biodiversity conservation, considering that the critical environmental issues lie elsewhere, in the farmlands, in the factories and, ultimately, in the atmosphere (O'Neill 1997).

Third, the true bad guys could be cast as the capitalists and neoliberals, who first organised the global plundering of nature in the name of economic growth and who now loudly call for the commodification of the last remnants that have resisted them (O'Neill 2001). The rise of market-based conservation approaches, for instance through payment for ecosystem services (Kosoy and Corbera 2010) or mitigation banks (Robertson 2004), can been seen as an attempt to internalise nature into the capitalist logic of markets (Maris 2014).

The dilution of nature in the technical, economic and bureaucratic spheres

The focus of this chapter is the science, management, policies and institutions for which nature is a central concern – that is, the world of biodiversity conservation. Obviously it is a fragmentary analysis, but it has a strong influence on the way biodiversity policies are designed and on the narratives conveyed from the scientific arena to the public.

The care for nature has long operated along two distinct lines: resource conservation and wilderness preservation. From a management perspective, these two ends have distinct sets of means and rationales – interventionism and economic efficiency for resourcism on one side, and *laissez-faire* and ecological processes for preservationism on the other.

With the concept of biodiversity the distinction is subsumed; nature and natural resources are reconciled. The coherent framework of the past, in which nature preservation calls for the fewest interventions and resource conservation necessitates active management, has been blurred. The optimisation of resource management sometimes appeals to *laissez-faire* supporters since it may be cheaper not to intervene; conversely, nature preservation could be the theatre of strong interventions in order to mimic nature, interventions that have the inherent paradox of working out how to design spontaneity. This reorientation of conservation goals and rationales is accompanied by the progressive absorption of nature in the technical sphere, the economic sphere and the technocratic sphere.

The technical absorption

Biodiversity conservation now has at its disposal a growing technical toolkit for the conservation, restoration or recreation of nature. Beside the traditional enclosure policies, natural habitats are subject to more and more intrusive conservation measures: exotic species eradication, population reinforcement by the reintroduction of animals raised in captivity, translocation, assisted colonisation, and so on.

With a much more technological flavour the new biotechnologies of reproduction are now part of conservation, with artificial insemination, the transplantation of wild species embryos into females of closely related domestic species, or even the so-far unsuccessful attempt to resurrect extinct species. For instance, in 2009 a Franco-Spanish research team managed to make a clone from the conserved genetic material of the Pyrenean Ibex, a species extinct for 2,000 years (Folch et al. 2009), and work is underway on genetic material from woolly mammoths and even Neanderthals. This intensification of intrusive and technology-dependent means to conserve or restore biodiversity makes it less and less easy to distinguish what is natural from what is artificial, including in those areas traditionally dedicated to nature.

The economic absorption

A second mutation observable in the field of biodiversity sciences and management is the multiplication of appeals to strictly economic rationality in order to incorporate nature's values to justify its protection or pay for its conservation. In the 1990s, monetary valuation of biodiversity and ecosystem services proliferated at varying scales and deployed a growing set of methodological devices, culminating with the well-known work of Robert Costanza and his colleagues published in *Science* in 1997 (Costanza et al. 1997). They estimated that the total value of the world's ecosystem services and natural capital amounted to US$33 trillion each year, which (if valid) equates to more than twice global gross national product. During the Nagoya meeting of the Convention on Biological Diversity in 2010 the United Nations Environment Programme (UNEP) published *The Economics of Ecosystems and Biodiversity*, the object of which was to estimate the economic costs of biodiversity loss and ecosystem services degradation, as well as to offer a comprehensive assessment of the various methods for the monetary valuations of biodiversity and ecosystem services (UNEP 2010).

The popularity of monetary valuations is not confined to academic economics but has been encouraged and appropriated by institutions. Within its *Horizon 2020* framework, the European Union requires all member states to provide a national economic valuation of their ecosystem services. This flow of monetary quantification, despite the insurmountable methodological and conceptual weaknesses of such exercises, reflects the idea that in order to protect nature, its benefits to humans and the costs induced by its degradation should be internalised into economic accounting systems. The trend is made visible in the changing vocabulary of conservation, which increasingly borrows jargon and metaphors from economics. Nature protection is now concerned with the management of natural capital and the optimisation of ecosystem services. For the proponents of this approach, 'conservation must pay for itself' (Daily 1997) or, better, conservation should no longer be viewed as a constraint but an *opportunity*. To achieve this goal new mechanisms of commodification have been developed, such as mitigation banks and payments for the use of ecosystem services (Gómez-Baggethun et al. 2010; Maris 2014).

The bureaucratic absorption

The third sphere that progressively digests the idea of nature is the bureaucratic one. Biodiversity sciences have proudly and enthusiastically embraced the era of Big Data. Everything looks as if scientists, unable to slow down the unprecedented rate of biodiversity erosion, are rushing to collect and to monitor any possible information, from the smallest scale – with, for instance, the new technical tools of barcoding – to the largest one – with global monitoring and the mapping of land cover, atmospheric composition and so on. A giant bio-panopticon is being constructed; trillions of data are collected every day, sometimes without the slightest idea of the way the information could be treated in order to extract usable knowledge or practical recommendations (Hampton et al. 2013; Kitchin 2014).

The 'Anthropocene' narrative as the ultimate assault

So now let's enter the Anthropocene era, whose narrative forms the ultimate assault on the idea that there could be something out there to be called nature. Previously, the ages of the Earth were stratigraphically recorded in its geological skin, making visible biogeological successions and the rhythm of its long life. Now, with Earth entering the era of humans, we are at home everywhere. We have become the powerful – although blind and planless – architects of the planet we inhabit.

I will not address the scientific relevance of the Anthropocene from a geological perspective but rather question whether this new narrative can become an effective lever to overcome the ecological crisis. To do so, I will focus on three features of the Anthropocene narratives – the Earth as a globalised planet, human beings as a species, and the ecological crisis as a techno-scientific issue. Each is problematic.

The scientific description of the Anthropocene throws us in spatial scales disconnected from political action and, even more, from individual choices and responsibilities. The main components of Anthropocene sciences are 'the atmosphere, the biosphere (including humans and their societies) and the oceans' (Leemans 2006, 246). The Anthropocene tells the global story of Earth as if observed from the sky, hardly a view to motivate local political action.

If humans have long been cultural and biological agents, it is only recently that they became known as geological agents (Chakrabarty 2009). But it is worth noting that the new agents are not of the same kind. Cultural and biological agents are individuals or, at least, social groups. The idea that humans could be geological agents refers to humans as a species. Individual or small group behaviours cannot interfere with the great geological processes. The anthropogenic influence on climate is not due to the action of anyone specifically, but to the cumulative effects of a multitude of actions across time and across people. It is humanity as a whole that is at stake in climate change sciences. Thus the Anthropocene has been described 'as an unintended effect of human choices' (Chakrabarty 2009, 210) where human beings are considered to be a homogenous species. Accepting that, as matter of fact, *Homo sapiens* is a geological agent leads one to seek solutions in the ability of humanity to use its geological agency in a more conscious and deliberate way. In their seminal article Crutzen and Stoemer wrote: 'An exciting, but also difficult and daunting task lies ahead of the global research and engineering community to guide mankind towards global, sustainable, environmental management' (Crutzen and Stoermer 2000, 17).

Philosophers such as Hans Jonas (1985) and, more recently, Dominique Bourg and Kerry Whiteside (2010) have defended the need to assign a special and privileged place to experts and scientists both in public debate and in decision making. Calls for a new kind of 'expertocracy' or even an enlightened despotism are common, especially in the scientific community.

These three features of Anthropocene sciences (their global scale, humanity as a species and the techno-scientific characterisation of the problems) all converge on the same dead-end – individuals are dispossessed of their moral responsibility and ability to be actors in the solutions. The future of the Earth now lies in the hands of global institutions, scientists and engineers. The public become powerless witnesses to the degradation of the planet. Every two or three years, over several days, the world's eyes turn anxiously toward climate negotiations at some international summit or other. The negotiations are typically judged to be unsatisfying in the face of the challenges at stake. Then we immediately turn back to real life, driving our cars, eating our steaks, and waiting for the next global warming summit to solve the problem.

Why do we need nature?

In this final section, I will not attempt to offer a ready-made operational conception of nature to replace the idealised old 'Nature', but I do suggest three characteristics that should be conveyed by a new concept, ones that provide the conceptual backdrop against which the ecological challenges should be sketched – the exteriority of nature, the otherness of nature and the agency of natural entities.

The exteriority of nature

Nature can be considered to be the part of reality that we have not created. We must cease to absorb and swallow everything around us, like unconscious macrophages or innocent bulimic babies. Recognising the exteriority of nature, accepting that we are not the designers of the Earth we inhabit and of the living things with which we share it is urgently needed to halt the tyrannical delirium that possesses us. Without such an external background, it is impossible to build and to reframe our own subjectivity.

The otherness of nature

Humanism and the consonant anthropocentrism are deeply rooted in reciprocity. Western traditional moral theories all depend on the recognition in the other of the same kind of fundamental interests or the same inherent autonomy as those of the moral agent. We are looking for ourselves in the others in order to grant them our moral consideration. This narcissistic feature of humanism, if able to ground morality inside quite homogeneous cultural groups like white enlightened Western men, has failed to create the genuine moral framework needed in the pluralist and globalised societies we now live in. We urgently need to find ways of rethinking morality from a different perspective. The recognition of the otherness of the others and the respect of differences, rather than the desperate seeking for resemblances could be fruitfully stimulated by the reconsideration of human–nature relationships that are grounded neither in assimilation nor in rejection.

The agency of nature

Since swallows breed under human roofs they are not independent of human activities. Yet swallows are not hybrid human-and-non-human objects; they are just swallows. They do not need us, and they do not care about us. To consider swallows as hybrid composites stemming from a long coevolution of birds and humans, carrying with them representations, symbols and cultural values (Latour 2004) is just ignoring the fact that swallows live their own swallow life, with feelings, intentions and potentialities that cannot be reduced to human ends and representations. A thorough consideration and respect for nature could be a real asset in reconciling ideals of autonomy and solidarity between humans and non-humans as well as between humans themselves. The universalist pretension of traditional humanist theories fails to offer a satisfying account of our moral bonds in a globalised world, where those who are affected by our daily choices and actions are so unprecedentedly remote in space and time that the reciprocity cannot tell us much about our responsibility toward them.

Final thoughts

In this new era of the Anthropocene, the worst approach would be to remain prostrate, gazing at nature's agony, both fascinated and terrorised by our own power. But there is also good news under the sky. While technophiles and environmentalists are chorusing a requiem for the late nature, nature itself comes back everywhere, and not only nature but, for better or worse, wild nature. The wolves have come back to the Alps. The otter, almost extinct in France in the 1980s, is recovering, and more and more of Britain's rivers are now hosting this elegant little mammal. Even big cities can become habitats for wildlife: coyotes stroll Chicago's streets and foxes forage in London's backyards; prairie dogs colonise Denver's suburbs; Peregrine falcons nest in the highest roofs of New York City, and so on. Obviously, these heartening stories are anecdotal compared to the strong evidence of biodiversity decline, but they offer perspectives on the possible cohabitation of human beings and wildlife. Reframing the ecological crisis at smaller scales so as to question our personal relationship with our fellow humans and with non-humans is a great occasion to reconsider the ways we can accommodate and welcome the otherness of others. At the global scale, the human imprint on the Earth might seem omnipresent and unprecedented, but at a smaller scale one just needs to let things go in a couple of square metres in the backyard to realise that nature is neither dead nor agonising. Nature is everywhere, latent, silent, waiting for the opportunity to burgeon and flourish, and there are many ways to protect it other than to subjugate it. These ways are explored by some restoration ecologists who are humble enough to consider their work as giving a push for degraded ecosystems to recover their natural trajectories, by biodiversity managers adopting a rewilding approach, and by urban wildlife activists campaigning for a peaceful cohabitation with nature.

References

Bookchin M 1995 *Re-Enchanting Humanity: A Defense of the Human Spirit Against Antihumanism, Misanthropy, Mysticism and Primitivism* Cassell, New York

Boyd R and Richerson P J 1988 *Culture and the Evolutionary Process* University of Chicago Press, Chicago

Bourg D and Whiteside K 2010 *Vers une Démocratie Ecologique. Le citoyen, le savant et le politique* Presses de Seuil, Paris

Callicott J B 1987 *A Companion to a Sand County Almanac* University of Wisconsin Press, Madison

Chakrabarty D 2009 The climate of history: Four theses *Critical Inquiry* 35 197–222

Costanza R d' Arge R de Groot R Farber S Grasso M and Hannon B 1997 The value of the world's ecosystem services and natural capital *Nature* 387 253–60

Crutzen P J and Stoermer E F 2000 The 'Anthropocene' *Global Change Newsletter* 41 17–18

Daily G C 1997 *Nature's Services: Societal Dependence on Natural Ecosystems* Island Press, Washington, DC

Descola P 2013 *Beyond Nature and Culture* University of Chicago Press, Chicago

Folch J et al. 2009 First birth of an animal from an extinct subspecies (*Capra pyrenaica pyrenaica*) by cloning *Theriogenology* 71 1026–34

Gómez-Baggethun E de Groot R Lomas P L and Montes C 2010 The history of ecosystem services in economic theory and practice: From early notions to markets and payment schemes *Ecological Economics* 69 1209–18

Guha R 1989 Radical American environmentalism and wilderness preservation: A third world critique *Environmental Ethics* 11 71–83

Halpern B S et al. 2008 A global map of human impact on marine ecosystems *Science* 319 948–52

Hampton S E et al. 2013 Big data and the future of ecology *Frontiers in Ecology and the Environment* 11 156–62

Jonas H 1985 *The Imperative of Responsibility: In Search of an Ethics for the Technological Age* University of Chicago Press, Chicago

Kitchin R 2014 Big Data, new epistemologies and paradigm shifts *Big Data & Society* 1 1–12

Kosoy N and Corbera E 2010 Payments for ecosystem services as commodity fetishism *Ecological Economics* 69 1228–36

Latour B 2004 *Politics of Nature: How to Bring the Sciences into Democracy* Harvard University Press, Cambridge

Leemans F 2006 Scientific challenges in anthropogenic research in the 21st century: The problem of scale, in Ehlers E and Krafft T eds *Earth System Science in the Anthropocene* Springer, Berlin 248–62

Maris V 2014 *Nature à Vendre: Limites des services écosystémiques* Quae, Paris

McKibben B 1989 *The End of Nature* Random House, New York

Merchant C 1980 *The Death of Nature: Women, Ecology, and the Scientific Revolution* Harper Collins, San Francisco

Mittermeier R A et al. 2003 Wilderness and biodiversity conservation *PNAS* 100 10309–13

O'Neill J 2001 Markets and the environment: The solution is the problem *Economic and Political Weekly* 36 1865–73

O'Neill M 1997 *Green Parties and Political Change in Contemporary Europe: New Politics, Old Predicaments* Ashgate Publishing Limited, Aldershot

Piña-Aguilar R E et al. 2009 Revival of extinct species using nuclear transfer: Hope for the mammoth, true for the Pyrenean Ibex, but is it time for 'Conservation Cloning'? *Cloning and Stem Cells* 11 341–6

Robertson M M 2004 The neoliberalization of ecosystem services: Wetland mitigation banking and problems in environmental governance *Geoforum* 35 361–73

Sylvan R 1973 Is there a need for a new environmental ethics? *Proceedings of the XVth World Congress of Philosophy* Sofia Press, Varna

Takacs D 1996 *The Idea of Biodiversity: Philosophies of Paradise* Johns Hopkins University Press, Baltimore

United Nations Environment Programme (UNEP) 2010 *Mainstreaming the Economics of Nature: A Synthesis of the Approach, Conclusions and Recommendations of TEEB* United Nations Environment Programme, Bonn

White L Jr 1967 The historical roots of our ecologic crisis *Science* 155 1203–7

Wilson E O 1975 Sociobiology: The New Synthesis Harvard University Press, Cambridge, Mass.

Wilson E O ed 1988 *Biodiversity* National Academies Press, Washington, DC

11

ACCEPTING THE REALITY OF GAIA

A fundamental shift?

Isabelle Stengers

At the origin of this text was the *Thinking the Anthropocene* conference held in Paris, 14–15 November 2013, the aim of which was to gather social sciences and humanities scholars 'with an intuition that something fundamental has shifted', meaning that their disciplines, as they rested on the 'social only' conceptions that define modernity, need rethinking. 'Gaia', it was written in the invitation circular, 'has reawakened'. While 'Anthropos', now defined as a 'geological force', has met a remarkable academic success, the name Gaia is liable to provoke a 'you can't be serious' reaction, asking for an 'it is only a metaphor' reassuring answer. For those who share 'the intuition that something fundamental has shifted', I will claim that the contrast between the 'Anthropocene' and the 'reawakening of Gaia' is significant and may indicate that the articulation between diverging conceptions of 'reality' is part of the shift.

In a way, the association between Gaia, a bastard child of climate sciences and ancient paganism, and the proposition to 'think the Anthropocene' seems unproblematic. Both are pointing to the very uncertain times we are entering. The Holocene, which would belong to the past, marked the end of the last glacial period, the beginning of a semi-stable climate regime, propitious to the development of what would be 'entirely new', including modern sciences. The geologists are proudly able to situate this novelty in Earth's timeline. Anthropocene would mean something new again, but the novelty would be that 'Anthropos' must now be considered as a 'geological force' in its own right, leaving all over the world the incontrovertible mark that something 'new' has happened. But just as with the looming climate disorder, those marks give no reason for pride to the one who would be responsible for them. They tell, and will go on telling in a far away future measured in geological time, about erosion, pollution, radioactive contamination, a monstrous accumulation of garbage, and, of course, a massive loss in biodiversity.

When I first heard about the Anthropocene proposal, I had mixed feelings, as I felt it was smoothing down a distinction that, I thought, should rather be dramatised. The damage, even injury, caused to the Earth is not something we 'discover'. The lasting character of it is certainly impressive but depredation, exploitation, rape, loss are words we are used to, and they may concern both 'ecosystems' (not to use the now ritually criticised term 'nature') and the many peoples on this Earth who were not aware that they did belong to the species called 'Man', or *homo sapiens*, or Anthropos. In contrast, what we have learned about the speed and possible irreversibility of the coming climate change creates a novel situation. 'Man', we realise, has not only been abusive but has also played the sorcerer's apprentice and may well provoke an awesome answer from something which can no longer be figured as a 'victim', something which gives a new meaning to the powerful being whom James Lovelock and Lynn Margulis baptised Gaia.

For the 'climate change' community, and in particular for one of its most central figures, Stephen Schneider, Gaia was never a simple metaphor; rather it was the questioning figure this community had to decipher (Schneider 1984). It is Schneider who, in 1988, organised the first Chapman Conference on the Gaia Hypothesis, which did much to get the issue discussed seriously by scientists. And right from the beginning the ethos of Gaia was at stake for him. Is Gaia the name for a living organism, or, at least, a homeostatic coevolutionary system, ensuring the optimal condition for the flourishing of life on the Earth? It was Lovelock's thesis, but Schneider had a rather different idea. For him, the 1980 Alvarez hypothesis, which had linked the famous extinction of the dinosaurs some 65 million years ago to the Earth being struck by a giant asteroid and the consequent global cooling due to a dust cloud enveloping the Earth, gave a taste of Gaia's capacity to destroy what she had previously sustained. The stability and stabilising power of Gaia could not be taken for granted.

The possibility of brutal extinction staged by the Alvarez hypothesis has been the starting point for a community of 'climate change' modellers with an inseparably political and scientific agenda. The 'nuclear winter' hypothesis of the 1980s, a time when there was perceived to be an increased possibility of a nuclear confrontation, was brought to public attention by alarm-bell ringers Paul Crutzen, Stephen Schneider and many others. They organised international cooperation, including Soviet scientific partners, in order to run computer simulations of the possible 'global' effect of even a 'limited' nuclear war, and called publicly for a ban on the use of nuclear weapons.

It is worth emphasising the difference between this new alarm-sounding role and the post-war movement of physicists against the prospect of a nuclear war and the famous mutually assured destruction (MAD) strategy. Physicists went public as those who bore responsibility for their science having produced the awesome possibility of destroying humanity, but they could also be heard as giving voice to human consciousness in general – physics had given the means but the decision to use them was in purely human hands. In contrast, during the 'nuclear winter' episode, computers (very, very slow by today's standards) were running very simplified models, insufficient data were gathered and worst-case scenarios were envisaged. Which means that the point was no longer the classical one, that of 'the power science gave to humanity'. The point was the *creation* of a knowledge the very sense of which was its relevance for – or intrusive interference with – political matters. The decision to go public with admittedly uncertain results – results, it must be emphasised, that could only be uncertain, whatever the power of the computers and the progress in modelling – meant that the concerned scientists were breaking with the traditional position of science of putting the weight of the facts' authority against the passions of sociopolitical conflicts and irrational public fears.

As humanities and social sciences specialists, we should be able to measure the very unusual position of our so-called hard science colleagues as they cast their lot with an alarming message that challenges the idea that a science which is not able to prove what it claims should wait for the proof before addressing public issues. This may put us in a rather unusual position ourselves. Concerned by the message, do we risk accepting that we are 'simply' part of the public, worrying like everybody else about the prospects of climate change? Or do we critically address this new figure of 'scientific power', unwittingly joining another part of the public, the deniers, like the readers of Michael Crichton's *State of Fear*? Merchants of fear or merchants of doubt: we are in the very uncomfortable position of having to choose.

The name Gaia clearly marks the refusal of the 'we need more research' refrain intoned by the merchants of doubt and we may share this refusal with arguments of our own, questioning, for instance, the number of accepted so-called scientific proofs that have for their first authority the agreement of stakeholders and public authorities. Clearly the evaluation of what counts as a proof has nothing neutral about it. Also, why not accept that Gaia 'exists' for her own sake at a time when the Market is accepted as such? This, however, protects our traditional critical or agnostic stance, claiming that 'true demonstrations' are not of this world, against the intuition that 'something fundamental has shifted'.

Going further I would insist on the difference between those two 'global' objects – Gaia and the Market – and the corresponding models they rest upon. The dynamics of climate modelling and of the gathering of empirical data presupposes that with better and more detailed models, more powerful computers, and more empirical observations, it is possible to learn about the ethos of Gaia. In a way, the original Lovelock's Gaia had some analogy with the Market – she was defined by the hypothetical role she was to endorse (Lovelock 1979). Learning about Gaia's ethos does not rest any longer on selected examples of couplings between processes that would illustrate Gaia's stabilising, homeostatic power. In climate models all couplings are potentially relevant and most are ambiguous, seemingly participating in the overall stability in some conditions but liable to amplify the temperature change if a tipping point, the nightmare of climate specialists, is passed.

The possibility of such a nightmare is the signature of a 'realist' science, a science the truth-value of which depends on successfully giving the reality it addresses the power to make a significant difference in the way it would be characterised. In contrast with experimental sciences, however, in climate science the power to make a difference is not aimed at turning this reality into a well-defined object, whatever the improved relevance and reliability of the models. Calling it Gaia is signifying that it is, and will remain, what can be called a 'being', existing in its own terms, not in the terms crafted to reliably characterise it. It is not a living being, and not a cybernetic one either; rather it is a being demanding that we complicate the divide between life and non–life, for Gaia is gifted with its own particular way of holding together and of answering to changes forced on it (here the charge of greenhouse gas in the atmosphere), thus breaking the general linear relation between causes and effects.[1]

In this sense, Gaia may be typical of a new kind of scientific being. As computer modelling makes it now possible to escape the ideal of 'linearisation' and to explore situations with strong nonlinear couplings (positive and negative feedbacks), such beings are bound to multiply, and the strong differentiation may dissolve between the language of compulsion or 'make do' (used for Baconian Nature) and the language of 'obtain from' (used by seducers, trainers and teachers for instance). Rather than fulfilling the engineering dream of synthetic biology, this perspective may communicate with a new kind of eco–ethology addressing what each such beings require, be it in order to maintain their existence or to 'behave' or to modify their behaviour. This would not be an 'innocent' or respectful concern, to say the least, but a new style of concern, demanding that the dream of control or mastery be given up, replaced by the need to pay attention to, to care about and to learn from what we are bound to coexist with.

Gaia is thus not the Earth, a resource to be exploited (hopefully in a sustainable way) or a vulnerable and unique wonder to be respected and protected. She is 'global', not in the sense of the famous 'blue planet' picture but because global computer models are required to grasp the intricate processual couplings which human activity has interfered with. As I underlined six years ago, writing about the 'intrusion of Gaia' (Stengers 2009), Gaia's reawakening is not to be associated with a 'crisis', such as a nuclear war would have brought with a transitory 'winter' or 'autumn', but with the need to take into account a protagonist that will never recede into the background, and whose the stability 'we' will never again be able to take for granted. In this sense Gaia is intruding not in general but in our 'human only' story-making. As a scientific being, furthermore, she conveys neither demands nor messages. Scientific models can only capture the indifferent relentlessness of the answer given to inconsiderate interferences. But the challenge of this answer has direct political implications because we are situated, scientists tell us, in the very short time period that is left before her full, irreversible awakening.

It was at the time when climatologists were becoming more and more impressed by the threatening speed of the awakening, and frustrated by the inertia of the political powers to whom they were relaying the threat, that Paul Crutzen launched the 'Anthropocene' motto, which has since invaded the whole scene. It has been loudly endorsed by many academics who, welcoming its geological credentials, used it to defend against what may well have been for them the *real* threat of Gaia, the opening of the door to hordes of irrational, catastrophists 'believers'. I do not think it is useful to criticise Crutzen's initiative. After having given the many reasons why the name is a highly disputable one, and emphasising that etymologically 'Anthropos' may derive from the 'upward-looking ones' (those who are fascinated by abstract ideals and pay no attention to earthly muddles), Donna Haraway (2014a) generously remarked: 'Eugene Stoermer and Paul Crutzen were not vexed by these ambiguities. Looking up, their human eyes were on the Earth's atmospheric carbon burden. But also, swimming in hot seas with the tentacular ones, they saw with the optic-haptic fingery eyes of marine critters the dying of coral symbioses.'

Gaia, as a scientific being, does not ignore earthly muddles. Rather those muddles are framed by the open, ceaselessly reworked question of how and to what extent they affect Gaia. Not so with Anthropos, who claims as his right and greatness not to pay attention. It may well be that Crutzen never really wondered about this petty distinction. For him and his colleagues the point was 'anthropogenic'. Obviously the hypothetical nuclear winter would be an anthropogenic event, while Alvarez's extinction was not. The claim that the already observable average temperature variation was to be related to 'human activity' was the crucial point to convey. Allying this point with the indisputable consequences of human activity irreversibly marking the Earth at a geological scale was a way to hammer it in, to impress on imaginations the novelty of the situation. But the paradox of this rhetorical move is that it allied two scientific communities – geologists and climatologists – that have a rather different relation with this novelty.

The great 'ages of the Earth' dating enterprise is part of the grand geopolitical-scientific-economic story of the conquest of the Earth and its resources. The geological time scale is the one part that may exhibit the prestigious 'universal-disinterested-knowledge-vanquishing-irrational-beliefs' stamp. I intend no easy irony here, no intention to debunk the achievement. As Stephen J. Gould (1990) once remarked, whatever its historical complication, the closure of the great Devonian controversy is pure joy in the collective memory of the geologists' community, a joy unadulterated by geopolitical concerns. It is a joy that must remain so; the time taken by the International Stratigraphy Commission to decide whether we are indeed living in the 'Anthropocene' may serve the geologists' wish not to follow their climatologist colleagues in their urgent alarm-sounding strategy. Further, the two communities do not share the same view of 'change'. The 'catastrophist' Alvarez hypothesis was first ferociously resisted by geologists, for whom the uniformitarian doctrine was synonymous with their own version of the victory of scientific rationality over belief. Certainly the situation has changed and the evidence testifying for a history punctuated by great extinction episodes is now accepted, together with hypotheses about the turn of events that brought them about. But the long-view story is still about a recovering Earth, and indeed naming our epoch is centre-staging virtual geologists of an unknown (recovered?) future who would gather and contemplate data from all over the Earth testifying for a change deserving a name, and who would come to the conclusion that this change was not, this time, caused by 'natural forces'. That those responsible for this change may or may not have survived in this future is not the geologists' business. Their business is to ensure that their virtual colleagues will confirm the verdict still under discussion – whether 'our' epoch indeed 'deserves' a proper name; whatever it may be, *it will have marked* a new age.

This 'future perfect continuous tense' is swallowing the time that remains 'now', a time that is not merely wasted but under attack because, far from diminishing, there is a rapid acceleration in the production of greenhouse gases. It is swallowing the question of 'what will happen', of how the virtual geologists will characterise this new 'age'. This is beyond the geologists' responsibility, which is precisely to keep their decision disinterested, protected from today's 'burning' concerns (which their colleagues in the field are busily stoking as they find promising new sources of so-called unconventional fossil fuels).

Anthropocene, for geologists, may well be 'just a name', but names have a power of their own. Today, witnessing the very success of this name, not only in the media but also in academic circles, we may hypothesise that this success is not unrelated to the comfort of the geologists' future perfect continuous tense, which frees up room for academic reflexive pondering and new theoretical turns. We even hear new voices 'celebrating' Anthropos as the one who will not only successfully find the way to neutralise the climatic threat (via geoengineering), but will go on, as a now self-conscious geological force reconfiguring the Earth and turning the Anthropocene into a 'good Anthropocene', so fulfilling its godlike destiny. We may be grateful for the vigorous alarm sounded by Clive Hamilton (2013) against the temptation to consider that we are only dealing with a ridiculous remake of an old refrain; the remake may well be the early announcement of the rhetoric that will flourish when the strategy of climate disorder denial will have done its time and 'we' will have to face the failure of what is officially 'plan A', the promised reduction of greenhouse gas emission. The apprentice sorcerer will claim there is no choice but to try and tame Gaia, and its minions will turn the attempt to do so into a logical accomplishment of human emancipation and mastery. There is no reason why we would submissively depend on mere 'natural forces'.[2]

I was a witness to a rather ominous scene in Brussels showing how easily the path towards this future may be initiated. Clive Hamilton was addressing an academic public about geoengineering as the looming plan B, already sustained by those whose money previously fed the 'merchants of doubt'. Following his talk, the only questions that broke the silence came from engineers and scientists emphasising that surely our fate should not be left in the hands of private companies, and calling for public research, if only to assess objectively (and with the sole general interest in mind) the feasibility and risks of the diverse possibilities. To them, working on such fascinating questions was clearly the rational answer, maintaining science in its usual position as the solution provider. I will not begin to enumerate what they abstracted away – from the rules of present-day knowledge economy to the insuperable tendency of the work 'on' a possibility turning into 'for' a possibility. Nor will I analyse what contradicts the 'rational answer' in terms of the obstacles to be downplayed or the dangers of putting it into the perspective of a cost–benefit analysis – the case of genetically modified organisms (GMOs) is eloquent, and we can be sure the benefits of geoengineering would appear to be overwhelming. In Brussels the dream was alive and well, and a scientist even remarked that the acquired knowledge would be quite useful if, as Steven Hawking claimed, 'we' had to leave an irreversibly messed-up Earth and terraform another planet. Hamilton's answer, however strong, was, I am afraid, unable to banish from the room haunting speculations about promising research projects. The ominous silence was rather a 'Yes, I know, but nevertheless . . .'

This scene will not astonish those of us who practise historico-critical studies. Have we not published enough about the political, ideological nature of scientists' claims that they produce 'disinterested' knowledge, transcending particular interests, political conflicts and ideological commitments? Nothing fundamental seems to have shifted here. And this may well be the point. Would we not also be ready to critically analyse the way climatologists insist theirs is a 'true' science, with the legitimate objective authority any science claims to impose? Do we not deal with the very example of big calculation centres scaling an abstract question that will be imposed on every people on this Earth, regardless of what may again be disqualified as 'matters of belief'? Here is the shifting ground: what if we accept Gaia's 'reality'?

Ten years ago, when Bruno Latour asked 'Why has critique run out of steam?', he invoked the example of the deconstructivist argument being hijacked by those whom we now call 'merchants of doubt'. He wondered: 'Can we devise another powerful descriptive tool that deals this time with matters of concern and whose import then will no longer be to debunk but to protect and care, as Donna Haraway would put it? Is it really possible to transform the critical urge in the ethos of someone who *adds* reality to matters of fact and not *subtract* reality from it?' (Latour 2004, 232). This proposition implies that matters of fact, such as the ones climatologists claim to obtain, are not as such something to be 'afraid of', as if some 'global' matter of concern could be derived from it. It should be sufficient to note that the leading and very specific concern of the specialists gathered in IPCC Working Group I is about the reliability of their working abstractions. Their models may well conclude that Gaia is a global threat, but in their case 'global' is no triumph over earthly local, frictional muddles. Gaia has no unifying power other than that of a 'real' claim to authorise sounding the alarm. It is 'mute' as to the answers to be given to the threat.

Latour's point implies giving up critique as an end in itself, but not critical *concerns*. And we may indeed be concerned at this point: Gaia, as defined by climate scientists, may well have no unifying power *but only as long as none is added* – if not by the 'upward-looking' Anthropos, certainly by those who refer to science in order to define what 'really matters'. If there must be critical attention, a need to protect and care, it is not a matter of debunking the illusions of objectivity and realism of what I will call globally 'group I' specialists. There are three working groups in the IPCC, and the third one is busy converting Gaia's question into a problem formulated for policy makers, that is, in terms that conform to the socio-economic parameters they consider relevant. Between groups I and III the definitions of 'abstraction' and 'realism' have almost nothing in common. While group I experts get nightmares when they obtain a new understanding of the intricate dynamics of the ice sheets, group III experts tell no such stories about the protagonists of their scenarios. They may 'neutrally' take note that greenhouse gas emissions are accelerating rather than slowing down, but they will not enter too much into the (politically explosive) reasons for why they are bound to continue doing so. If the motto of a 'good' Anthropocene is to worm itself into and gain credibility in the public debate, it will be through the 'make-believe' formulations of group III – not 'adding' inconvenient reality to matter-of-fact Gaia but postulating that nothing is real but the (global) business–as–usual approach of policy makers.

I am not proposing that group I specialists are innocent, disinterested scientists. I am just emphasising that references to objectivity and reality in no way constitute the common denominator of the three groups but crucially depend on their respective specific matter of concern. As for the alarm-sounders' own conception of their role, it may well be that many trusted the fable that when scientists have shown the 'facts', consequences should follow, forgetting that this only applies when facts authorise new possibilities for what is called development. Others may have trusted democracy, or even the market. Some have maintained their 'we give the facts' neutrality façade because they were aware that their enemies were just waiting for any fissure in this façade to appear – as in the French child's play song '*I hold you, you hold me by our little goatee. The first one of us two who will laugh will get a wee slap!*' But some others are now bluntly (that is realistically) heralding their (objective) conclusion. When, in December 2012, geophysicist and complex systems specialist Brad Werner crossed the abyss between the 'realities' of groups I and III, it resulted in a talk titled 'Is Earth F★★ked? Dynamical Futility of Global Environmental Management and Possibilities for Sustainability via Direct Action Activism' (Werner 2012).

Werner insists he is speaking as a geophysicist, in the name of a model he is constructing. The problem, he says, 'cannot be left just to the social scientists or the humanities'. As a matter of fact, they play no role in his model, while the influence of 'Direct Action Activism' – through 'indigenous peoples, workers, anarchists and other activist groups' who demonstrate to others that it is possible to resist 'capitalist culture' – appears as the only chance for a future. We in the social sciences or humanities may feel it is a typical example of 'objective science' imperialism. But let us now imagine Werner suddenly turning towards critical thinkers with a 'Hey guys, the situation is *really, objectively*, a fucked up mess. Can you help?' Here we may feel that 'something fundamental' is indeed shifting. What Werner calls 'capitalist' or 'dominant' culture we know well, and we are quite ready to discuss it and dispute each other's definitions. But is this knowledge liable to add rather than subtract reality from other people's concerns, including those of climatologists? Is it liable to sustain or help or delay activism? Or is it rather activism? Or is the critique of illusions more important so that it deciphers the hold of capitalist culture over us in such a way that imagining the end of humankind on this Earth is easier (or academically safer) than imagining that it can be defeated?

In his *Inquiry into Modes of Existence*, Bruno Latour demands that we resist the temptation to 'attribute too much power to this monster' (Latour 2013, 384), that is, that we do not attribute to Capitalism the unifying power that is denied to Gaia. In other words, Capitalism should not be ceded the power to authorise the formulation of the 'one' problem to which every other matter of concern must be subordinated (It's Capitalism, stupid!). Today, both Jason Moore (2013) and Donna

Haraway (2014b) nevertheless claim that if our geological epoch were to acquire a name of its own, this name should be the Capitalocene, not the Anthropocene. Perhaps many frustrated climatologists would now agree. The challenge for us may then be to use descriptive tools that do not give to Capitalocene the power to explain away the entanglement of earthly, resilient matters of concern, while adding that no Capitalocene story, starting with the 'long sixteenth century', can go very far without being entangled with the on-going invention/production/appropriation/exploitation of what Jason Moore calls 'cheap nature'.[3] In other words, we should not indulge in the very Capitalocene gesture of appropriation, of giving to an abstraction the power to define as 'cheap' – an inexhaustible resource that may be dismembered or debunked at will and reduced to illusory beliefs – whatever escapes its grasp as we do with theoretical abstractions.

The common point between those groups practising what Brad Werner characterises as 'Direct Action Activism' is that they do not act in the name of a theory. They experiment with practices that refuse theoretical abstractions authorising to define as 'cheap' their collateral damage (whether they be ecological or social, a distinction which is itself a Capitalocene one).[4] This requires the reclaiming and cultivation of cooperative collective intelligence, the art of giving voice to powers, human and non-human, that must be addressed if they are not to turn into destructive ones, the art of caring for the unfolding of the matter of concern that gathers them. Such activist groups do not need to become a new general model for academics to ponder. There is no collective intelligence in general (*pace* Negri). The experimental, reclaiming practices called for (re)generating what Capitalocene has systematically eradicated are always situated and precarious. The only generalities are about what inhibits, poisons or destroys such practices and academic critical pondering may well be part of the poison, debunking as mere beliefs what does not conform to their standards, subtracting reality from the experimental assemblages which sustain the never to be taken for granted creation of collective intelligence.

'Can you help?' I have imagined Brad Werner could ask us this question in order to trouble us, to make us think, to turn the question into an arrow maybe hitting its target. If we look at academic production we must admit that none of our sophisticated critical and analytical tools have produced knowledge that helps others, those 'activist' groups who need to cultivate cooperative, ongoing collective intelligence. Rather we have been critically dismembering as illusory fictions that which they have learned empowers them to think and act.[5]

Curiously enough, what could be demanded from us, humanities and social sciences academics, as from many others, may be to enact what Bruno Latour rather daringly called the 'admirable injunction' of liberalism – 'Don't let anything go, don't let anything pass!' (*Ne pas se laisser faire, ne rien laisser passer!*) (Latour 2013, 471–2). A formidable injunction indeed, which may well go to the core of the question that Gaia imposes on the Capitalocene, and which has nothing to do with the mythic Anthropos. It rather cruelly emphasises the despondency we may feel regarding all that we academics have let go and let pass in our own institutions. What is clear is that this injunction can be addressed neither to the anonymous 'subject', be he (rather than she) knowing or critical, nor to any of the self-sustaining '*homos*' who populate modern pseudo-sciences.

What is also clear is that any confusion between this injunction and the demand for 'reflexivity' would be as gross a misunderstanding as the idea that critical 'deconstruction' is a way not to let anything go or anything pass. Becoming able not to let anything go or anything pass is not playing the princess and the pea; it implies rather the reverse, tolerating no mattress of abstraction allowing a comfortable escape from the messiness of a situation. Rather, the injunction gives to the trouble the power to trouble us, as what we have to live and think with. This may be a meaning for those 'earthly' sciences Latour occasionally alludes to, sciences that would fully accept the need to protect and care for the situations they are concerned with, learning how to betray the Capitalocene regime of appropriation.

In brief, if 'something fundamental has shifted' for us, if we have to accept thinking and feeling and imagining with the question Gaia imposes on us, it might well demand that we dare to be 'realists', no more and no less than climatologists but in our own ways. Not letting go but actively discarding the norms of distance and detachment that act as mattresses protecting us against what Donna Haraway calls response-ability, the need to become able to respond to what our work adds to the world, for the way we, as we propose it, are casting our lot for some ways of living and dying and not others. Not letting pass what we consider matters of critical concern, but doing it in such a way that the matters are liable to be shared with the concerned people, liable maybe to add new dimensions to the issues they struggle for.

Those issues are *real*, and we have to protect this reality against 'our' enemies. Not the enemies of climatologists but our own. It may well be that the time has come to not let pass the role playing of academic civility, the indifference regarding the poisons so many among our dear colleagues add to the world, not just politely stating our intellectual disagreement, as if they were in need of enlightenment, but politically and publically analysing the way the poison is working, the way it participates in the Capitalocene regime of appropriation.

Notes

1 Another model to be resisted is that of 'autopoietic beings', whose 'own terms' and 'own particular way' indicate an 'owner', a being maintaining its formal identity through its exchanges with its outside, unilaterally assigning its meaning to what affects it. Donna Haraway proposes to speak about 'sympoiesis', which escapes the face-to-face opposition between heteropoiesis and autopoiesis, a bit like the way an enlightening conversation escapes the two extremes of a 'command/obey' relation and a 'dialogue of the deaf'.

2 Suddenly the seemingly delirious ravings of accelerationist Reza Negarestani speculating about our ultimate task, 'to evade the limits posed by the solar economy' rings prophetic (Negarestani 2011, 201).

3 '"Cheap nature" in the modern sense encompasses the diversity of human and extra-human activity necessary to capitalist development but not directly valorised ("paid") through the money economy. The decisive historical expression of Cheap Nature in the

modern era is the Four Cheaps of labor-power, food, energy, and raw materials' (Moore 2013, part I 21). As Moore emphasises, appropriation (enclosure, destructive exploitation and colonisation) is then part and parcel of the Capitalocene, well before the celebrated steam engine. See Linebaugh on the destruction of the commons in England and then all over the world (Linebaugh 2008) and Starhawk's telling of the burning of the witches as part of the destruction of the peasant communities (Starhawk 1997).

4 The principle of non-separation between social and ecological concerns is at the very basis of what is now called 'commoning'. 'No commons without commoning', it is said, no common good or resource without the social creation needed to 'make it common'. Thinking 'like a commoner' (Bollier 2014) is no innocent thinking, no dreaming of an unspoilt wilderness. It is rather consequential thinking, with the fragility and need for on-going maintenance of the social, cultural and ecological interdependence.

5 I am thinking among others of 'pagan' versions of Gaia and of the fate of eco-feminism, the academic branch of which turned against the 'spiritualist' or 'essentialist' activism of those who went so far as to create rites empowering them to 'do the work of the Goddess' (Starhawk 1997).

References

Bollier D 2014 *Think Like a Commoner* New Society Publishers, Gabriola Island, Canada

Gould S J 1990 The power of narrative, in his *An Urchin in the Storm* Penguin Books, London 75–92

Hamilton C 2013 *Earthmasters: The Dawn of the Age of Climate Engineering* Yale University Press, New Haven

Haraway D 2014a Staying with the Trouble: Sympoiesis, String Figures, Multispecies Muddles, Manuscript of the talk given at the encounter 'Gestes spéculatifs' in Cerisy, France, 29 June–5 July

Haraway D 2014b Anthropocene, Capitalocene, Chthulucene: Staying with the trouble 5/9/14 (http://vimeo.com/97663518). Accessed 23 July 2014

Latour B 2004 Why has critique run out of steam? *Critical Inquiry* Special issue on the Future of Critique 30 225–48

Latour B 2013 *An Inquiry into Modes of Existence* Harvard University Press, Harvard

Linebaugh P 2008 *The Magna Carta Manifesto* University of California Press, Berkeley

Lovelock J 1979 *Gaia: A New Look at Life on Earth* Oxford University Press, Oxford

Moore J 2013 The Capitalocene, Online manuscript in three parts (http://jasonwmoore. wordpress.com/2013/05/13/anthropocene-or-capitalocene/) Accessed 23 July 2014

Negarestani R 2011 Drafting the Inhuman: Conjectures on capitalism and organic necrocracy, in Bryant L Srnicek N and Harman G eds *The Speculative Turn* Re.press, Melbourne, 182–201

Schneider S 1984 *The Coevolution of Climate and Life* Sierra Club Books, San Francisco

Starhawk 1997 *Dreaming the Dark* Beacon Press, Boston MA

Stengers I 2009 *Au temps des catastrophes. Résister à la barbarie qui vient* Les Empêcheurs de penser en rond/La Découverte, Paris; forthcoming Open Humanities Press

Werner B 2012 Is Earth F★★ked? Dynamical Futility of Global Environmental Management and Possibilities for Sustainability via Direct Action Activism, Presentation to the conference of the American Geophysical Union, San Francisco, December (http:// climate-connections.org/tag/brad-werner/) Accessed 23 July 2014

12

TELLING FRIENDS FROM FOES IN THE TIME OF THE ANTHROPOCENE

Bruno Latour

To Clive Hamilton

Those among you who have seen *Gravity*, the film directed by Alfonso Cuarón, will have noticed, I am sure, that once again a blockbuster's special effects offer a powerful symbol of a drastic change of mental state. For the human race there is *no space* anymore, at least no durable occupation of outer space. That is, there is no way to escape from the Earth. The main character, Dr Ryan Stone, confesses it at one point: 'I hate space,' she says while trying to run from one destroyed space station to the next. Even more forcefully than in Cameron's *Avatar*, the characters, and with them the spectators, realise that there is no longer any Frontier; no escape route except back to Earth. The direction is not forward, *Plus ultra*, but inward, *Plus intra*, back home. When Ryan, the sole survivor of the space adventure, reaches the shore of the lake where she has finally landed and grabs a handful of dirt and mud, she has, literally, been metamorphosed from a human to an Earthbound, while the old-fashioned American hero played rather clownishly by her teammate George Clooney has vanished forever in outer space, debris among the debris of the European and Chinese space stations. Much as in von Trier's *Melancholia*, in *Gravity* we witness the step-by-step destruction of the old Galilean idea of the Earth as one body among other spatial bodies. We are forced to turn our gaze back to sub-lunar Gaia, so actively modified by human action that it has entered a new period that geologists-turned-philosophers propose to label the Anthropocene.

In spite of its pitfalls (Bonneuil and Fressoz 2013), the concept of the Anthropocene offers a powerful way, if used wisely, to avoid the danger of naturalisation while ensuring that the former domain of the social, or that of the 'human', is reconfigured as being the land of the Earthlings or of the Earthbound. Like Aesop's tongue, it might deliver the worst – or worse still, much of the same; that is, the back-and-forth movement between, on the one hand, the 'social construction of nature' and, on the other, the reductionist view of humans made of carbon and water, geological forces among other geological forces, or rather mud and dust above mud and dust. But it might also direct our attention toward the end of what Whitehead (1920) called 'the bifurcation of nature', or the final rejection of the separation between Nature and Human that has paralysed science and politics since the dawn of modernism.

The jury is still out on the staying power of this concept of the Anthropocene (its half-life might be much shorter than I think). Right now, however, it is the best alternative we have to usher us away from the notion of modernisation. Like the concept of Gaia, the risk of using such an unstable notion is worth taking. Especially if we wish, as we do in this book, to probe the philosophy and theology of such a novel concept. The dreams that could be nurtured at the time of the Holocene cannot last in the time of the Anthropocene. We might say of those old dreams of space travel not 'Oh, that is sooo twentieth century,' but rather 'Oh, that is sooo Holocene!' In this sense, the use of this hybrid term combining geology, philosophy, theology and social science is a wake-up call. What I want to do here is to probe in what sort of time and in what sort of space we do find ourselves when we accept the idea of living in the Anthropocene.

But, just as it was for Dr Ryan Stone, the problem is that it is difficult for those who have been moderns (that is, for those who have *never* been modern) to find their ways back to Earth! Just like Dr Ryan, they *miss* and they *lack* gravity. . . Especially because most of our ways to map where we are, where we are heading and what we should do, have been defined by a division of labour between science and politics – what I have called the unwritten Constitution (Latour 2014). This Constitution is totally ill-equipped to handle the conflicts we have to navigate. In fact, it is so ill-adapted that even the notion of conflict, or rather, to call a cat a cat, the *state of war*, that is the defining trait of the Anthropocene, is constantly downplayed or euphemised. In such an epoch, both science and politics assume a totally different shape.

§

The spurious debate about climate science is a good indicator of that new shape. On the one hand, there is no debate whatsoever, and no question of natural history has been better settled than the anthropic origin of climate change. With the last IPCC report, all nations, it appears, are bracing themselves for a world 4°C warmer by perhaps 2070 (and that might be the optimistic scenario!). And yet, it is useless to keep saying that 'there is no discussion'. No matter how spurious a controversy, it remains that for a large part of the population, there *is* a controversy, the effect of which we may witness everyday through the total inertia – I might use the word 'quietism' only to reassure myself – of governments as well as of civil societies that are supposed to exert a pressure on their elected proxies.

You will not find a single bookshop in France that would put a book by Claude Lanzmann on the Shoah side by side on a table with a book by an arch *negationnist* like Faurisson. A few days ago, however, my friend Clive Hamilton was horrified to see his book, *Requiem for a Species* (Hamilton 2013), together with one of the newest pamphlets (Gervais 2013) by a climate denier '*L'innocence du carbone*' (amazing title, I will come back to that). And the worst is that Clive would have appeared unfair and dogmatic if he had taken the manager to task for keeping such an absurd and scandalous balance. If he had protested, no doubt the manager would have answered that this is a 'rational debate' and that 'both sides' have to be heard. There is a law (in France) against Faurisson, but not against climate *negationnism*.

And that is one of the problems that paralyse politics in the Anthropocene. This is not a rational debate. Or rather, it is a debate in which the climatologists of the IPCC who *would have been considered* rational in another climate are being rendered powerless. They are portrayed as irrational by those who use the power of reason and appeal to the freedom of scientific inquiry to pollute not only the atmosphere but also the public sphere, to use James Hoggan's expression (Hoggan 2009). Why? Because both sides – and this is what produces the idea that there are two sides – use the *same science-versus-politics repertoire*.

This repertoire has two parts. First, both sides imply that Science is about distant, dispassionate facts of nature while politics is about ideology, passions and interests whose intrusion into Science cannot do anything but *distort* the plain facts. Second, both sides agree that policy should *follow* scientific expertise and that we cannot make decisions based on uncertain science. Part one: science is about incontrovertible and indisputable facts; part two: policy follows science. The difficulty is that this repertoire (disproved by fifty years of historical case studies) is shared by most of the public as well. It means that if any lobbyist paid by the mining or oil industry, or any physicist with his own pet version of what the laws of nature tell him, manages to introduce the smallest grain of doubt into the expertise, the whole policy train stops. Since this is what all politicians, as well as every onlooker believe, and since it is also the way TV shows organise debates as if they were judges in a courtroom, it is incredibly easy to make *two sides* emerge even when there is only one.

To give credit where credit is due, this should be called the Luntz strategy to honour Frank Luntz's infamous memo to the Republican Party: 'Should the public come to believe that the scientific issues are settled, their views about global warming will change accordingly. Therefore, you need to continue to make the lack of scientific certainty a primary issue.'[1] His success speaks volumes about the mass of money spent to foster climate deniers but it also speaks to the fragility of the immunological system of those who use the science-*versus*-politics repertoire. It appears that the slightest virus is enough to make them doubt and stop policy in its tracks. Because of this weird – though common-sensical – vision of science *versus* politics, there is no way to immunise the public against such an infectious form of 'scepticism' – a grand adjective that has been most maliciously appropriated.

Of course, it would be welcome if we could imagine that at some point, because of the many public debates about the issue, the two sides would become one. Case settled, let's now move on to the policy. The apparently innocuous term 'scepticism', used so intently by deniers, might seem to lead in such a direction. Let us have a 'fair and balanced' debate, as they say on Fox News. But there is not the slightest chance that this closure will ever occur, since the deniers' success is not to win any argument, but simply to make sure that the rest of the public is convinced that there *is* an argument. How could the poor, helpless climatologists ever win in such a kangaroo court where the point is not to reach a verdict (the verdict has been reached in the IPCC report already anyway). The new discipline of 'agnotology', to use James Proctor's expression (Proctor and Schiebinger 2008), is the willful production of ignorance that has functioned marvelously for cigarettes as well as for asbestos, and, with more resistance, for extermination camps. It will work much better, and for much longer, for climate science, and for one additional reason: it is about the daily life of billions of people. The chance to ever reach closure is nil. And yet waiting for closure before drafting policy is not an option either.

This is the Achilles' heel of Mr Luntz's strategy. Not in trying to achieve closure by reasonable debate – the dice are loaded as long as there appear to be two sides – but in opposing the science-*versus*-politics repertoire with a much more reasonable, and on the whole much more rational, alternative repertoire. There are two sides, it is true, but the dispute is not between climatologists and climate deniers. There are two sides: those who stick to a traditional science-*versus*-politics version and those who have understood that this older *political epistemology* (to give it the more accurate label (Latour 2004)) is what renders both politics and science weak when the issues at stake are too large for too many interested people directly affected by their decisions. This is where there is a real distinction to be made between a Holocene and an Anthropocene settlement. What might have been good for Humans (and I doubt it ever was the case) has lost any sense for the Earthbound.

The great limit of the old settlement was to make impossible any connection of science *with* politics and not *versus* politics. For this, of course, one has to abandon the idea that the only thing politics may do is to distort facts! Although this version of politics is as old as Socrates fighting against Calicles, it flies in the face of everything we expect from politics: building a collective polity on a precisely defined soil or land – now, more precisely and more extensively, a polity that has an Earth under its feet, so to speak. Politics has gravity when it has a territory to defend.

But one should also abandon the idea that science is about incontrovertible and indisputable facts. Science, always with a small s, is about producing, through the institutions of many disciplines and the monitoring of many instruments, robust access to a great number of entities with which the polity has to be built. In this view both science and politics are mundane, rather humble, frail and pedestrian activities, open to doubt, revision, and prone to mistakes as soon as their delicate operations are not constantly supported.

As I have shown in *Politics of Nature* (Latour 2004), the only thing *they cannot afford to do is to work separately*. Their skills are obviously and fortunately totally distinct, but they have to exercise themselves on the same new entities whose disturbing novelty they have to learn in common how to handle. Without the instruments of science, the body politic will never know how many strange entities it has to take into account. And without politics, the same body politic will never know how to array, grade, and rank those bewildering number of agencies with which it has to progressively compose a common world – which is the definition I proposed for politics-with-science. The great paradox of the Moderns is to have granted, to the absolute distinction of Science and Politics, the task of maintaining facts and values as clearly separated as possible. Unfortunately, the common-sense opposition between facts and values is everything but common sense since the notion of 'facts' covers what is still uncertain just as well as what is undisputable (what triggers *perplexity* and what has been well *instituted*) while the notion of 'values' is supposed to designate who should allocate the dispute as well as the order in which all the objects of values should be ordered (what requires a *consultation* as well as what demands to be put into a *hierarchy*). To be sure there is a difference, but it runs along an exactly orthogonal direction to the calamitous one between facts and values. It should bring science and politics (plus many other trades) to bear on the two essential tasks: defining *how many entities* have to be taken into account (namely perplexity and consultation); and *how they can stand together* in a livable form (that is hierarchy and institution).

There is perhaps one comforting thing to say about the Anthropocene. It has demonstrated that the ancient settlement was rendered useless as soon as issues became too touchy or concerned too many people. The old settlement worked – if it ever did – only in the rarefied air of outer space, for distant problems that interested only a few people and had indirect, remote consequences. This ancient settlement has certainly not worked for what concerns us in the present – or worse, concerned us in the past – where the background and foreground have merged. This is exactly what the word Anthropocene underlines so well. When action modifies the very framework in which history is supposed to unfold, the idea of distant, disinterested facts becomes less relevant than that of highly disputed matters of concern.

§

To shift from a science-*versus*-politics to a science-with-politics is, of course, not without its dangers. At first glance, climate deniers will have a field day, clamouring that their adversaries have finally confessed what they, the deniers, have always said: *climate science is politics*. To which the only reasonable answer is: 'Yes, of course, where have you been? And what are you doing yourself?' After a minute of hesitation because of the loss of the old settlement – it is not easy to lose confidence in the Maginot line of fact-versus-value! – those who fight against the deniers should quickly grasp how to redraw the lines of conflict. Not between two sides of an epistemological debate (on one side the climate science and, on the other, the climate sceptics), but between two sides – and they will be soon more than two – with a completely different view of what you may expect from science as well as from politics. There is no conflict between science and politics. But there is a conflict between two radically opposite political epistemologies, each with its own definition of what science and politics are, and how they could collaborate.

Of course, there exist plenty of reasons for imitating what feminists call 'strategic essentialism' and to employ, whenever necessary, a form of 'strategic positivism' as if we could confine to a settled science of the climate the task of serving as an incontrovertible premise for policy. But even if this strategy could succeed (and the weak response to the last IPCC report indicates that it has failed this just the same as all previous attempts to 'convince' the public), it would not solve the question because it would remain a *pedagogical* gain – not a *political* one. More people would know for sure, which is always good, but they will not be moved an inch out of the situation of just knowing. We are not dealing here with indisputable 'matters of fact', but with 'matters of concern' to be disputed. It is a question of knowing 'uncomfortable facts' about pressing issues that concern the very soil on which every body resides.

It should have become clear that expressions such as 'the innocence of carbon' as well as 'uncomfortable facts' straddle the distinction between facts and values. How could it be otherwise since we are talking here about conflicts that pit against one another different definitions of the land to which the various polities are attached? How could anyone, I beg you, defend one's territory quietly and dispassionately when it is under attack? The only result of the older settlement of fact-*versus*-politics is that, in such a conflict, one side fights with all the forces at its power while the other side, the rational and reasonable climatologists, must fight with their hands tied behind their backs by the injunction that they, and they alone, should protect the sanctity of Science (capital S) against any encroachment of ideology and interest.

In the old days, such an alternative political epistemology could have smacked of 'relativism'. But today it is much clearer that when opponents reach for their guns and mention the 'science wars' it is much fairer, and, once again, more rational to say: 'Not a science war, but for sure, *a war of the worlds.*' Or rather, a war for the occupation and definition and composition of what the world, at least this sublunary planet, Gaia, is like. How could we agree on this composition since, depending on the answer, each of us has to move literally to another place? How could we settle the issue when, depending on the response given, we ally with other people and break sides with others? Paradoxically, capitalists seem to know what it is to grab, to possess and to defend a land more than their space-less adversaries who have to defend Science and its View-from-Nowhere for inhabitants of no place. At least they know to which soil they pertain better than those who keep defending themselves by an appeal to the extraterritorial authority of Science. Remember the Bushist's war cry: 'Americans are from Mars, Europeans are from Venus'? Well, it seems that those traditionally defined nations are neither from Mars nor from Venus, but some are from an Earth which has a specific shape and some are from *another Earth*, or, perhaps, from a land of no land called 'utopia', the utopia that the Moderns have imagined as their only future (Danowski and de Castro 2014). A future that now looks just like the destroyed space stations from which Ryan Stone tries to escape in *Gravity*.

§

In addition to 'strategic positivism', there is fortunately another resource we could use to clarify the conflicts we must confront living in the Anthropocene. It is not true that the general public, the one that is so easily contaminated by Luntz's viral infection (a dangerous metaphor, I agree), is endowed with the sole repertoire of science-*versus*-politics. Most of them are ordinary people who act most of the time in a universe made of uncertain facts that concern them a lot. Before investing in a company or having children or buying travel insurance, they don't wait for completely incontrovertible evidences and only *then* leap into action. If there is one thing everybody can understand, it is that when their life is put into question, when the territory on which they live is threatened, when they are attacked by other people who want their place, their land, their soil, their cherished plot of earth, what used to be called their 'mother land', they certainly don't wait for experts to agree. They need to quickly identify those who can help and those – is there another word for it? – who risk *betraying* them. Making decisions amongst contradictory evidence about pressing issues, this attitude is common to scientists, politicians and ordinary members of the public. Such a common-sense attitude takes full force when their territory is under threat. What could be called *mobilisation* is an uneasy, worrisome, dangerous feeling, a source of ill-defined consequences, but one thing is certain: in case of war, the attitude is not of complacency, appeasement and delegation to the experts.

It is bizarre that militants as well as 'concerned scientists' (a venerable label from the former fights around the virtual nuclear holocaust) could simultaneously complain about the lack of mobilisation of the public and of their elected representatives, while trying to euphemise the conflict by shying away from the word 'war'. Their adversaries have no such qualms. For them, it is a forceful *land grab*: the land is theirs and they hold to it fast. That they try to hide behind the mantle of Science is a simple ploy (they are actually the ones playing the game of strategic positivism! And they do it to its limit). We should not be surprised by this appeal to Science. That 'Gott Mitt Uns' has always been embroidered on the banners of earlier war parties, does not mean that God ever sided with any of the warring factions. Even though it might be perilous to speak of war – when there is a state of peace – it is even more dangerous to *deny* that there is a war when you are under attack. Appeasers would end up being the deniers – not by denying climate science, this time – but by denying that there is a war for the definition and control of the world we collectively inhabit.

There is indeed a war for the definition and control of the Earth: a war that pits – to be a little dramatic – Humans living in the Holocene against Earthbounds living in the Anthropocene. What I take to be the clarifying effect of stating this, is that it makes possible for the various camps to fly 'under their own colors' (to use Walter Lippmann's expression (Lippmann 1925 [1933])), and not under the flag of 'Gott' or, rather, 'Natur Mitt Uns'. When you meet climatosceptics who have the nerve to call the IPCC 'a lobby', it would be much more powerful to answer: 'Of course it is a lobby, now let us see how many are you, where does your money come from. And, since we are at it, since you are accusing us of being biased by "an ideology", let's put everything on the table: in what world do you live, where, with what resources, for how long, what future do you envision for your kids, what sort of education do you wish to give them, in which landscape do you wish them to live.' And, step by step, the whole set of differentiated power relations that are so blatantly missing from the common notion of the Anthropocene would be brought back. Such a counter-attack is exactly the opposite of retreating behind the Maginot line of a Science unpolluted by politics.

Of course, this geo-graphy or, rather, this *Gaia-graphy* requires a description of the front lines. For such delineation, we need to draw on all the resources of all the disciplines, be they social or natural. 'Please, delineate what you are defending, what do you think the land is worth, with what other organisms, what sort of soil, what sort of landscape, what sort of industry, what sort of commerce you wish to survive with.' For instance, let us pit 'Innocent carbon' against 'Carbon democracy', the title of Timothy Mitchell's crucial book (Mitchell 2011), since both straddle the fact/value distinction. In both accounts, carbon does not play the same role, does not receive the same qualifications, and does not have the same properties. Fine. This does not prove any distortion of scientific facts. It means that there are many ways for carbon to be composed into a common word. If the same atoms can generate materials as different as graphite and diamond, should we be surprised that the same carbon in the hands of a climate denier has different arrangement and virtues, that is, different agencies, than in those of an historian of the Middle East? 'Innocence' and 'guilt' are properties of atoms that, very exactly, very literally, depend on their composition.

All those connections, what John Tresch calls 'cosmograms' (Tresch 2012), can be made explicit only if we don't break them according to the science-*versus*-politics divide. Of course, such geopolitics, or rather such *Gaia-politics*, does not correspond to the old coloured maps over which so many wars have been waged (Elden 2014). The borderlines are difficult to detect, but it does not mean that it is not about territories, that those new maps don't have to be drawn and that it is not about conflicts. How could we introduce the concept of the Anthropocene and not draw the consequences in terms of politics of the Earth? Mines, rivers, pollution, oceans, fish, fowl, grass, insects, clouds, rain and floods, they are all there.

What is a *territory* if not that without which you would not be able to live? Well, list all those beings, those agencies you say you can do without. We will do ours. Then we will draw the territories that are under attack, those that are worth defending, and those that could be abandoned. Once this is done, we might compare our chances of losing or of winning. Since appeals to Nature known by Science and its Laws – the older *State of Nature* – does not bring peace even in the case of such a hardened fact as that of the anthropic origin of climate change, then we should accept living in a declared state of war. And anyway, our opponents are more attuned to what is at stake, better versed in what the words 'possession' and 'defense of one's possessions' mean. They, our adversaries, mobilised long ago.

§

The real advantage of making the state of war explicit instead of undeclared is that it might be the only way to begin to envisage *peace*. Not a *pedagogical* peace obtained through the older science-*versus*-politics repertoire – as if we could begin to discuss policy now that we have all learned the natural sciences so that we necessarily agree with one another about what makes up the world. But instead a *political peace*. One negotiated by the camps who, having exhausted all other options, and knowing that neither the 'God' nor the 'Nature' embroidered on their banners are really behind them, attempt a settlement as if there was *no arbiter* above their heads. The main difference between the two forms of peace is that the pedagogical one comes *before* any war. Then war is simply the irrational mistake of those who have not understood the laws of nature or of economics; peace will be restored once everyone has learned the truth about what things are and always have been. Pedagogical peace is akin to police intervention or to what is today called 'governance'. By contrast, political peace comes *after* the war has exhausted the warring parties, who end up composing what is exactly named a *modus vivendi* – that is, an entangled set of makeshift arrangements to survive.

It is because the political peace is not dictated by what is already there but by what should be progressively realised that there is no way to *delay* it any longer. Delay is part of the Modernist dream. Actually, it is their definition of the future. A future made of nothing but a flight from the past and 'eyes wide shut' to what is coming. This is where the concept of the Anthropocene meets not only a philosophy of science – the politics-with-science repertoire instead of politics-*versus*-science, not only a definition of the ground on which polities are built – but also a 'Gaia-politics' of highly contested grounds. And, so important theologically: the Anthropocene meets another *time*, as different from the modernist one as its spatial rooting. This inclusion of theology into ecology is formulated in many ways, from the more secular version offered by Jean-Pierre Dupuy – 'enlightened catastrophism' (Dupuy 2003) – to the more spiritual version proposed by Michael Northcott (Northcott 2013) – what I have called a 'carbon theology'!

What they have in common is that, in the same way as they propose a different *spatial* grounding for each warring camp, they offer another *temporal* rhythm for action. Action cannot be delayed because time does not flow from the present to the future — as if we had to choose between scenarios, hoping for the best – but rather from what is coming ('*l'avenir*' as we say in French to differentiate from '*le futur*') to the present. Which is another way to consider the times in which we should live as 'apocalyptic'. Not in the sense of the catastrophic (although it might be that also), but in the sense of the revelation of things that are coming *toward* us. This odd situation of living 'at the end of time' in a different type of hope, the hope that has been made one of the three theological virtues and that the French, once again richer than English, calls '*espérance*' to make sure it is not confused with '*espoir*'. Clive Hamilton has wisely advised us to jettison this '*espoir*', this hope, because, as long as we rely on hope, we still expect to escape from the consequences of our action. It is only once we have radically changed our relation to time – what is called living in 'apocalyptic times' – that we might be spurred into action without delay (Anders 2007). 'The times are fulfilled.'

§

Historians of ecology are right to say that there is probably nothing completely new in the concept of the Anthropocene since conflicts about territories and their resources are as old as the human race and since warnings about the consequences those 'land grabs' have on the environment are as old as the industrial revolution (Bonneuil and Jouvancourt 2014). What I take to be really new in this Anthropocene label (apart from the unusual collaboration between geology, history – or rather geo-story – politics and philosophy) is that it modifies simultaneously the spatial and temporal frames in which action is being situated; and, moreover, that this frame has modified the two main pillars on which the metaphysics of Science has been established since the 'bifurcation of nature', to use Whitehead's famous description.

How odd it has been for the Moderns to imagine that their materiality could be made of atomic points without spatial extension and of instants without duration. It is this most idealistic definition of matter that is now showing its utopian and toxic character. It is such an odd conception that has been so constantly at odds with the experience of space and of time. It has rejected every impulse that insisted on being 'from a place and having duration' as being nothing but mere subjectivity, poetry, theology or philosophy.

To the point that the Modernist dream may be defined as a constant fight to replace the 'subjective' space and time by a really rational view of a space belonging to no space and a time made of timeless instants. It is fair to say that civilisation has been a long fight, mainly lost, of resisting, for good and bad reasons, such a definition of the modernising frontier. Well, now, through a completely unexpected inversion of the respective positions of every field of inquiry, the many disciplines of natural history are calling for a return to the spatial conditions of the Earth and for an urgent sense that 'times are fulfilled'. Gaia is not nature; and it is not a polity either. Scientists are fighting many other battles. They discover totally different friends and foes. And so do we all. There is no modernising frontier any more. Instead there are so many new lines of conflicts that a totally different Gaia-politics is now redrawing all the maps (Stengers 2009 and this volume). So by remixing all the ingredients of what used to be distinct domains of subjectivity and objectivity, the very notion of the Anthropocene is indeed an enormous source of confusion – but a welcome source. Like that of Dr Ryan Stone, our collective return to Earth is a rather traumatic one. But at last we know where we are and what we should fight for. Ah! But should we not have known that all along? '*Memento, homo, quia pulvis es, et in púlverem revertéris*'; 'Remember, man, that thou art dust, and unto dust thou shalt return.'

Note

1 In a 2002 memo to President George W. Bush titled 'The Environment: A Cleaner, Safer, Healthier America', obtained by the Environmental Working Group http://en.wikipedia.org/wiki/Frank_Luntz#Global_warming (accessed 4 July 2014).

References

Anders G 2007 *Le temps de la fin* Editions de l'Herne, Paris

Bonneuil C and Fressoz J-B 2013 *L'évènement anthropocène: La Terre, l'histoire et nous* Editions du Seuil, Paris

Bonneuil C and Jouvancourt P D 2014 En finir avec l'épopée. Récit, géopouvoir et sujets de l'anthropocène, in Hache E ed *De l'univers clos au monde infini (textes réunis et présentés)* Editions Dehors, Paris

Danowski D and de Castro E V 2014 L'arrêt de monde, in Hache E ed *De l'univers clos au monde infini (textes réunis et présentés)* Editions Dehors, Paris

Dupuy J P 2003 *Pour un catast rophisme éclairé: Quand l'impossible est certain* Editions du Seuil, Paris

Elden S 2014 *The Birth of Territory* University of Chicago Press, Chicago

Gervais F 2013 *L'innocence du carbone* Albin-Michel, Paris

Hamilton C 2013 *Requiem pour l'espèce humaine* (traduit par Jacques Treiner et Françoise Gicquet) Presses de Sciences-Po, Paris

Hoggan J 2009 *Climate Cover-Up: The Crusade to Deny Global Warming* Greystone Books, Vancouver

Latour B 2004 *Politics of Nature: How to Bring the Sciences into Democracy* (translated by Catherine Porter) Harvard University Press, Cambridge, MA.

Latour B 2014 War and peace in an age of ecological conflicts *Revue Juridique de l'Environnement* 1 51–63

Lippmann W 1925 [1993] *The Phantom Public* Transactions Publishers, New Brunswick, NJ

Mitchell T 2011 *Carbon Democracy: Political Power in the Age of Oil* Verso, New York

Northcott M S 2013 *A Political Theology of Climate Change* Eerdmans Publishing, Grand Rapids, MI

Proctor R and Schiebinger L 2008 *Agnotology: The Making and Unmaking of Ignorance* Stanford University Press, Stanford, CA

Stengers I 2009 *Au temps des catastrophes. Résister à la barbarie qui vient* Les Empêcheurs, Paris

Tresch J 2012 *The Romantic Machine: Utopian Science and Technology after Napoleon* University of Chicago Press, Chicago

Whitehead A N 1920 *Concept of Nature* Cambridge University Press, Cambridge

13

A MUCH-NEEDED RENEWAL OF ENVIRONMENTALISM?

Eco-politics in the Anthropocene

Ingolfur Blühdorn

Introduction

Eco-politics in advanced liberal consumer democracies is in a most perplexing state. On the one hand, the seriousness of the sustainability crisis (social, economic, ecological) and the urgency of truly transformative action are virtually uncontested. Talk about sustainability is ubiquitous, and there is commitment not only to protecting the biophysical environment but also to the goals of social justice, inclusion, empowerment, diversity and so on. On the other hand, the structural transformation of the capitalist growth economy and the consumer culture which the more radical currents of environmentalism, in particular, have always demanded, and which many climate scientists now regard as indispensable if large-scale catastrophe and social collapse are to be averted, is nowhere in sight. Instead, critical intellectuals are lamenting the post-democratic and post-political condition of eco-politics, in which governing bodies and even transnational corporations have 'taken over our language' and thereby destroyed 'our capacity to say what we want, to know what we want . . . even [to] dream' any alternative to the socio-economic order that prevails (Dean 2009, 10).

In this impasse, the concept of the Anthropocene has reinvigorated and theoretically enriched eco-political debates. Suggesting, as it does, that we have entered a new geological epoch in which the impact of human activity on the Earth has become so strong that it has evolved into a key parameter influencing or even changing the trajectory of planetary development, it further increases human responsibility and the pressure to take effective action. Its underlying hypothesis, that in view of human activity now impacting on even the remotest geographical area and eco-system, the traditional distinction between *nature* and *civilisation*, *society* and its *environment*, *eco-systems* and *social systems*, *subject* and *object*, is no longer viable has triggered fresh hopes that the 'post-natural' condition may offer a unique opportunity to bring about 'the much-needed renewal of environmentalism' (Arias-Maldonado 2013 1). Yet others have immediately rung the alarm bells, claiming that the emerging 'new environmentalism will lead us to disaster' (Hamilton 2014). So, what does the Anthropocene imply for eco-politics? What potentials for eco-political renewal does it entail? What kind of renewal might this be?

This chapter suggests that the arrival of the Anthropocene is most unlikely to facilitate the 'much-needed renewal' envisaged by those who are frustrated with the current mainstream of depoliticised sustainability policy (Bulkeley et al. 2013), who are hoping for 'a massive escalation of truly disruptive action' (Crouch 2004, 123) that will 'change everything' (Klein 2014), and who are trying to convince themselves that already 'more and more people are starting to participate in the search for alternative ways of living and working' (Novy 2014, 42). Nor, however, are the ecological *cum* societal conditions of the Anthropocene likely to be experienced as the disaster, the warnings of which have always been constitutive to eco-political discourse, but which curiously never materialised. Trying to move beyond the activist juxtaposition of *U-turn or disaster*, and sharing neither the new optimism nor the pessimism which the concept has triggered, this chapter takes the notion of the Anthropocene as a conceptual lens that focuses attention on the abovementioned dualisms which have underpinned all eco-political discourse so far and that pushes us to explore the condition of eco-politics *beyond* this model of dualist thought. The chapter distinguishes between eco-political approaches in the science- and technology-oriented *mode of objectivation* and eco-politics in the culture- and identity-oriented *mode of subjectivation*. It reveals how, for the purpose of generating legitimacy and authority for their diagnoses and prescriptions, both of these approaches fundamentally rely on the nature/society dualism. Yet at the point where society is on the verge of fully colonising nature, thereby pushing the sustainability crisis potentially to its extreme form, this strategy of generating legitimacy and authority collapses, leaving eco-politics self-referential and eco-political theory and activists disoriented vis-à-vis the prevailing *politics of unsustainability* (Blühdorn 2011, 2013, 2014, 2015). This is the condition and predicament of eco-politics in the Anthropocene.

Eco-politics in the mode of objectivation

The short film *Welcome to the Anthropocene* opened and was supposed to set a re-energising tone for the UN Rio+20 Summit in 2012, which aimed to breathe new life into the *sustainable development* agenda that already at the 2002 World Conference on Environment and Development in Johannesburg had shown clear signs of fatigue. Yet, in retrospect, the event revealed more clearly than ever that, in the wake of the global financial crisis, in particular, 'there is little political appetite' among political leaders for any fast or sweeping change, however unsustainable the prevailing order of neoliberal consumer capitalism may be acknowledged to be (Linnér and Selin 2013, 983). Indeed, sustainable development – which, following the original Rio Summit of 1992, had become the beacon and big promise of global environmental politics – today seems an exhausted paradigm. It 'no longer exerts the pulling power it once had'; 'both sustainability governance and the sustainable development concept are under growing pressure amid a perceived failure to deliver change' (Bulkeley et al. 2013, 958f).

In the early 1990s, the concept had stimulated tremendous hope and enthusiasm, not least because it came with the promise that environmental policy can be placed on a much more solid, reliable and *objective* footing than it had been so far, whilst at the same time extending the focus on the 'bounds of the ecologically possible' (integrity of nature) to include attention to the 'needs' of present and future generations of human beings (wellbeing of society). The Brundtland Report, which famously established these points of reference, had itself not undertaken any major attempt to specify these criteria. Yet, subsequently, academic sustainability research made huge efforts to spell out where and what the 'bounds of the ecologically possible' may be, and which human 'needs' would have to be met in the present and beyond. Crucially, where earlier environmental movements had invoked aesthetic norms (preserve the beauty of nature), religious imperatives (protect divine creation) or the ethical principle to respect the integrity and dignity (intrinsic value) of nature, sustainability research aimed to establish indicators and criteria based on science and economics alone. It aimed to emancipate eco-political thinking and environmental policy from their earlier dependence on soft and *subjective* criteria, putting them, instead, on a foundation of hard facts and *objective* knowledge. In the effort to avoid 'being trapped in some of the *idea-ends* of the environmental movement' (Jänicke and Mol 2009, 1; my emphasis), *ecological modernisation* was promoted as the policy-oriented counterpart to scientific sustainability research. As 'a technology-based and market-oriented strategy focusing on the efficient use of resources and providing co-benefits for both ecology and economy' (Jänicke and Mol 2009, 1), it was expected to re-energise environmental politics and render it much more effective than it had ever been before.

This attempt to reconceptualise environmental issues as a matter of scientific knowledge, technological innovation, economic incentives and administrative efficiency – that is, to *depoliticise* and *objectivate* environmental policy – proved successful in that it built communicative bridges between, for example, radical environmental movements and representatives of industry, who had previously been divided by deep ideological rifts. It also paved the way for a wide range of policies addressing specific problems such as river pollution or sulphur emissions from coal power plants. Yet, given that 'revolutionary system change' and any 'move beyond a modern market economy' were not on their agenda (Jänicke and Mol 2009, 19), the sustainability paradigm and ecological modernisation predictably failed to deliver a structural transformation of industrial capitalism and the consumer culture. Effectively, they just expanded the life expectancy of the established socio-economic order that, at its core, still remained inherently unsustainable.

Even more importantly, being fully preoccupied with the effort to measure, map, quantify and then calculate the limits of the ecologically possible, sustainability research discounted or even denied the fact that the accumulation of scientific knowledge, however detailed and exhaustive, can never be a substitute for normative judgement. Ecological modernisation, on its part, conveniently ignored that the pursuit of resource efficiency is predicated on assumptions about what qualifies as a *resource* deserving protection and what should be used as a benchmark for *efficiency*. Yet the fact remains that science on its own cannot define sustainable limits to resource use because 'normative judgements are essential to give social and political meaning' to the notion of limits. Nor can it define 'the positive social goods that are to be secured through the recognition of such limits' and related policies of resource efficiency (Meadowcroft 2013, 988). Science can gather empirical information, but empirical facts and scientific findings never speak for themselves. Ultimately, environmental politics and policy are powered by *concerns*, that is, *values*, and the relationship between facts and concerns is very intricate indeed.

So, while science is surely essential to describe and understand conditions in the biophysical world and to measure and explain phenomena of environmental change, the empirical data it delivers never immediately qualify as problems or trigger any form of social action. For that to happen, they must be put into relation to, and be perceived to conflict with, established social values, expectations and aspirations. Put differently, what are commonly referred to as environmental problems are, ultimately, perceived violations of malleable social norms, and, as such, they are not easily accessible to scientific enquiry. Talking in terms of limits, one might say that *ecological* limits in the biophysical sense do not exist or are not politically relevant. Instead, what eco-political discourse is, ultimately, all about are *limits of social acceptability*, that is, concerns about violations of established social norms that are deemed unacceptable. If applied to the notion of sustainability itself, this implies that the unsustainability of particular physical conditions or processes of biophysical change is, as such, not problematic. It turns into a problem only if, and in so far as, it challenges established social norms and expectations. Thus, the problem is actually not the unsustainability of an empirically measurable condition or process, but the perceived unsustainability (in view of this condition or process) of established social norms and the social order they underpin.

Therefore, with its fixation on science and its strategy of objectivation, the sustainability paradigm did not simply neglect the irreducibly normative character of environmental policy and politics; rather, it systematically failed to grasp the actual core of eco-political discourse. With their false promise that issues of society–nature relations and climate change can be dissolved into issues of scientific knowledge and technomanagerial innovation, the proponents of ecological modernisation manoeuvred environmental politics into a condition where the availability of knowledge and technologies by far outstrips the political ability and will to specify criteria (norms) for their socially legitimate and efficient application. And as the negotiation of what may constitute social efficiency – and whether, how and for what objectives scientific research and new technologies should best be used – lags way behind, technological development and application is left to be ruled by its own dynamics, and that of the market. Yet the more this eco-politics in the mode of objectivation acquired the hegemonic status it today maintains, the more did contemporary societies lose their ability to conceptualise their concerns, to articulate eco-political demands, to even *think* what they might want in terms other than those of technological innovation, individualised consumer choices or emissions trading, all of which reinforce rather than challenge the logic of liberal consumer capitalism.

Eco-politics in the mode of subjectivation

Thus eco-politics in the mode of objectivation has reached its limits. Its distinction between the social, subjective realm and that of the natural sciences, which can, allegedly, deliver objectively valid problem diagnoses and define requirements for remedial action, has proved unviable. Its underlying assumption that the acquisition of scientific knowledge and the dissemination of factual information will either automatically trigger commensurate action, or at least translate relatively easily into policy programmes for the transformation of the established order of unsustainability, is profoundly wrong. Critical observers following the tradition of post- or neo-Marxist critical theory have interpreted the fact, that this – invariably insufficient – eco-politics in the mode of objectivation has, nevertheless, become essentially hegemonic as the victory of the neoliberal right which, they argue, have strategically pursued an agenda of de-politicisation and post-democracy in order to consolidate their rule (Klein 2008, 2014). From their perspective, not only are the prevalent forms of contemporary eco-politics a 'perfect expression' of the post-political order, but neoliberals have turned the environmental crisis itself into a major catalyst for the post-political consensus (Swyngedouw 2007, 18; 2009, 610). Eco-political issues, Swyngedouw suggests, enter the political machinery framed in ways which already imply the neoliberal patterns of addressing them and 'do not tolerate dissent', about either the formulation of the problem or the political and social solution (Swyngedouw 2007, 11). Thus, eco-political debate becomes a means to reinforce and consolidate the post-political condition and its forms of post-democratic governing.

Accordingly, post- or neo-Marxist critics are proposing to once again 'enhance the democratic content of socio-environmental construction by means of identifying the strategies through which a more equitable distribution of social power . . . can be achieved' (Swyngedouw 2010, 32). Their objective is to recentralise the notions of equality and freedom and to explore 'perspectives for re-vitalising the political possibilities of . . . the emancipatory project' (Swyngedouw 2011, 370). Indeed, in eco-politics as elsewhere, the neo-Marxist agenda is, ultimately, to reinstate the emancipatory project and reinstall the notion of the *autonomous subject* as the centre of an authentically democratic politics. As the depoliticising and objectivating strategies of mainstream sustainability policy have proved not only unable to deliver structural change, but actually aggravate the multiple sustainability crises, re-politicisation and re-subjectivation are presented as the obvious antidote. Somewhat nostalgically, the suggestion that the sustainability crisis 'is upon us because democracy has been corrupted' and that it can be resolved only by 'reclaiming democracy for the citizenry' (Hamilton 2010, 223) harks back to *radical ecologism* and its programme of eco-politics *in the mode of subjectivation*. Yet, whilst it is certainly true that political, economic and scientific elites are much more likely to reinforce than suspend the established logic of unsustainability, this argument disregards, first, that radical ecologism also depended on strategies of depoliticisation and objectivation and, second, that modernisation-induced shifts in prevalent notions of identity and subjectivity render the re-politicisation and re-subjectivation of eco-politics a rather unpromising strategy.

The thinking of *ecologism* (Dobson 2007) that emerged and had its greatest political purchase in the 1970s and early 1980s (for example, Commoner 1971; *The Ecologist* 1972; *Die Grünen* 1980; Bookchin 1982; Porritt 1984) was built around the belief in categorical eco-imperatives, the intrinsic value of nature, threats to the survival of the human species or apocalyptic fears for *spaceship Earth*. There were significant differences between, for example, *eco-centric* and *anthropocentric* strands, but these different varieties of radical eco-political thought all had in common that they were based on normative *fundamentals* that were assumed to be non-negotiable, incontestable and exempt from the imperative of political justification. Armed with such essentially pre-political norms, eco-fundamentalists radically critiqued – politicised – the established socio-economic order and the prevailing conceptualisations of the nature–society relationship. They employed the universalising (*We are all equally affected by this crisis!*) and allegedly uncompromising (*U-turn or apocalypse!*) logic of ecological integrity and human survival as a lever to crack the hegemony of the post-war 'growth–security alliance' (Offe 1985, 818) and to politicise the wide range of previously uncontested beliefs which underpinned the established order of liberal democratic consumer capitalism. Referring to the apocalyptic threats of eco-system collapse and the extinction of human and other life, they insisted that *there is no alternative* to the radical restructuring of the established socio-economic order. In other words, they mobilised the TINA logic long before it was identified as the hallmark of ideological neoliberalism.

In these eco-fundamentalist discourses the intrinsic value of nature, categorical eco-imperatives and the demand to respect the integrity of the *Other* featured prominently. Ultimately, however, the diverse strands of radical ecology always centred on the modernist notion of the *subject* or *Self* and its constitutive norms of autonomy, integrity and identity. Even those eco-political currents which conceived of themselves as eco-centric, ultimately, based their critique on, and justified their demands with, the belief that nature must be accredited the same autonomy and dignity, that is, the same status of a *subject*, that modernist Enlightenment thought had installed as the inalienable right and attribute of all human beings. Thus, the political force and normative authority of radical ecologist thinking, in fact, never derived from any objective necessities, incontestable physical conditions or categorical imperatives of survival, but from the modernist norm of the autonomous subject which provided the yardstick for the critique of the established order and shaped the contours of the envisaged alternative. By projecting the constitutive norms of modernist subjectivity (autonomy, dignity, integrity, equality) onto nature, eco-fundamentalists externalised the normative foundation of their demands so as to safeguard them against political contestation. Reference to the intrinsic value of nature, to supposedly categorical eco-imperatives and apocalyptic threats to the human species helped to provide *objective* legitimacy for an essentially very *subjective* (subject-centred) emancipatory agenda. Thus, depoliticisation and objectivation were indispensable tools even for this eco-politics in the mode of subjectivation; for ecologism, too, always remained subject to the principle that 'political authority can be stable only as long as it is . . . complemented by self-sustaining non-political spheres . . . which serve both to exonerate political authority and to provide it with sources of legitimacy' (Offe 1985, 819). But this eco-fundamentalist legitimation strategy of *objectivated subjectivity*, and thus the critique and project of radical ecologism, had, of course, only as much purchase as the modernist norm of subjectivity had itself.

Into the Anthropocene

So, radical political ecology, too, relied on the dualistic model that has, in ever new varieties, underpinned all eco-political thinking so far. Traditional *conservationism* had distinguished between pristine nature and human civilisation and based its demands to protect the former precisely on its conceptualisation as being untouched and unspoilt by human civilisation, that is, on its framing as society's *external* counterpart. Modern environmentalism no longer understood nature as radically distinct from society, but saw it rather as the biophysical context into which the latter is embedded. But analytical frames such as the *nature–society metabolism* (Haberl et al. 2004) or the *ecological footprint* (Wackernagel and Rees 1998) as well as its distinctions between, for example, natural and man-made capital, non-renewable and renewable resources, eco-system services that can or cannot be substituted and so forth, reveal to what extent the dualistic model remained essential and bear witness to the attempt to specify normative criteria which are located beyond society and are, therefore, objectively valid. In an attempt to take a *holistic* approach, radical or deep ecology aimed to move beyond the dualisms of modernity, yet in that it invoked a supposedly *transcendental* norm of subjectivity and a transcendental right to *authentic* autonomy, integrity and dignity it simply reproduced the dualistic model on a different level. And just as the technomanagerial eco-politics in the mode of objectivation assumed that information about the violation of supposedly objective biophysical imperatives would automatically trigger appropriate counter-action, fundamentalist eco-politics in the mode of subjectivation assumed that information about the violation of these supposedly transcendental norms of subjectivity would automatically initiate commensurate counter-action.

Yet, they were fundamentally wrong. As the environmental issue incrementally established itself on political agendas, and the range and diversity of eco-political

actors steadily increased, the principle of difference invaded ecological communication and unhinged the depoliticising, authority-generating logic of *one nature,
one planet Earth, one human species, one human survival*. The supposedly pre-political,
extra-societal, equalising and objective imperatives of environmental integrity and
human survival became themselves subject to processes of pluralisation, contestation and politicisation. Different notions of nature and norms of the natural were
positioned against – and had to compete with – one another. While cultural and
environmental sociology revealed that despite its portrayal and perception as the
opposite of civilisation and culture, nature is an irreducibly *social* category (see,
for example, Latour 1993; Eder 1995; Macnaghten and Urry 1998) and, as such,
never a source of *categorical* imperatives, the natural sciences demonstrated how
human civilisation impacts on even the most remote areas of *wilderness*, leading Bill
McKibben to his famous hypothesis of *The End of Nature* (McKibben 1990).

At the same time, the new social movements' drive for emancipation, plurality
and diversity propelled not only the differentiation of prevalent norms of subjectivity and identity, but also their transformation towards inherent unsustainability.
Political ecology and the more radical currents of the new social movements had
been driven by the longing for, and the belief in, the *authentic Self* and identity
beyond the individualised and predominantly materialist consumer lifestyle, *real ful-
filment* beyond the alienating treadmill of competitiveness and efficiency, *pacified
social and natural relations* beyond social and ecological instrumentalisation, exploitation and destruction, and *genuinely empowering forms of political and economic organisation*
beyond the only formally democratic order of liberal consumer capitalism. Yet, in
the wake of a value and culture shift which elsewhere I have conceptualised as *second-
order emancipation* and the *post-ecologist turn* (see, for example, Blühdorn 2011, 2013,
2014), this profound unease with the *alienating* order of scientific-technological-
industrial modernity has largely evaporated – or at least it seems to have lost the capacity
to organise itself into really potent actors of change. Concerns about the accelerating
pace of modern life, the spiralling complexity of modern society, the unmanageable
wealth of information or the social and environmental implications of modern lifestyles do, of course, persist. Yet the promise that more authentic happiness and
self-realisation may be found beyond the capitalist, high-tech consumer culture has
become strangely outdated; and the desires for deceleration, simplicity or social and
ecological responsibility are commercially serviced in 'theme-park' style by yoga
classes, Transition Towns or 'green' consumerism.

As a vision for a comprehensive alternative at the level of individual life or
even society at large, ecologist ideals – small-scale, low-tech, steady-state, localised,
non-consumerist, self-sufficient – retain less and less of their earlier appeal. Ever-
expanding needs in terms of, for example, mobility, technology, protein intake,
travel, communication or shopping opportunities have become essentially non-
negotiable. Prevalent notions of well-being and quality of life imply that ways *must*
be found to meet them. They demand that the supposedly categorical imperatives
(ecological and social) which ecologists had believed in *must* be reviewed; environmental policy and eco-political action *must* be amended to conform to, rather

than challenge, liberal consumer capitalism. Sustaining the established socio-economic order has itself evolved into a categorical imperative. Indeed, in a number of respects, *unsustainability* has become a constitutive feature of contemporary ideals of subjectivity and self-realisation: (a) notions of identity are inherently plural, flexible and fluid – they are neither *identical* nor intended to be sustained, but are expected to be remoulded in line with changing life–world requirements (Bauman 2000); (b) as self-construction, self-expression and self-experience are, more than ever, located in the further expanding consumer market, accelerated resource consumption is – despite new efficiency technologies – an almost inevitable side-effect; and (c) under conditions of modern low-growth economies, these patterns of self-realisation inherently rely on ever-increasing social inequality and exclusion.

So, in the wake of this value and culture shift, the norm that political ecologists had used as their ultimate point of reference, the *autonomous subject*, has lost its suitability as a signpost and yardstick for society's transformation towards sustainability. The ecologist version of the TINA principle – which was the assertion that there is no alternative to the ecologist understanding of autonomy and integrity – no longer has its plausibility or its ability to mobilise. By implication, the same applies to ecologist narratives of alienation, disaster and apocalypse. In view of the inherent unsustainability of prevalent norms of subjectivity and self-realisation, the re-politicisation and re-subjectivation of eco-politics seems a rather unpromising route toward structural change. Indeed, de-politicisation and objectivation now seem more legitimate and urgent than ever. Yet, as demonstrated above, eco-politics in the mode of depoliticisation and objectivation is not a viable alternative either.

Conclusion

This dilemma – the simultaneous exhaustion of both eco-politics in the mode of subjectivation *and* eco-politics in the mode of objectivation – is the predicament of eco-politics in the Anthropocene. Of course, the collapse of the dualistic model of thought is not a categorically new discovery. Environmental sociology has been grappling with the implications of 'the boundaries between nature and society becoming blurred' (Beck 1992, 154) and 'no simple . . . distinction between nature and society' (Macnaghten and Urry 1998, 28) being sustainable for some considerable time. For environmental activists and policy makers, however, this idea remained unpalatable and they fiercely held on to their narratives of objective ecological necessities, threats to the survival of the human species and catastrophic social and ecological developments. Yet, with the new notion of the Anthropocene, the collapse of the dualistic model is now entering the discursive mainstream and delivering a fatal blow to these narratives.

In the Anthropocene the lack of external, and hence objectively valid, eco-political norms, and thus the self-referential quality of all eco-political discourse, has become more evident than ever before: ecological communication and environmental politics are neither about any *nature out there* nor any objectively measurable bio-physical constellations, but are, as noted above, ultimately about systems of social values, symbolic meaning and notions of subjectivity. Accordingly, the notion of categorical ecological imperatives or necessities becomes obsolete; the *catastrophic threats* which eco-political activists have always invoked in order to legitimate and mobilise eco-political action are, ultimately, the threat that established systems of social norms and the social order they support will not be sustainable and will, most probably, collapse.

In the wake of the *end of nature*, eco-politics in the Anthropocene requires 'post-natural' ways of defining and legitimising its agenda (Arias-Maldonado 2013, 11). But, as we have seen, it is dangerously naïve to suggest that 'adopting a post-natural stance with regard to sustainability' may be 'a key part of the much-needed renewal of environmentalism' – with sustainability turning into 'an inherently open principle for guiding social action' and 'discussing the kind of society we wish to have' (Arias-Maldonado 2013, 17). Equally, the claim that 'the real political problem today is that the left accepts capitalism' and instead of viewing 'capitalism and its effects as evil', 'has surrendered the state to neoliberal interests' (Dean 2009, 15) resorts to categories and explanations which are outdated and fail to grasp the condition of eco-politics in the Anthropocene. More than anything, such suggestions provide evidence of the helplessness of (eco-)political theory vis-à-vis the collapse of the dualisms of modernist thought. Disturbingly, in the wake of the value shift outlined above, the prevalent politics of unsustainability in fact *is* exactly about 'the kind of society we wish to have' or, as the Rio+20 report put it, *The Future We Want*.

Whatever its declared commitments, this politics of unsustainability is no longer powered by the attempt to change individual lifestyles and societal structures so as to make them comply with any categorical eco- or social imperatives. Instead, its focus is on managing the inevitable consequences, social and ecological, of the resolve to sustain the established value preferences and the related socio-economic order. Rather than trying to suspend – or even reverse – the prevailing logic of unsustainability, it confines itself to promoting societal *adaptation* and *resilience* to sustained unsustainability. For this purpose, the introduction of new technologies and nudging consumers towards specific product choices are important tools. But given that they are embedded into a context where increasing consumer demand and stimulating economic growth remain the highest priorities of any government, their effect will invariably remain marginal. More effective and powerful, how-ever, is a different strategy: In view of the fact that eco-political discourse is not primarily about empirically measurable conditions but about the social concerns which the latter may or may not trigger, strategies of adaptation and resilience can also focus on managing the *social perception* and *communicative processing* of changing societal and biophysical realities. It is precisely this that the *governance of unsustain-ability* (Blühdorn 2013, 2014) is all about. It entertains narratives of participatory governance and celebrates values like inclusion, empowerment, responsibility and sustainability – whilst resolutely pursuing a politics of social inequality and exclu-sion. And this not simply a matter of 'our enemy' having 'taken over our language' (Dean 2009, 10), but of a broad coalition of societal actors engaging in the discursive maintenance of norms that in the Anthropocene have lost their foundations but are, more than ever, essential for the preservation of social peace.

References

Arias-Maldonado Manuel 2013 Rethinking Sustainability in the Anthropocene *Environmental Politics* 22 428–46

Bauman Z 2000 *Liquid Modernity* Polity, Cambridge

Beck U 1992 *The Risk Society* Polity, Cambridge

Blühdorn I 2011 The politics of unsustainability: COP15, post-ecologism and the ecological paradox *Organization & Environment* 24 34–53

Blühdorn I 2013 The governance of unsustainability: Ecology and democracy after the post-democratic turn *Environmental Politics* 22 16–36

Blühdorn I 2014 Post-ecologist governmentality: Post-democracy, post-politics and the politics of unsustainability, in Wilson J and Swyngedouw E eds *The Post-Political and its Discontents: Spaces of depoliticisation and spectres of radical politics* Edinburgh University Press, Edinburgh 146–66

Blühdorn I 2015 Sustainability, post-sustainability, unsustainability, in Gabrielson T Hall C Meyer J M and Schlosberg D eds *The Oxford Handbook of Environmental Political Theory* Oxford University Press, Oxford (in press)

Bookchin M 1982 *The Ecology of Freedom* University of Michigan Press, Ann Arbor, MI

Bulkeley H Jordan A Perkins R and Selin H 2013 Governing sustainability: Rio+20 and the road beyond *Environment and Planning C: Government and Policy* 31 958–70

Commoner B 1971 *The Closing Circle* Knopf, New York

Crouch C 2004 *Post-Democracy* Polity, Cambridge

Dean J 2009 *Democracy and Other Neoliberal Fantasies: Communicative Capitalism and Left Politics* Duke University Press, Durham, NC

Die Grünen 1980 *Das Bundesprogramm* Die Grünen, Bonn

Dobson A 2007 *Green Political Thought* Routledge, London

Ecologist, The 1972 *A Blueprint for Survival* Penguin, London

Eder K 1995 *The Social Construction of Nature* Sage, London

Jänicke M and Mol A 2009 The origins and theoretical foundations of ecological modernisation theory, in Mol A Sonnenfeld D and Spaargaren G eds *The Ecological Modernisation Reader* Routledge, London 17–27

Haberl H Fischer-Kowalski M Krausmann F Weisz H and Winiwarter V 2004 Progress towards sustainability? What the conceptual framework of material and energy flow accounting (MEFA) can offer *Land Use Policy* 21 199–213

Hamilton C 2010 *Requiem for a Species: Why We Resist the Truth About Climate Change* Earthscan, London

Hamilton C 2014 The New Environmentalism Will Lead Us to Disaster *Scientific American* June 19 http://www.scientificamerican.com/article/the-new-environmentalism-will-lead-us-to-disaster (Accessed 15 December 2014)

Klein N 2008 *The Shock Doctrine: The Rise of Disaster Capitalism* Allen Lane, London

Klein N 2014 *This Changes Everything: Capitalism vs. the Climate* Simon & Schuster, New York

Latour B 1993 *We Have Never Been Modern* Harvard University Press, Cambridge, MA.

Linnér B O and Selin H 2013 The United Nations Conference on Sustainable Development: Forty years in the making *Environment and Planning C: Government and Policy* 31 971–87

Macnaghten P and Urry J 1998 *Contested Natures* Sage, London

McKibben B 1990 *The End of Nature* Penguin, London

Meadowcroft J 2013 Reaching the limits? Developed country engagement with sustainable development in a challenging conjuncture *Environment and Planning C: Government and Policy* 31 988–1002

Novy A 2014 The democratisation of all areas of life *Green European Journal* 9 40–4

Offe C 1985 New Social Movements: Challenging the boundaries of institutional politics *Social Research* 52 817–68

Porritt J 1984 *Seeing Green: The Politics of Ecology Explained* Basil Blackwell, Oxford

Swyngedouw E 2007 Impossible/undesirable sustainability and the post-political condition, in Gibbs D and Krueger R eds *The Sustainable Development Paradox: Urban Political Economy in the United States and Europe* Guilford Press, New York 13–40

Swyngedouw E 2009 The Antinomies of the postpolitical city: In search of a democratic politics of environmental production *International Journal of Urban and Regional Research* 33 601–20

Swyngedouw E 2010 Apocalypse forever? Post-political populism and the spectre of climate change *Theory, Culture & Society* 27 213–32

Swyngedouw E 2011 Depolitized environments: The end of Nature, climate change and the post-political condition *Royal Institute of Philosophy Supplement* 69 253–74

Wackernagel M and Rees W 1998 *Our Ecological Footprint: Reducing Human Impact on the Earth* New Society Publishers, Gabriola Island, BC

14

THE ANTHROPOCENE AND ITS VICTIMS

François Gemenne

Politics in the Anthropocene

What is most remarkable about the Anthropocene is the way a concept derived from geology has entered the realm of social sciences. It is certainly not the first concept to cross over from natural to social sciences: adaptation, a key issue in the climate negotiations, is derived from biology, after all. But what sets the Anthropocene apart is that it might well have a life of its own among the social sciences. Even if the International Commission on Stratigraphy decides that we have not yet entered the Anthropocene, the term is likely to remain a useful one in social sciences, for the Anthropocene is now as much a political statement as a geological epoch. And it is a statement well suited to social sciences: the world, which was traditionally conceived as the social and political organ of the Earth, can no longer be thought separately from the Earth. Both the world and the Earth need to be thought of as one global system – a concept dear to James Lovelock and Gaia.

For political science, it signals a new age of geopolitics, in the true meaning of the term; geopolitics is no longer about power over territories, about land and sea, but about the Earth as a whole. Geopolitics is transformed into Gaia-politics – the Politics of the Earth. But there's another way to see this. We also need to be aware that the Anthropocene could be seen as an operation of depoliticisation of subjects. The Anthropocene, the 'Age of Humans', should indeed rather be described as the Oliganthropocene – the age of few men and even fewer women – to borrow an expression coined by Erik Swyngedouw (2014). If humans have indeed become the principal agents of changes on this planet, overwhelming natural forces of change, most humans are actually the victims of these changes rather than their agents. While some have become the main agents of changes on this planet, these very changes have also become the main agents of the transformation of the daily lives for a majority of the people living on the planet.

In 2013, natural disasters forced 22 million people to flee their homes – a figure that is higher than the number of political refugees forced to cross a border because of violence and persecutions (16.9 million) (Yonetani 2014). The number of those fleeing natural disasters does not include the many more who are displaced because of the slow, creeping and incremental impacts of climate change, and who are not accounted for in any kind of statistical database (Gemenne 2011). Environmental changes – human-induced or not – have now become a major driver, if not the major driver, of migration and displacement on the planet. The focus of this chapter is on those very people whose lives have been altered dramatically – the victims of the Anthropocene.

Displaced by environmental changes

Environmental changes have always been a major cause of migration. Since prehistorical times, the geographical distribution of the population on the planet has been shaped largely by environmental conditions. This explains, for example, why so many people live around coasts and deltas, and why Europe was settled about 40,000 years ago (Beniston 2004). Throughout history, there have been numerous examples of migrations associated with environmental changes. In 1755, for example, the Lisbon earthquake destroyed most of the city, inducing mass displacements to other parts of Portugal, with some of those displaced later returning to Lisbon (Dynes 1997). The 1930s Dust Bowl migration in the southwest United States is a classic example of mass migration associated with environmental events, though such events often cannot be disentangled from their broader socio-economic context. The Dust Bowl consisted of devastating dust storms that followed severe droughts and poor agricultural practices that depleted the soils. Thousands of farmers from Oklahoma, Texas and Arkansas had no choice but to sell or abandon their farms and move westwards.

In recent years, however, environmental changes have become an increasingly important factor in displacement worldwide. Over the period 2008–12, more than 140 million people were displaced as a result of natural disasters (Yonetani 2014), a figure that does not include those who have been displaced as a result of slow-onset environmental changes such as desertification and rises in sea levels. Their number remains unknown. Thus there are today at least as many people displaced by environmental changes as there are people displaced by wars and violence.

The concept of 'environmental migrants' encompasses a wide diversity of environmental changes, but also of migration patterns. Among the major environmental disruptions that can induce migration are flash floods, earthquakes, droughts, storms and hurricanes, but also slow-onset changes such as sea-level rise, desertification and deforestation. Large development or conservation projects, such as dams and natural reserves, are sometimes included as well. Many of these disruptions will be aggravated by climate change. They lead to varied forms of migration requiring different policy responses. Empirical research shows that most of these movements occur over short distances, often within national boundaries

(Foresight 2011). Contrary to a frequent assumption, those who migrate are usually not the most vulnerable populations. These are often trapped and immobile in the face of environmental changes, as they do not have access to the resources, networks and information that would enable them to relocate to safer areas (Foresight 2011). Though most of these migrations occur in developing countries, and particularly in South Asia, Southeast Asia and Sub-Saharan Africa, developed countries can also experience them, as evidenced by the massive population displacements resulting from Hurricane Katrina in the southern United States, which led to the evacuation of about 1.2 million people in the Gulf Coast region, or by the Fukushima disaster in Japan, which displaced around 470,000 people.

Far from being a conjectural phenomenon, environmental migration has become an essential component of migration dynamics worldwide. This is largely due to the impacts of climate change, but also to creeping deforestation and natural disasters. The major development over recent decades, however, is that an increasing proportion of environmental disruptions are human-induced. The impacts of climate change, in particular, have dramatically altered the environment–migration nexus; not only has the magnitude of environmentally-induced population movements increased dramatically, but the issue of the responsibility for these movements has also entered the policy debates.

A 'Copernican revolution'

For a long time, policy debates turned a blind eye to environmental migration. The forces driving migration were assumed to be political or economic in nature; environmental causes were largely ignored by scholars and policy makers alike. Environmental migrants do not exist in international law, and no specific UN agency or international body has been tasked with providing them with assistance and protection, though organisations such as the UN High Commissioner for Refugees and the International Organization for Migration have conducted regular interventions to protect and assist such migrants.

Migration related to environmental changes, and to climate change in particular, is often perceived as a decision of last resort that people take when they have exhausted all possible options for adaptation in their place of origin, and are left with no other choice. Reports on climate change impacts are indeed replete with the idea that climate-induced migration should be avoided at all costs, and would represent a failure of both mitigation and adaptation policies (Myers 2002; Stern 2009). Over time, 'climate refugees' have become the human face of global warming, being at the same time the first witnesses and the first victims of climate impacts such as sea-level rise or melting permafrost. This has been particularly true for populations from small island states, described as the 'canaries in the coal mine', which are alerting the rest of the world to the dangers of climate change, and are themselves left with no other choice than relocate abroad (Farbotko 2010).

However, many scholars, including myself, insisted that this depiction of the migrants did not match the reality, and that migration was often a *strategy* used by migrants to deal with environmental changes (Rain 1999; Black et al. 2011). We insisted that migrants should be perceived not as resourceless victims of climate change, but rather as resourceful agents of their own adaptation. We argued that migration could indeed prove a powerful adaptation strategy: migrants could diversify their incomes, alleviate environmental pressures in the region of origin, send remittances, or simply put both themselves and their families out of harm's way. Many institutions and organisations, including the international negotiations on climate change, quickly embraced this view. In 2010, the Cancun Adaptation Framework included, in its Article 14 (f), 'measures to enhance understanding, coordination and cooperation with regard to climate change induced displacement, migration and planned relocation . . .'.

This was a 'Copernican revolution'. Migration in the context of climate change was no longer a disaster to avoid at all costs, but a strategy that ought to be encouraged and facilitated. This led to a drift towards seeing the climate negotiations as the best platform for discussion of the issue. The movement of people was no longer a matter of migration policies, it was seen instead as an aspect of environmental policies. It had become an adaptation strategy.

But what about those who were *forced* to flee as a result of environmental disruptions, those who would have liked to stay but had no other choice? These displacements were now considered to be a form of collateral damage, one that could be addressed through the Loss and Damage mechanism, the agreement made at the 2012 Doha negotiations of the UNFCCC at which rich countries agreed to compensate poor countries for the loss and damage caused by human-induced climate change (Kreft 2013). Migration related to climate change had become something that was no longer taboo , but rather something we could enable, facilitate and manage. And this is something that we, as a research community, had pushed forward and wished for.

How we let migrants down

On further reflection, however, I have come to realise that we had missed something in this process of the 'de-victimisation' of migrants: we had used environmental changes as a Trojan horse to 'depoliticise' migration. In our quest to make research policy-relevant, we had let policies take over politics, we had let governance replace government. In a nutshell, we had forgotten what we were doing to the victims of the Anthropocene. In our attempt to stress the agency of the migrants, we had forgotten the responsibility that we (in the West) had towards them. Because the Anthropocene is first and foremost a war, a war that we are waging against the most vulnerable populations of this planet. If we, humans (and especially those in industrial nations), have become the main agents of transformation of the Earth, the result of this transformation has been to make the Earth increasingly uninhabitable for a growing number of people.

A fundamental difficulty in collective action against climate change is that those who need to undertake most of the effort to cut greenhouse gas emissions, the industrialised countries, are also those who will be comparatively less affected by the impacts of global warming. From a rational, neoliberal perspective, industrialised nations thus have little incentive to act; our agency is denied by our interest. If climate change is rooted in the inequalities between rich and poor, migration is the lens through which these inequalities materialise. Early theories on migration, such as those of Lee (1966), assumed that migrations could be an adjustment between inequalities; yet they are the symptoms rather than the cure.

Depoliticising migration

Two examples of recent policy debates attest to this process of depoliticising migration through an environmental perspective. One is related to the way we name these migrants; the other is about how we regard them.

In the press and in public debates, those uprooted by climate change are often referred to as 'climate refugees'. Legal scholars and international organisations, however, have been keen to dismiss the term, which had no legal grounding (McAdam 2009). They are right: the 1951 Geneva Convention sets out various criteria one needs to fulfil to qualify as a refugee, and 'climate refugees' clearly do not meet them. Most scholars have therefore agreed not to use the term, and to use more clinical terms such as 'climate-induced migrants', 'people on the move in the context of climate change', and so on. I was one of them, and I think I was wrong. By forgoing the term 'climate refugee' we had depoliticised the reality of these migrations. A central element in the concept of 'refugee' is persecution; in order to qualify as a refugee, one needs to flee persecution or a well-founded fear of persecution. And forgoing the term 'climate refugee' is also, in a way, forgoing the idea that climate change is a form of persecution against the most vulnerable. Yet climate impacts are indeed a form of persecution: now that the causes of global warming are unequivocal and its impacts well-known, the emission of greenhouse gas should be treated as a form of political oppression. Conisbee and Simms developed this idea in 2003, arguing that climate-induced migration is a very political affair rather than an environmental one. For this very reason, and despite the legal difficulties, I think this is a strong reason to use the term again, for it recognises that these migrations are first and foremost the result of a persecution to which we are subjecting the most vulnerable.

The second example deals with resettlement, a policy of increasing popularity with governments seeking to anticipate the effects of climate change. Many populations are highly exposed to these impacts, and some governments are in the process of relocating them to safer zones in order to reduce their geographical exposure to hazards (De Sherbinin et al. 2011). Although these may appear to be rational, sensible solutions, these resettlement processes raise a number of ethical issues, and, in particular, with regard to the human rights of the resettled populations. The government of Vietnam, for example, is implementing a policy called 'Living with Floods', which is about resettling villages located in the Mekong delta, a zone increasingly subject to floods and sea-level rise (Danh and Mushtaq 2011).

Though this resettlement process reduces the geographical exposure of the populations, it has resulted in greater vulnerability because of the disruption to their livelihoods and networks induced by the process, one in which they had very little say. Resettlement processes often treat people as commodities that can be uprooted from one place and settled in another, in order to accommodate the anticipated impacts of global warming.

Keeping the Earth habitable

In April 2013, Bangladesh was struck by the Rana Plaza tragedy, the collapse of a garment factory that resulted in the death of more than 1,000 workers. At the time, I was struck by the international reaction to the disaster: not only was there a widespread outcry at the working conditions in these factories, but many people held clothing companies responsible for the calamity. Some stopped buying clothes from the high-street retail chains implicated and called for a boycott. Others demanded, sometimes successfully, better working conditions for the garment workers in Bangladesh. People had suddenly realised that buying clothes had consequences for people in other parts of the planet.

Bangladesh is also a country at the forefront of climate impacts, where displacements are already commonplace. Yet the connection between the action of some and the suffering of others, which was made on the occasion of the Rana Plaza disaster, does not seem to be realised with regard to climate change. Indeed, the biggest challenge of the Anthropocene is perhaps the challenge of cosmopolitism. The concept of the Anthropocene might produce the false impression of a unified humanity, where all humans are agents of planetary change. Yet the Anthropocene is also rooted in inequalities, where the actions of some cause the suffering of the others. And in that regard, the Anthropocene can also lead to the depoliticisation of subjects, where the 'environmentalisation' of politics would actually end up in a depoliticisation of the environment. That is what has happened, to a certain extent, in the case of climate refugees, and it is why the Anthropocene is first and foremost a matter of keeping the Earth habitable for the most vulnerable.

References

Beniston M 2004 Issues relating to environmental change and population migrations: A climatologist's perspective, in Unruh J Krol M and Kliot N eds *Environmental Change and its Implications for Population Migration* Kluwer Academic Publishers, Dordrecht 1–24

Black R Bennett S Thomas S and Beddington J 2011 Migration as adaptation *Nature* 478 447–9

Conisbee M and Simms A 2003 *Environmental Refugees: The Case for Recognition* New Economics Foundation, London

Danh V and Mushtaq 2011 Living with Floods: An evaluation of the resettlement program of the Mekong Delta of Vietnam, in Stewart M and Coclanis P eds *Environmental Change and Agriculture Sustainability in the Mekong Delta* Springer-Verlag, Berlin

De Sherbinin A et al. 2011 Preparing for resettlement associated with climate change *Science* 334 456–7

Dynes R 1997 The Lisbon Earthquake in 1755: Contested meanings in the first modern disaster, in *Preliminary papers*, University of Delaware Disaster Research Center, Newark (DE): Disaster Research Center, University of Delaware

Farbotko C 2010 The global warming clock is ticking so see these places while you can: Voyeuristic tourism and model environmental citizens on Tuvalu's disappearing islands *Singapore Journal of Tropical Geography* 31 224–38

Foresight 2011 *Migration and Global Environmental Change. Final Project Report* The Government Office for Science, London

Gemenne F 2011 Why the numbers don't add up: A review of estimates and predictions of people displaced by environmental changes *Global Environmental Change* 21 S41–S49

Kreft S 2013 *Addressing Climate Loss and Damage* Germanwatch, Berlin

Lee E S 1966 A theory of migration *Demography* 3(1) 47–57

McAdam J 2009 From economic refugees to climate refugees? *Melbourne Journal of International Law* 10 579–95

Myers N 2002 Environmental refugees: A growing phenomenon of the 21st century *Philosophical Transactions of the Royal Society B* 357(1420) 609–13

Rain D 1999 *Eaters of the Dry Season: Circular Labor Migration in the West African Sahel* Westview Press, New York

Stern N 2009 *The Global Deal: Climate Change and the Creation of a New Era of Progress and Prosperity* Public Affairs, New York

Swyngedouw E 2014 Anthropocenic promises: The end of nature, climate change and the process of post-politicization, Lecture at the Center for International Studies and Research (CERI), Sciences Po, Paris 2 June

Yonetani M 2014 *Global Estimates 2014: People Displaced by Disasters* Internal Displacement Monitoring Centre, Geneva

Epilogue

COMMISSION ON PLANETARY AGES

Decision CC87966424/49:
The onomatophore of the Anthropocene

TO ALL TO WHOM THIS NEWS SHALL COME, BE IT KNOWN:

that there appeared before the Commission on Planetary Ages a creature of the species called Anthropos, a species which has achieved the fourth of the thirty-six known levels of sentience;

and that this creature announced that the world in which it has its origin, known as Earth, has entered a new stage in its journey from the nothing that was, through the something that is, to the nothing that will be;

and that the creature proclaimed that its kind was starting to understand the laws governing the becoming of worlds, and that these have revealed the role they have played in moving the Earth to a new state;

and that the creature laid a claim before the Commission, on behalf of all its kind, asserting that the new age of its world should therefore be named 'the Anthropocene', after its own kind;

and that this creature thereby claimed for its whole species the status of the onomatophore, the name-bearer, of their planetary age;

and when it had finished speaking, it struck its chest once, a sign which in some of our cultures signifies truth, in others pride, in others shame;

Planetary ages

and having regard to the powers granted to this Commission to determine the names of the ages of all worlds throughout the galaxy, according to the principles of endokairology, the science of the times that grow within self-organising things, and that out of this growth produce other times from within themselves, thus generating the lacework of times that connect the 10,000 things;

and having regard to the *first* law of endokairology, which states that a world or any other self-positing thing generates its *own* time out of its particular way of enduring, and that this time is not the time of *chronos*, the extensive time of mere succession, but the time of *kairos*, the intensive time of singularities and qualities;

and having regard to the *second* law of this science, which means that planetary ages are determined not by the visible signs that are written on the face of a world, but by the hidden signs and communication within it, between mantle and crust, crust and ocean, ocean and atmosphere, atmosphere and life;

and having regard to the *third* law, which means that the immanent time that a world generates through its own mode of becoming folds back on itself, so that the way a world changes changes, that a world undergoes radical leaps in its mode of becoming;

and having regard to the *fourth* law, which means that the immanent time of worlds has other immanent times curled within them – that within the aeons of a world, whose edges mark the great changes in planetary becoming when time begins anew, lie the eras of that world, and within the eras lie the periods, and within the periods the epochs, and so on;

and having regard to the consequence of the first three laws that the ages of a world cannot be laid side by side – that because the time of worlds is produced from within, and because each age has its own internal time, there is no time which can comprehend all the ages of a world; each age starts but never finishes; the time of each age is finite but eternal, which means that it can make itself felt long after other ages have started;

and having regard to the relationship of the Commission on Planetary Ages with those lower commissions responsible for the times of ecosystems, species and organisms, of objects, molecules and atoms, of bosons, leptons and quarks; and with those higher commissions responsible for the times of planetary systems, of galaxies, clusters, superclusters and filaments, of cosmoses and multiverses;

Onomatophores

and having regard to the regulations on onomatophores, which recognise that, while all agents in a planetary age are named by that age, one agent can have a special relationship to that age, and its name to the name of that age, and this is because they are the 'cause' or subject of that age, and this agent is known as the onomatophore or 'name-bearer' of that age;

and having regard to the powers granted to this Commission to determine the onomatophores of the ages of all worlds throughout the galaxy;

and recognising that to be decreed an onomatophore the agent must be the 'cause' of an age in the sense of at least one of the nine recognised kinds of cause:

- the forward cause that pushes from the earlier or
- the backward cause that pulls towards the later,
- the upward cause of part to whole or
- the downward cause of whole to part,
- the first cause that initiates or
- the last cause that completes,
- the universal cause that is always or
- the singular cause that is now, or
- the emblematic cause that summarises;

and recognising that being a cause is always relative to a particular age; that each age of a world defines and distributes agency in particular ways; and that transitions between ages redefine what an agent is and how it can act;

and having regard to the duty of the Commission, when presented with a claim by a potential onomatophore, to inform all other agents of the age under consideration that a claim has been lodged, and to consider any counterclaims received;

The Palace of the Ages

and having regard to the Palace of the Ages, where all onomatophores abide;

and recognising that this palace has many dwelling places, each of which correspond to a single age of one or other kind of body or assemblage, and that these dwelling places are arranged in ranks and lines and layers:

- from the time of the smallest particle to the time of the multiverse,
- and for each of these, from the shortest class of ages to the longest class,
- and for each of these, from the first of ages to the last of ages;

and that each of these dwelling places, one for each unit of time, is a throne;

and recognising that to become an onomatophore is to be elevated to one of these thrones alongside the other geological forces and events that determine the ages of a world – alongside magma, comets and tides; eruptions, collisions and evolutionary leaps – and alongside all the forces and events that determine the ages of every kind of body and assemblage;

and that for a being to be enthroned in the Palace of the Ages is to be made αιωνον [aionon], 'of the ages', which means to belong not just to the time of that being but also to an age of deep, planetary time;

and that being enthroned in the Palace of the Ages is also to be made αιωνιος [aionios], which means 'eternal', beyond time, because each age has its own time that begins but does not end;

so that to be made onomatophore is to be placed beyond time, beyond normal agency and responsibility;

The Earth's specific planetary endokairology

and noting that the creature's world is so far following what is called the 'main sequence', the most common trajectory in the development of rocky worlds;

and noting that the Earth has thereby exhibited the radical transitions in its mode of becoming which mark the bounds between the great **aeons** of a world, such as the establishing of continents that are not pulled down into the magma, or the taking of control over the chemical and thermodynamic balance of the world by living things;

and that the long aeons of the Earth so far number four, and are called by Anthropos the Hadean, the Archaean, the Proterozoic and the Phanerozoic;

and noting that, within a given aeon, transitions between **eras** such as the emergence of an atmosphere with free oxygen, or the rise of the terrible lizards, are the result of a dialogue between the balancing of intensive forces within a world and forcings from outside;

and that at the finer kairological level of **periods** a world moves between different points of stability within an era – often between times of great heat and of unimaginable cold;

and that at the even finer level of **epochs** a world, pressed by intensive gradients and forcings, explores the different possible states that are available to it within a given period;

and noting that the Earth has recently undergone significant changes: that the surfaces of the continents and the floors of the oceans have been profoundly altered; that the planet's subsystems, the flows of sunlight, water and nitrogen, have been captured and directed into the house of the Anthropos; that layers laid down in earlier periods have been mined and spread around the world or vented into its atmosphere; that the gifting of heat between sun and earth and space has been transformed, so that the world is warming;

and noting also that the way that the Earth's own distinctive time emerges from its internal intensive differences is also changing; that just as Proterozoic life learnt how to take the inorganic systems of the Earth up into itself, and to move the world far from equilibrium, so too have the complex organisms of Phanerozoic life learned how to take assemblages of inorganic matter and give them their own kind of life — are creating what are known as technics or machines — and that these are altering the processes through which the Earth organises itself;

The Anthropos

and noting that at the heart of these changes is the species of the claimant, known as Anthropos;

and noting furthermore that the claim of the claimant has been challenged: that alternative onomatophores — other beings and forces which also claim the status of the name-bearer of the new planetary age of the Earth — have presented themselves to the receiving chambers of the Commission:

- the coal which laid itself down in the Carboniferous period;
- but also the fungi which held back their appearance in the Earth and permitted the coal to accumulate;
- the machines, those excrescences of vitality whose needs drive the transformation of the Earth;
- but also the economies that drive the needs of the machines

and many more candidate causes of the new epoch, of all nine kinds of 'cause';

and noting that the species of the claimant has many members and that some of these — the poor, the different, the not yet born — say that they have not been cause of the new epoch in any of the nine senses of 'cause', and that they do not pretend the title of onomatophore;

BE IT KNOWN THAT THE COMMISSION HAS DECIDED:

that the world of the claimant is indeed entering a new age;

that the epoch of human civilisation, the Holocene, is closing: its time can never end, but it will no longer define the Earth, and the agents of the Earth;

but that the proposal to name the new age 'the Anthropocene', a denomination which would locate this closing as a mere shift of epoch within the Quaternary period, itself within the Cenozoic era, must be rejected;

because the closing of the Holocene to which the Anthropos testifies is also the closing of the Quaternary period, the end of the gentle oscillation of the Earth between glaciations and interglacials, which slow music will always echo down the ages of the Earth but will no longer determine them;

and the closing of the Quaternary period is also the closing of the era of mammals — the onomatophores of the Cenozoic, who did not push that era into being from the past, but willed it into being from the future, who will not die and will eternally be onomatophore but will no longer be emblematic, as their era has closed;

and that the closing of the Cenozoic era is also the closing of the Phanerozoic, the whole great aeon of visible life, as living matter starts to shed the limits of the organism: that multicellular organic life will continue, but will no longer be definitive of the time of the Earth;

and that the closing of the Phanerozoic aeon is also the opening of a new aeon in the Earth's immanent time, which the Commission decrees shall be called the Phanerotechnic: the aeon of technological life, of organised inorganic matter, which in the deep time of the main sequence will surely be succeeded by the Aoratotechnic, the aeon of invisible machinery, of pure organisation, when technology will finally shed its material form;

and that the opening of this new Phanerotechnic aeon is also the start of the first era of that aeon: the Proterotechnic, the era of early machines, still primitive, still tied to organic life for their purposes, not yet truly autonomous, not yet their own independent life;

and that the opening of the Proterotechnic era is also the start of the first period of that era, the period in which machine life will escape the Earth and refashion the planetary system of which it is a part, will capture the flows of energy from its sun, convert matter into energy and energy into information;

and that the opening of this period is also the start of the first epoch of that period, an epoch which is already seeing the refashioning of the home world, the enframing of its energies, the mining of its stocks, the capturing of its flows, the overturning of its layers, the fabrication of a new surface of the Earth, and the casting of a new machinic layer of the Earth far above that surface;

AND BE IT ALSO KNOWN THAT THE COMMISSION DECREES:

that the Anthropos, the species of the claimant, has indeed been cause and agent within these developments in the time of the Earth;

but that the Anthropos is only the last, the proximate cause in the pushing of the Earth into its new epoch, its new period, its new era and its new aeon, and that other agents have stronger claim to the status of onomatophore for these new units of Earth time;

and that this first new epoch that the Earth is entering feels the hand of the Carboniferous period, which closed 3,000,000 Earth years ago but whose time, like those of all past ages, still unravels in the becoming of the Earth; and that it is the machinic assemblages of engines, currencies and markets, that bring ages together, that bloom across the Earth and that govern its transformation;

and that neither will the Anthropos be emblematic of the new epoch of the Earth, though it may survive it;

but that the Anthropos *is* the onomatophore of the epoch that is closing, the last epoch of the Quaternary period and the Cenozoic era and the Phanerozoic aeon, for it has been the emblematic species of this closing chapter of the era of mammals and of the very aeon of complex life on the Earth;

and thus that the Holocene epoch, the epoch that is now closing, should henceforth be called the Anthropocene;

and that as one age is succeeded by the next, as the time of the world changes, as its becoming becomes, then agency itself is changing, and the agency of the human is changing; the Anthropos will always be onomatophore of the epoch which is closing, will be enthroned in the Palace of the Ages for ever, to the ages of the ages, so that the time of the Anthropos is eternal and its role not over; yet it is no longer the primary agent of Earth's becoming, since that role has passed to the machines.

The Commission is now in communication with the higher commissions, to whose jurisdiction this case will now be passed.

INDEX

Marx- "metabolism"

Made in the USA
San Bernardino, CA
13 January 2018